This book is an investigation of the methodological and epistemological foundations of macroeconomic theory, based on an examination of the theories of Keynes and Lucas. It is divided into two parts. In the first Professor Vercelli discusses the methodological issues which lie behind the conflict among different schools of thought in macroeconomics (equilibrium and disequilibrium, risk and uncertainty, rationality and causality). These issues are central to the current debate not only in many branches of economics, but also in other scientific disciplines. The traditional point of view of science based on equilibrium, stability and determinism has been increasingly challenged by a new point of view in which disequilibrium, instability and uncertainty play a crucial role. This, the author argues, is bound to put macroeconomics in a new, more promising position.

In the second part of the book the author compares the two main alternative research programmes in macroeconomics: that outlined by Keynes in his *General Theory*, and that suggested by Lucas, the leader of the new classical economists. He maintains that a thorough understanding of the methodological underpinnings of these main conflicting views helps to give a deeper knowledge of the crucial macroeconomic issues and to clarify the future prospects of macroeconomic research.

Professor Vercelli concludes that the Keynesian conception of macroeconomics as a discipline autonomous from microeconomics and open to theoretical and methodological innovation should be defended and further developed, excluding any fundamentalism either of the Keynesian or new classical varieties.

Methodological foundations of macroeconomics: Keynes and Lucas

Methodological foundations of macroeconomics: Keynes and Lucas

ALESSANDRO VERCELLI

Dipartimento di Economia Politica,
University of Siena

The right of the
University of Cambridge
to print and sell
all manner of books
was granted by
Henry VIII in 1534.
The University has printed
and published continuously
since 1584.

CAMBRIDGE UNIVERSITY PRESS

Cambridge
New York   Port Chester   Melbourne   Sydney

Published by the Press Syndicate of the University of Cambridge
The Pitt Building, Trumpington Street, Cambridge CB2 1RP
40 West 20th Street, New York, NY 10011–4211, USA
10 Stamford Road, Oakleigh, Melbourne 3166, Australia

First published 1991

Printed in Great Britain at the University Press, Cambridge

British Library cataloguing in publication data

Vercelli, Alessandro
Methodological foundations of macroeconomics: Keynes and
Lucas.
1. Macroeconomics. Theories
I. Title
339.301

Library of Congress cataloguing in publication data

Vercelli, Alessandro.
[Keynes dopo Lucas.   English]
Methodological foundations of macroeconomics: Keynes and Lucas /
Alessandro Vercelli.
p.   cm.
Translation with revisions of: Keynes dopo Lucas. I fondamenti
della macroeconomia, with four new chapters added.
Includes bibliographical references and index.
ISBN 0 521 39294 2
1. Keynes, John Maynard, 1883–1946.   2. Lucas, Robert E., Jr.
3. Macroeconomics.   I. Title.
HB103.K47V3813   1991
339 – dc20   90-36075   CIP

ISBN 0 521 39294 2 hardback

SE

In memory of my parents

Contents

Contents

Contents

Preface

This book originated from the translation of a book published in Italian: *Keynes dopo Lucas. I fondamenti della macroeconomia*, Rome, NIS, 1987. However, the present version is much more than a simple translation as I have added four new chapters (3, 5, 10 and 12) and I have revised all the others, adding sections, appendices, notes, and references. I have also tried whenever possible to improve the argument by rearranging and shortening the original text.

The preliminary plan for this monograph was conceived more than ten years ago, and I have worked on it continuously, though not exclusively, for all these years. In the meantime the original project has undergone a number of changes and ramifications, which constantly widened the gap between the text I was gradually building up and the goal I had set myself.

A few years ago I realized that the process was not converging towards the objective, and indeed could not converge without interrupting the evolution of my ideas. At that point I decided – so to speak – to 'take a snapshot' of the work at its present stage. In a few months I produced a very concise draft in which I set out certain essential points of my reflections on the foundations of macroeconomics, leaving further developments to be argued in articles.

The disadvantage of this selective procedure is that the treatment is summary and incomplete: the result can at best be considered as a 'blueprint', not as the building itself. The advantage, on the other hand, lies in the greater agility and accessibility of the argument. I have thus tried to keep the language as plain and comprehensible as possible. In particular, in the main text I have almost completely avoided the use of any formalized language, relegating it to the appendices, the reading of which is not indispensable for the understanding of the essential structure of the discussion.

I do not mean, however, to question the usefulness of formalization in political economy. The formalism now endemic in our discipline has been subjected to criticisms which are largely justified and increasingly significant; but one should not go so far as to deny the utility of formalized languages, provided they are used with due critical awareness. Authors such as Marshall and Keynes probably went too far in their criticism, and thereby weakened their arguments. Therefore I have tried, in the appendices, to construct a few bridges – however fragile and temporary – towards formalized economic theory.

From what I have said it follows that the language used in the main text of this book should be accessible to readers with a university education and some knowledge of economics. I will not deny that the problems discussed here are very arduous and complex; but I have made a great effort not to add avoidable difficulties of language to the intrinsic difficulties of the subject.

This book, therefore, will lend itself to didactic use, either as a supplement to a course in macroeconomics or as the nucleus of a course in economic methodology. But the aims of the book are not purely didactic: it argues, from a well defined point of view, in defence of a conception of macroeconomics as an *autonomous* and *open* discipline. Today this conception is threatened and therefore must be courageously supported and developed. The abandonment of this conception would have devastating consequences for the possibility of solving not only theoretical and methodological problems, but also the economic problems that beset us.

The preface to the Italian edition contains a long list of acknowledgments, which of course apply also to this version but do not need to be repeated *in extenso* here. I will thus limit myself to expressing my gratitude to all the friends and colleagues who helped me in the transition between the Italian version and this English version.

First of all I would like to thank all those who wrote reviews or comments on the Italian version. Most of them were very perceptive and contributed greatly to the improvement of the English draft. In particular, I would like to mention R. Bellofiore, M. Cini, F. Filippi, G. Lunghini, F. Saltari and S. Zamagni.

Preliminary drafts of the English edition have been read by T. Asimakopulos, S. Bowles, M. De Vroey, N. Dimitri, F. Hahn, J. Harcourt, P.A. Klein, M. Landesman, H. Minsky, U. Pagano, S. Sordi, H. Varian and three anonymous referees. Their comments and criticisms have been invaluable, although I was not always willing, or able, to follow their suggestions. Of course none of them is responsible for the remaining mistakes, omissions and opacities of my arguments.

My special thanks go to Mrs J. Hall and V. Catmur who with great skill helped me to translate the Italian version and to improve the English style.

Abbreviations

AM	Abraham, R., and Marsden, J.E., *Foundations of Mechanics*, 2nd edn, Reading, Mass., Benjamin and Cummings, 1980.
C-D gap	gap between competence and difficulty
CW	Keynes, J.M., *The Collected Writings of J.M. Keynes*, edited by Moggridge, D.E. and Johnson, E., London, Macmillan, 1971– .
EBC	equilibrium business cycle
G-causality	Granger causality
GT	Keynes, J.M., *The General Theory of Employment, Interest and Money*,1936, reprint as vol. 7 of CW.
KP	Kydland, F.E. and Prescott, E.C., 1982, Time to build and aggregate fluctuations, *Econometrica*, 50, 1345–70.
k-uncertainty	'strong' uncertainty (in the sense of Knight and Keynes)
MBC	monetary business cycle
MMEU	maximin criterion for expected utility
MRBC	monetary–real business cycle
RBC	real business cycle
s-instability	structural instability
s-stability	structural stability
TP	Keynes, J.M., *A Treatise on Probability*, 1921, reprint as vol. 8 of CW.
VAR	vector autoregression

Introduction

My present aim, then, is not to teach the method which everyone must follow in order to direct his reason correctly, but only to reveal how I have tried to direct my own. One who presumes to give precepts must think himself more skilful than those to whom he gives them; and if he makes the slightest mistake, he may be blamed. But I am presenting this work only as a history or, if you prefer, a fable in which, among certain examples worthy of imitation, you will perhaps also find many others that it would be right not to follow; and so I hope it will be useful for some without being harmful to any, and that everyone will be grateful to me for my frankness. (Descartes, 1637, p. 21)

1.1   The crisis of macroeconomics

For many years macroeconomics has been in a state of crisis. Since the end of the sixties Keynesian macroeconomics[1] has been staggering under a series of attacks on many fronts: on the empirical side (instability of the Phillips curve, and generally of the parameters of Keynesian econometric models), on the theoretical side (absence or weakness of microeconomic foundations), and also in the area of economic policy (inadequacies of public intervention emphasized by the world economic crisis).

In the course of the seventies a new orthodoxy began to coalesce, particularly in the USA.[2] This was called 'new classical economics' as it was

[1] The Keynesian orthodoxy, embodied in the so-called 'neoclassical synthesis', gradually consolidated itself during the forties and became pre-eminent in the course of the fifties and sixties, first in the academic world and then even in the political milieu (where it became known as the 'new economics'). The dominance of the 'neoclassical synthesis' did not remain unchallenged in that period; its validity was questioned mainly by the monetarists led by Milton Friedman, as well as by heterodox schools of Keynesian and/or radical orientation which did not accept the neoclassical component of this alleged synthesis.

[2] The famous Presidential Address to the American Economic Society, given by Friedman in 1968, may be seen as a watershed between the two periods. That paper announced the breakdown of the Phillips curve in its original Keynesian version, as well as what was to

inspired by the aim of giving rigorous foundations to macroeconomic propositions on the 'classical' principles of general equilibrium. The impact of this school spread, as in the Keynesian case but with a shorter lag, from academic circles to public opinion and eventually to the political milieu, where it influenced macroeconomic policies adopted at the end of the seventies and at the beginning of the eighties.

During the eighties, however, the new orthodoxy has been increasingly questioned. A number of unsettled empirical, theoretical and methodological problems have gradually emerged together with significant differences and counterpositions among new classical economists.[3] At the same time there has been a new emergence of ideas referring back to Keynes. Such contributions open up a wide range of possible alternative research programmes, including hybrid forms crossing Keynesianism with new classical economics, more or less updated versions of the neoclassical synthesis, and new attempts to construct a macroeconomic theory able to restate the basic insights of Keynes in rigorous terms.

1.2   Methodology and economics

The macroeconomic debate is extremely complex and fragmented, and it covers methodological, empirical, theoretical and policy problems. Methodological issues play a decisive role in the debate since explicitly or implicitly they enter most arguments in a crucial way. Unfortunately confusions and misunderstandings often emerge precisely on methodological issues, and these make the scientific debate slippery and often barren. It is thus important to clarify concepts and problems involved in the methodological foundations of macroeconomics. That is one of the main aims of this monograph.

Methodological literature is not greatly esteemed by most economists. This attitude is partly justified, because there are contributions in this field which appear pedantic and pretentious; often they just mechanically import concepts from other disciplines (philosophy of science, epistemology, logic or natural science) which remain extraneous to the economic argument and hence sterile. But this should suggest a justified mistrust of bad economic methodology, not of economic methodology as such.

---

become the characteristic feature of the subsequent anti-Keynesian counter-revolution, i.e. the emphasis on the microfoundations of macroeconomic propositions on general equilibrium theory. However, in the early eighties, the profound differences between new classical economics and traditional monetarism became altogether clear (see chapter 10).

[3] A significant example is given by the theory of the equilibrium business cycle which is at the heart of new classical economics. In Lucas's own theory economic fluctuations are seen as essentially monetary, whereas in most recent theory, equilibrium business cycles are considered real (see chapter 10). A recent contribution by Lucas (1987) attenuates but does not eliminate this divergence.

Economics aims to describe, explain and forecast the behaviour of economic agents, which crucially depends on expectations about the future behaviour of the relevant variables. The process of expectations formation depends in turn on the economic theory adopted by the agents and on its revision rules. At the very moment when we elaborate a theory or a model we have to make assumptions about the cognitive methodology adopted by economic agents (see e.g. Muth, 1961 and Hahn, 1973). We are thus bound to deal with economic methodology, whether we like it or not. Today this must be accepted as an established principle. In particular it is implicit in the literature on rational expectations, although there the use of this principle has often been reductive if not misleading.

Economic methodology should thus be conceived as a discipline entirely within the scope of economics. We might say that economic methodology and economic theory should be not simply juxtaposed but connected in a 'chemical synthesis'. This does not mean it may not be possible, and sometimes even opportune, to make excursions into methodologies of other disciplines, or into the general methodology of science, or into epistemology itself; but the particular demands of economics should never be overlooked.

1.3 Keynes and Lucas

Macroeconomics has come to an awkward crossroads. Several paths ahead look promising, but we do not know which one may carry us further. Some of the alternative routes have been only partially explored, others are barely glimpsed, others may yet be discovered. In order to find the right direction we must identify a wide spectrum of possibilities, whose extreme poles may be approximately represented by Keynes and Lucas.

A discussion of these two authors, though certainly limited, may go a long way towards establishing proper coordinates for choosing the most promising research programme in macroeconomics. It is preferable to analyse single authors, like Keynes and Lucas, rather than 'schools' which are always very difficult to define. It is not by chance that the choice falls on these two authors. The work of Keynes is still the main single point of reference, either positive or negative, for all the schools in macroeconomics. They still define themselves in relation to Keynes's ideas, either as a development of some version of his thought or as a restoration of some version of pre-Keynesian 'classical' thought. This implies perhaps that macroeconomics is not yet a mature discipline, since it has not managed to emancipate itself completely from its founding father. However, it is better to accept this reality than to claim a wishful 'maturity' which would misleadingly relegate Keynes to the history of economic thought. I believe that we still have to deal very seriously with his thought, and particularly with his methodological contributions, which only now can be completely appreciated.

As far as Lucas is concerned, there are many reasons for focussing attention on his thought. He is recognized as the intellectual leader of new classical economists,[4] who have in a way managed to weaken the dominance of Keynesian economics, and sometimes (particularly in the USA) to overcome it. He also developed a methodological approach, at variance with that of Keynes, putting in particular the emphasis on substantive rationality, equilibrium, demonstrative methods, and 'risk' (in the sense of Knight and Keynes). Lucas refines and organizes these methodological tendencies – which were already creeping into the 'neoclassical synthesis' – in a 'pure form', i.e. in a particularly coherent though extreme form. This makes it easier to evaluate the scope and limits of the 'classical' methodology, old and new.

As leader of the new classical school Lucas launched the most radical challenge to Keynesian macroeconomics. Friedman's monetarism shares with Keynes many theoretical and methodological premises which are rejected by Lucas. For example, according to Friedman (1968) the readjustment process in disequilibrium may last over a decade and profoundly affects the economic behaviour, whereas it is considered unimportant by the new classical economists either because it is thought to be instantaneous or because it is judged a non-intelligible process.

According to Lucas Keynes's contribution has been completely superseded, not only from the point of view of economic policy but also from that of theory and methodology. It is reduced to little more than a source of epigraphs: 'economists who find Keynes's style congenial will continue to use his writings as Dennis Robertson did Lewis Carroll's, but surely there is more to the cumulative nature of economics than this!' (Lucas, 1981, p. 276). Lucas has thus tried to launch a radical anti-Keynesian counterrevolution. Since this attempt has enjoyed a remarkable success, it is very important to assess the soundness of its key arguments and to see whether Keynes, after Lucas, still leads to a viable research programme.

1.4   Scientific paradigm and heuristic model

A thorough comparison of the scientific paradigms of Keynes and Lucas has to emphasize methodological problems. In fact both authors see the

---

[4] This is the prevailing opinion (see e.g. Tobin, 1980a and b, and Klamer, 1984). There are many other important representatives of the school such as Sargent, Wallace, Barro and Prescott. Lucas, however, is considered by many to have been particularly successful in providing a general framework, both conceptual and methodological, for this school of thought.

essence of their own contributions, and of the contrast between the two research programmes, as mainly methodological. According to Keynes, economic theory must be conceived not as a doctrine but as a method. In his opinion the crucial error of classical theory lies essentially in its method, which cannot provide an answer to crucial problems like those raised by the Great Depression of the thirties (see e.g. Keynes, *General Theory*, from now on abbreviated GT). Lucas in turn agrees that the 'Keynesian revolution has been a revolution in method' (Lucas and Sargent, 1979, p. 296). New classical economists interpret their own counter-revolution in methodological terms, as a 'strategy of model construction' (see e.g. Townsend in Klamer, 1984, p. 85, and Taylor, *ibid.*, p. 172).

The comparison between the two theoretical points of view is simplified by a further important similarity. In each case a general model is developed to coordinate the set of models elaborated to cope with specific problems, and to suggest instructions for their proper use and for the construction of new ones. This general framework, which gives unity and an overall meaning to the set of specific models characterizing a certain theory, will be called the *heuristic model* of that theory.

It occupies an intermediate position between the two classical levels of Schumpeter's historiography: the *vision* and the *analytical model* (see Schumpeter, 1954, in particular pp. 41–2, 114, 561–2, 1171).[5] The heuristic model is a representation of the vision of a certain author in a sufficiently simplified and operative way to permit continuous direct control of the use, construction and revision of analytical models. Since its role is a strategic one in any research programme, our attention should be focussed on it whenever alternative theoretical paradigms are appraised. In fact, as soon

---

[5] The Schumpeterian distinction between 'vision' and 'analysis' has been very successful and has become common usage among economists. However, its interpretation has undergone an unconscious change as the line of demarcation between the two concepts has gradually shifted. In fact the semantic range of 'vision' has gradually broadened, while the semantic range of 'analysis' has gradually narrowed. This originated, in my opinion, from the growing spread of formalization in economics, and thus from the growing influence of the mathematical concept of analysis. Today an 'analytical model' is taken to mean a mathematical model having an analytical solution, whereas Schumpeter considered any model, in whatever language, as part of economic analysis. In particular Keynes's model, expressed in ordinary language in the first 17 chapters of the *General Theory* and summarized in the same language in chapter 18, is considered by Schumpeter as a typical example of economic analysis: 'the *General Theory* presented an analytical apparatus which the author summed up in chapter 18' (1954, p. 41; see also pp. 1171–84).

On the contrary, 'vision' is for Schumpeter only 'the first perception or impression of the phenomena to be investigated' which helps to 'single out the set of phenomena we wish to investigate, and acquire intuitively a preliminary notion of how they hang together' (*ibid.*, pp. 570 and 562). Today the term is used in the broader sense, borrowed by Kuhn, of a 'scientific paradigm' or in the analogous sense, borrowed by Lakatos, of a 'research programme'.

as an analytical model is severed from its context it loses most of its meaning, whereas the pre-analytic vision often exerts no clear and direct influence on analytic models. The heuristic model provides the necessary bridge between the two poles, which gives a general meaning to the specific analytical models and clarifies how each of them is affected by the vision.

The conceptual cleavage between vision and analytical models is reflected by a disciplinary cleavage between the 'history of economic thought' and the 'history of economic analysis'. This dual gap should be bridged. The heuristic model is meant to play precisely this role.

The main purpose of this book is a comparison and appraisal of Keynes's and Lucas's heuristic models. My task is made less difficult because both of them are lucidly aware of the crucial role played by what I have called the 'heuristic model' and put a lot of effort into making it clear and explicit. The *General Theory* aims expressly to construct a new 'heuristic model' to set against that of the classical economists. Lucas in turn feels the need to make explicit the heuristic model that underlies the analytical models of the new classical economists (see Lucas and Sargent, eds., 1981, 'Introduction', and Lucas, 1987).

1.5   The structure of the book

This work is divided into two parts. In the first part (chapters 2–7) I will discuss a few crucial concepts involved in the recent debate on the foundations of macroeconomics and on the appraisal of alternative research programmes. In the second part (chapters 8–14) I will reconstruct and compare the heuristic models of Keynes and Lucas. Readers can thus choose between two possible itineraries. The first part can be seen as a methodological premise for the appraisal of the two alternative paradigms analysed in the second part; the second part can be seen as an emblematic application of the concepts discussed in the first. Both readings make sense. The first part, though not an end in itself, is more general than the second; in fact it could also be applied to research programmes different from those of Lucas and Keynes. However, the choice of these two authors is not at all arbitrary for the aims of the book, since in many respects they represent the two extreme conceptions among those hitherto developed in macroeconomics. It is thus particularly important to compare and appraise them, and this presupposes the detailed methodological investigation carried out in the first seven chapters.

The detailed structure of the book is as follows. The first part contains a fairly summary discussion of the basic methodological issues that haunt macroeconomics: equilibrium and disequilibrium (chapter 2), dynamic and structural instability (chapters 3 and 4), uncertainty and predictability (chapter 5), rationality and expectations (chapter 6). In these chapters I shall classify the main meanings of these concepts and explain the choice of an apparatus of definitions which I consider particularly useful for my purposes. In the seventh chapter I will try to throw some light on the concepts of causality employed by Keynes and Lucas in building their own heuristic models.

The second part contains a description and discussion of Lucas's heuristic model (chapter 9), reconstructed in the context of his general research programme (chapter 8). Then I will briefly consider the evolution of the new classical macroeconomics and of Lucas's own point of view with regard to the equilibrium business-cycle model (chapter 10). In chapter 11 I will describe the heuristic model put forward by Keynes in the *General Theory*, without giving a systematic account of his own research programme as it is too well known to require it. I will examine in chapter 12 the distinction between a 'monetary economy' and a 'barter economy' comparing it with the Schumpeterian dichotomy between 'circular flow' and 'development' in order to clarify the deepest foundations of Keynesian thought. In chapter 13 I will discuss the crucial features of Keynes's heuristic model in comparison with those of Lucas's heuristic model.

Chapters 8 and 11 may be skipped by a hurried reader possessing a good background in macroeconomics, but they may offer a few basic concepts for readers who need to refresh their memories. In addition these chapters make explicit my own interpretation of both Keynes and Lucas.

In the final chapter (chapter 14) I will sum up the main conclusions of the study. Keynes remains, after Lucas, a fundamental source of inspiration for macroeconomics, not particularly for his 'vision' of the capitalist system, nor for his strictly analytical contributions, but for his conception of macroeconomics as an autonomous and non-demonstrative discipline and for the methodological implications of his heuristic model.

Methodological foundations of macroeconomics

Equilibrium, disequilibrium and economic theory

A real economy is always in disequilibrium. (Hicks, 1982, p. 32)

2.1   Introduction

Concepts of equilibrium and disequilibrium have long been involved in controversies over alternative macroeconomic theories. The debate on these issues has been rendered largely sterile because of confusion between the different meanings of these terms, which are often not even explicitly defined. In the present discussion, for instance, we may observe that what Keynes calls under-employment equilibrium is interpreted as disequilibrium by Lucas, whereas if we adopt the Keynesian meaning of equilibrium Lucas's 'equilibrium business cycle' necessarily implies the introduction of a dynamic mechanism operating in disequilibrium (see chapters 8, 9 and 13). As this example shows, there can be no serious and constructive debate among different trends in economic theory until the different meanings of the concept of equilibrium are defined clearly and precisely and the reciprocal relations are understood in sufficient depth.

We will try to introduce some order into this question by distinguishing three basic concepts of equilibrium: the syntactic (or logical) concept, briefly discussed in section 2.2, the dynamic concept analysed in section 2.3, and the family of specific semantic concepts considered in section 2.4. In section 2.5 I will briefly survey a few basic reasons underlying the importance of equilibrium analysis. Then, in section 2.6 I shall discuss the relativity of the distinction between equilibrium and disequilibrium. Although this distinction is theory-dependent and model-dependent we cannot renounce the analysis of both equilibrium and disequilibrium states without impoverishing and distorting the semantic implications of the model. A pure-equilibrium model raises awkward paradoxes which will be briefly mentioned in section 2.7. Conclusions follow in section 2.8. In the first appendix (appendix 2A) I will sketch a semantic interpretation of the solution procedure of dynamic functional equations in order to clarify the relationship between the syntactic and the semantic implications of equilibrium and disequilibrium. In the second appendix (appendix 2B) a brief discussion of Nash equilibrium, a specialized concept very popular today with macroeconomists, will confirm the necessity of a thorough dynamic foundation of the equilibrium concepts utilized in macroeconomics.

2.2   The syntactic concept of equilibrium

The solution of an equation or system of equations is often defined as an 'equilibrium'. Examples abound in the literature.[1] But this definition is unacceptable because it cannot provide a criterion by which to distinguish between equilibrium and disequilibrium. For example, in a dynamic functional equation, disequilibrium also must be interpreted as a solution (see appendix 2A).

From the strictly syntactic point of view, the solution of a system of equations is simply that set of values which makes the equations of the system logically compatible. From this purely formal point of view the distinction between equilibrium and disequilibrium has no content. In fact any set of values which does not satisfy the system of equations – i.e. which does not correspond to a solution of the system – implies a logical contradiction and cannot be accepted as an object of scientific analysis. Thus both equilibrium and disequilibrium must be considered, within a formal system, as possible solutions of the system.

Hence whenever the solution of a system of equations is interpreted as an 'equilibrium' we must assume the intervention of a criterion which is not syntactic but semantic in nature. Usually the argument involves an explicit or implicit dynamic model.[2] A typical case is Walras's approach: the parable of a *tâtonnement* process converging towards equilibrium serves, among other purposes, to introduce a dynamic context that justifies the use of the term equilibrium to indicate a solution of the model.

2.3   The dynamic concept of equilibrium

According to the dynamic concept, a system is in equilibrium whenever it is not characterized by an *endogenous* dynamic process (i.e. which would persist even if the system were to be isolated from the environment).

---

[1] A few examples are offered by Lucas who defines an equilibrium as a solution of a system of stochastic difference or differential equations (see e.g. 1981, p. 178, n. 14) or as a Nash solution of an economic game (Lucas, 1987).
[2] Recently Hahn (1984) and Fisher (1983) have convincingly insisted on the crucial importance of this traditional requirement.

The concept of equilibrium in its dynamic sense may be explored through an apt semantic interpretation of the procedure for solving a basic dynamic equation (see, for example, Gandolfo, 1983). For the sake of simplicity let us consider a first-order linear finite difference equation (i.e. one characterized by a maximum delay of one period). As is well known, the general solution is obtained by summing a particular solution with the general solution of the homogeneous equation. The particular solution is found immediately, if the known terms are constant, by assuming that the unknown function is stationary. Whenever the known term is a function of time the mathematical textbooks suggest 'trying', as a solution, a function of time qualitatively similar to that characterizing the known term. The general solution of the homogeneous equation is then obtained by excluding the known term (i.e. the possible exogenous dynamic influence) and studying the dynamic behaviour of the deviation from equilibrium, or disequilibrium.

The rationale of this solution procedure is easy to understand when it is considered from the semantic point of view. The particular solution represents the equilibrium path, in that by definition it represents the behaviour of the system when one excludes the endogenous dynamics. The equilibrium is either stationary (i.e. constant through time), or mobile (i.e. a function of time) according as the influence of the environment on the system is constant or a function of time. In the latter case the dynamic behaviour of the system depends strictly, even in its functional qualitative characteristics, on the dynamic impulse exerted by the environment on the system. This is not surprising as a system in equilibrium is by definition passive, and thus cannot react to an external impulse: in other words its dynamic behaviour depends exclusively on exogenous influences.

On the other hand the general solution of the homogeneous equation is obtained by completely excluding the known term, i.e. the influence of the environment on the system. This makes it possible to analyse the endogenous dynamics of the deviation from equilibrium and thus the system's properties of stability.

The general solution, then, expresses the dynamic behaviour of the system as the sum of the exogenous dynamic behaviour in equilibrium relative to external coordinates (particular solution), and the endogenous dynamic behaviour in disequilibrium relative to the equilibrium value (general solution of the homogeneous equation).

This semantic interpretation of the solution procedure of a dynamic functional equation has a broad validity. It applies first of all to a first-order differential equation, which can be obtained from a first-order finite-difference equation by means of a simple passage to the limit which does not alter the basic formal and semantic properties of the solution procedure. It is also applicable, whether time is considered a discrete variable or a continuous one, to an equation of higher order. In fact, as is well known, a dynamic functional equation of the nth order can be reduced to a system of n first-order equations. Moreover the introduction of coefficients which are functions of time makes it more difficult to find a solution but does not alter the basic formal properties of the system. A few problems arise, on the other hand, from non-linear dynamic equations – but generally only in the sense that in this case the endogenous dynamics and the exogenous dynamics are no longer separable in additive form.

This dynamic interpretation suggests some guidelines regarding the use of the concepts of equilibrium and disequilibrium. These guidelines can be further specified according to the theoretical context and the particular application of the analysis, but they cannot be violated without creating serious internal inconsistencies and obscurities. One important consequence is that a necessary and sufficient condition for a dynamic system to be said to be in disequilibrium is that the system should exhibit an endogenous dynamic behaviour. Thus if we are able to detect an endogenous dynamic behaviour in a system it cannot be legitimately said, from the dynamic point of view, that the system is in equilibrium. These assertions should appear obvious, yet each of them has been – and as we shall see (in particular in chapters 8, 9, and 10) still is – a source of confusion and misunderstanding.

2.4   Semantic concepts of equilibrium

The dynamic concept of equilibrium is the least common denominator of various concepts of equilibrium specified from the semantic point of view, in relation to the dynamic forces which characterize a certain system according to a particular theory. Thus, for example, rational mechanics defines equilibrium as a state in which the total 'virtual work' within a system adds up to zero; if the system is not perfectly balanced in this sense, then according to this theory the virtual work expresses the virtual endogenous dynamics of the system. Similarly, according to the semantic concept typical of the Walrasian theory of general economic equilibrium, equilibrium is defined as a state in which excess supply and demand are absent, these being the only endogenous dynamic forces considered in the economic system.

By way of example I shall now examine the semantic concepts of equilibrium which characterize the theories of Keynes and Lucas. Keynes's concept is mainly of the dynamic type: under-employment equilibria are properly called equilibria because Keynes's theory assumes that the only endogenous force which can directly modify employment is effective demand. The 'equilibrium level of employment' is consistently defined by

Keynes as 'the level at which there is no inducement to employers as a whole either to expand or to contract employment' (GT, p. 27). Keynes's concept of equilibrium is thus methodologically sound; the results of his analysis may be criticized for possible theoretical defects, but not for the inadequacy of that concept. Yet strangely enough this sort of criticism is extremely widespread. One source of it is Patinkin, who has maintained several times that Keynes's concept of under-employment equilibrium assuming flexible money wages is a contradiction in terms, since the usual concept of equilibrium implies that 'nothing changes in the system' (1965, p. 643).

Even if we assume that money wages are flexible and that there is unemployment, that does not necessarily imply a change in the state variables characterizing the labour market, i.e. real wages and employment. In fact, as Keynes suggests, prices might vary in the same direction and to the same degree as money wages, while leaving real wages unchanged. More generally, however, Keynes's dynamic concept of equilibrium, which can very well be called the 'usual' concept of equilibrium, does not imply that 'nothing changes in the system', or that the equilibrium must be stationary. There may be dynamic processes which – as in the preceding example – involve variables different from state variables, whose influence on the latter adds up to zero through reciprocal compensation. Moreover, equilibrium may be mobile because of exogenous variables, as in the case of equilibrium growth models.[3] Nevertheless Patinkin's argument has been repeated many times, and particularly insisted upon by Lucas and other new classical economists. In a deterministic model, like those of Keynes and the classical economists during the thirties, they consider the concept of equilibrium suggested by Patinkin to be the only one possible. In their opinion the use of this concept of equilibrium was what caused the traditional incompatibility, which became evident during the Great Crisis, between classical theory and economic cycles. Hence they introduced stochastic models which they believed could overcome the impasse.

Lucas's concept of equilibrium is based on two requisites:

(a)   it must emerge as an optimal decision on the part of economic agents acting in their individual interest;
(b)   there must be no excesses of supply or demand.

---

[3] This is recognized also by Sargent (1979, p. 3):

> A model is said to be in static *equilibrium* at a particular moment if the endogenous variables assume values that assure that [the] equations [of the model] are all satisfied. Notice that it is not an implication of this definition of equilibrium that the values of the endogenous variables are unchanging through time. On the contrary, since the values of the exogenous variables will in general be changing at some nonzero rates per unit of time, the endogenous variables will also be changing over time.

If both these requisites are satisfied the two possible sources of endo-genous dynamics typical of general-equilibrium models are ruled out. The concept is applied to stochastic processes, which allow a further type of exogenous dynamics induced by random shocks; this is compatible with a given 'equilibrium' conceived as a stationary stochastic process. The use of dynamic functional equations of the stochastic type may accentuate the degree of analogy between the results of the model and reality, as Lucas and Sargent have often stressed. However, this modifies some semantic details of the concept of equilibrium, but it does not substantially affect the dynamic concept of equilibrium.

2.5 The epistemic reasons for equilibrium

The concept of equilibrium performs a number of extremely valuable functions for scientific analysis in general and for economic analysis in particular. It is dangerous if uncritically used, however, as it can lead to erroneous conclusions.

The following are some of its most useful functions:

(a)   It serves as a point of reference for the dynamics of a system. The endogenous dynamic behaviour of a system is studied in relation to coordinates centred on its equilibrium value. Exogenous dynamic behaviour is studied as the dynamic behaviour of the equilibrium configuration, in relation to coordinates which are also considered to be in equilibrium with respect to the observer. This is not surprising: the degree of permanence or temporal invariance of an equilibrium value is by definition greater than that of any other value the system may assume, since in disequilibrium exogenous forces for change are added to the endogenous ones;[4]

(b)   it serves as a criterion by which the dynamic behaviour of a system can be divided into two components: one endogenous in relation to the equilibrium position, and the other exogenous, determining the dynamic behaviour of the equilibrium value itself. In the case of linear systems, in particular, the concept of equilibrium allows a clear additive separation between the two components. Breaking down a complex problem into a number of simpler problems is a well known useful problem-solving strategy;

(c)   the hypothesis of equilibrium permits considerable simplifications in the functional structure of a system. In particular:

---

[4] More in general we may say that an equilibrium may be a precious conceptual reference for the analysis of an economic system. In this sense its role may be even 'negative' as underlined by Hahn (1984, p. 65): 'Debreu and others have made a significant contribution to the understanding of Keynesian economics just by describing so precisely what would have to be the case if there were to be no Keynesian problems.'

(i)   a feedback is represented in equilibrium by a single relation (for example the interaction between income and expenditure may be represented by a single relation, the multiplier);

(ii)   certain variables become equal in equilibrium (for example supply and demand, income and expenditure, etc.), thus reducing the number of unknowns;

(iii) certain terms become zero (for example derivatives when the equilibrium represents a maximum or minimum value);

(iv)   the equilibrium often maximizes or minimizes a certain function, which makes it an important reference point for analysis, particularly for the explanation and prediction of rational economic action.[5]

For these and other reasons, by comparing the equilibrium configuration of a system with the 'dynamic' configuration that permits the analysis of both equilibrium and disequilibrium, one can easily see that the former is a good deal simpler, which greatly facilitates the analysis.[6] It should never be forgotten, however, that the equilibrium configuration takes in much less information than the 'dynamic' representation. Any conclusion drawn from the subset of information which characterizes the equilibrium configuration may be gravely misleading unless the real system is guaranteed to be and remain in equilibrium.

All the properties mentioned above, which give the equilibrium concept much of its methodological appeal, are indissolubly linked with the dynamic concept. This is not necessarily true for the last property listed, i.e. the property of optimality. But a non-dynamic definition of equilibrium laying stress on the last property would conflict with the other properties, which are no less important methodologically. Hence one may legitimately conclude that in general a methodologically correct equilibrium concept must be compatible with the dynamic meaning.

Finally, we should note that if we wish to avoid an undue reification of equilibrium, the syntactic concept of equilibrium should not be confused with the semantic concepts, including the dynamic one, which is the least common denominator of the different semantic concepts.

---

[5] This does not imply that an equilibrium is always Pareto optimal or the most desirable state. As Machlup clearly stated long ago (1963, p. 59): 'Equilibrium as used in positive economic analysis – as distinguished from welfare economics – should not be taken as a value judgment, nor as a reference to a "desired state of affairs". Equilibrium is not a Good Thing, and disequilibrium is not a Bad Thing.'

[6] This explains why in the history of science, not only in economics, an equilibrium theory has very often preceded a fully fledged dynamic theory. This is as true for mechanics as for the theory of value (see e.g. Schumpeter, 1954).

From the semantic point of view equilibrium is a particular case of dynamic behaviour, but from the logical point of view any form of dynamic behaviour, even outside the equilibrium, must be reduced to equilibrium structures in order to be intelligible. This has to do with the need for coordination of the operative structures of a rational individual, which are completely independent of the type of dynamics represented by the formal model.[7]

Thus one can understand the temptation to reify equilibrium, in other words to project onto reality the equilibrium characteristics of our logical and formal structures. The reification of equilibrium has characterized several currents of philosophical thought (in particular the rationalist notions criticized by Voltaire in *Candide*), and it has also influenced scientific thought in various disciplines including economics. Keynes has often criticized this form of 'rationalism', which he saw as part of the classical mode of thought. Even today this attitude is quite widespread among economists. We shall see that the new classical economists, in particular, are not alien to this form of reification.[8] It can be avoided only by maintaining a full awareness of the possibility of disequilibrium and of its impact on the set of opportunities a rational agent faces.

2.6 Relativity of the distinction between equilibrium and disequilibrium

The definition of disequilibrium is as tricky as that of equilibrium. This is not surprising since a disequilibrium is nothing but a position which does not coincide with a given equilibrium. However, in this case the syntactic point of view obviously will not do. A value different from the solution (whether single or multiple) would involve a logical contradiction and therefore could not represent a real position.

An acceptable definition of disequilibrium must then be semantic. This is not yet a significant step forward, as there exist as many disequilibrium concepts as semantic equilibrium concepts. However we can avoid going into a discussion of semantic concepts of disequilibrium by observing that here again we should consider the dynamic concept of disequilibrium as ranking hierarchically above the single semantic concepts. We will thus refer to it throughout this book whenever it is not otherwise specified.

Even though we have chosen a dynamic point of view, the distinction between equilibrium and disequilibrium is still not without ambiguities, because it is not only theory-dependent but also model-dependent.

[7] This point has been clarified by the school of Piaget (see e.g. Piaget, 1967).
[8] This argument has been developed by Buiter (1980). Sargent (1984, p. 409) argues that this criticism applies to vector autoregression (VAR) econometrics rather than to rational-expectations econometrics. On this and related topics see chapters 8, 9 and 10.

For the sake of simplicity let us suppose we have a certain formal system in which there is a unique equilibrium. Its value is sensitive to any variation in the quantitative and qualitative characteristics of the endogenous and exogenous variables which define the system. A change in any of these characteristics, even in a single detail, will lead to a change in the equilibrium. In this case, what was an equilibrium in the old system becomes a disequilibrium *in the new system*. It follows that the distinction between equilibrium and disequilibrium is relative to the model used to define the economic system, and hence to the assumptions on which it is based.

These points are certainly obvious.[9] But there is one particular case of the foregoing argument, very important for economic theory, which has been even recently a source of considerable confusion. I am referring to the distinction between 'periods' of different 'length' which often enters economic analysis. In all these cases we find a plurality of models 'nested' one within the other, in the sense that one goes from the innermost one to the one just outside it by assuming that a certain constant becomes a variable. For example in Keynes's distinction between the short and the long period (influenced by Marshall's more complex and articulated distinction), while capital stock is assumed to be constant in the short period it can vary in the long period.

Clearly a short-period equilibrium generally turns out to be a disequilibrium from the long-period point of view. Confusion and misunderstanding arise unless one precisely establishes which type of 'period' one is referring to. For example the so-called theorists of disequilibrium (Benassy, Malinvaud, etc.) use the term 'disequilibrium' for what other economists prefer to call 'temporary equilibrium' or 'non-Walrasian equilibrium'. Both groups are right from different points of view: they are speaking of a temporary equilibrium which must be interpreted as a disequilibrium from a longer-period perspective.

We must avoid falling into linguistic traps. If we place ourselves in a syntactic framework, then we must adopt a different terminology. Dynamic behaviour in disequilibrium has to be reformulated through a hierarchy of concepts of equilibrium in the double sense that:

(a)   the dynamic behaviour of the lower-order equilibrium (e.g. that of the short period) depends on its divergence from the higher-order equilibrium (e.g. long-period equilibrium);

(b)   the dynamic behaviour of the lower-order equilibrium is therefore unavoidably influenced by that of the higher-order equilibrium, whereas the reverse is not necessarily true.

[9] One author who long ago insisted on the relativity of the distinction between equilibrium and disequilibrium is Machlup, 1963, pp. 57–8, 65–72.

The possibility of reformulating a succession of disequilibrium states as a succession of equilibrium states should not suggest the idea that disequilibrium analysis is just 'a more complex equilibrium analysis'. This point of view has been recently expressed by Lucas (1981) and other new classical economists (see Klamer, 1984). If it is so, the argument goes, there is no point in abandoning a pure-equilibrium analysis, such as the one advocated by new classical economists, which is qualitatively similar but simpler. This argument is misleading. The equivalence may be apparent from a strict syntactic point of view, but from the semantical point of view it does not hold. As conditions (a) and (b) above suggest, the equivalence is complete only if we postulate a precise network of dynamic relationships between different orders of equilibrium. In addition, by using a pure-equilibrium analysis we would completely lose sight of the distinction between endogenous and exogenous dynamics. We would thus interpret the succession of equilibria as shifted by forces exogenous to the system (as it always is by definition when we have a moving equilibrium), while in reality it could not be the case. This would affect our judgment as to whether it is desirable to change the structure of the system or not. First, since we have an equilibrium dynamics we are biased towards believing that it expresses an optimal response of the system to external shocks.[10] Second, if something undesirable is detected in the dynamic behaviour of the system we are biased towards blaming exogenous factors (e.g. policy rules). A pure-equilibrium method may thus be dangerously misleading.

2.7   Paradoxes of a pure-equilibrium method

In the history of thought, intelligibility has often been linked with an exclusive focus on equilibrium. According to a tradition in western thought going back to Greek philosophy, the essence of phenomena is defined by invariant equilibrium structures (*logoi*) and reason (*logos*) is seen as their faithful reflexion. Thus anything that could not be reduced to such equilibrium structures was considered as a non-intelligible appearance. In the extreme versions, time and even any kind of movement was considered as mere illusion (as in the well known paradoxes of Zeno).

A similar point of view has re-emerged on many occasions in the history of philosophy. In particular, the so-called 'rationalists' of the seventeenth

---

[10] This presupposes that an equilibrium is considered an optimum, which is not always true. However, the fans of pure-equilibrium methods often indulge in this identification. This is why, for example, the equilibrium business cycle (of both the monetary and the real varieties) is typically considered as an optimal response to exogenous shocks (see chapter 10).

and eighteenth centuries (Descartes, Spinoza, Leibniz) worked out a new version of this concept of rationality.[11]

This point of view has also influenced modern sciences. An extreme example in physics can be seen in the theory of general relativity, where time and dynamics are reduced to equilibrium topological structures.[12] However, the natural sciences in recent decades have emancipated themselves, to a considerable extent, from this too-strict umbilical link between rationality and equilibrium, focussing on disequilibrium phenomena, irreversible processes, phase transitions, etc. (see Prigogine and Stengers, 1984, for an extensive survey of these new developments).

By contrast, this link has become progressively tighter in mainstream macroeconomics. An extreme case is that of Lucas, who has repeated on many occasions that disequilibrium is non-intelligible, and has advocated a pure-equilibrium method. This point of view has to be firmly rejected. A method based on pure equilibrium is intrinsically one-sided, as is clearly shown by a host of embarrassing paradoxes.[13] I will here briefly recall three well known instances.

Arrow noticed long ago (1958) that the standard definition of a competitive equilibrium is self-contradictory because the assumption of cleared markets requires a prompt adjustment of prices to the equilibrium level, whereas the assumption that all the agents are price-takers, implied by perfect competition, leaves no one entitled to change prices and thus to adjust them to the equilibrium levels. In order to understand perfect competition we have to get out of equilibrium and look at how agents react to a disequilibrium situation. Only in this way can perfect competition become fully intelligible, in the sense that we can understand how a perfect-competition equilibrium may be established and can persist.

A second example, closely connected to the first one, is the paradox pointed out by Grossman and Stiglitz (1980). They noticed that the hypothesis of efficient markets is contradictory if it is formulated in the usual way as a pure-equilibrium hypothesis. If markets are efficient, the prices of assets fully reflect available information. But if that were the case no agent would have any incentive to collect and process information[14] and

---

[11] See an excellent brief account of the rationalists' thought in Cottingham, 1988.

[12] For an interesting discussion of these aspects of relativity theory see Piaget and Garcia, 1971.

[13] I use the word paradox in the same meaning as that specified by Machlup (1963, p. 269): 'A paradox is a seemingly self-contradictory statement, or just any unexplained or surprising contradiction, sometimes merely an apparent contradiction which disappears upon closer inspection or reflection, sometimes a statement or "phenomenon that exhibits some conflict with preconceived notions of what is reasonable or possible".'

[14] Grossman and Stiglitz (1976 and 1980) stress that this incentive comes from the possibility of obtaining extra profits in the course of the arbitraging process.

we could not understand how prices would be made to reflect market fundamentals. This second paradox may be seen as an implication of Arrow's paradox. If agents are defined in a perfect-competition equilibrium as information-takers, who is left to collect and process information?

A third related paradox is that pointed out by Sims (1982, 1987). If the rational-expectations hypothesis implies that agents perfectly forecast the systematic part of the future,[15] then we cannot modify it through policy interventions. This would demonstrate the impossibility of economic policy whenever we assume a rational-expectations equilibrium.

These and other paradoxes of a pure-equilibrium approach are not logical paradoxes but semantic paradoxes, since they express not a logical contradiction but a semantic contradiction. Generally speaking, as these paradoxes show, there are semantic implications of equilibrium which would remain unintelligible unless we interpret this equilibrium as a limiting state of a dynamic process.[16] In the Arrow paradox it is pointed out that a pure-equilibrium account of perfect competition would leave unexplained how agents adjust prices to their equilibrium value, which is so central an issue in any semantic conception of perfect competition. Similarly, in the Grossman–Stiglitz paradox it is pointed out that a pure-equilibrium account of perfect financial markets would leave unexplained how it occurs that prices convey full information on market fundamentals. Finally, Sims's paradox points out that a rational-expectations equilibrium in its strong interpretation is not suitable for studying the effects of policy interventions.[17]

These paradoxes suggest that equilibrium is not fully intelligible unless it is interpreted within a dynamic framework. Therefore we must study the dynamic behaviour of a system not only in equilibrium but also in disequilibrium. Moreover, as is well known but too often forgotten, only the analysis of the dynamic behaviour in disequilibrium can provide the necessary foundation for equilibrium analysis (in particular for comparative statics; see sections 3.2 and 3.3). This is the only way to make an equilibrium fully intelligible. New classical economists have asserted that

---

[15] This is true only of the strong substantialist interpretation of the rational-expectations hypothesis which excludes systematic mistakes *ex post* in the indefinite future (see chapter 6).

[16] Another important example has been clearly illustrated by Hahn (1984, p. 4): 'imposing the axiom that the economy is at every instant in competitive equilibrium simply removes the actual operation of the invisible hand from the analysis. By postulating that all perceived Pareto-improving moves are instantly carried out all problems of co-ordination between agents are ruled out. Economic theory thus narrowly constructed makes many important discussions impossible.'

[17] Sims's own interpretation is different. The contradiction between rational-expectations equilibrium and Lucas's definition of policy change is solved by suggesting a definition of policy change different from that of Lucas. In chapter 10 I will argue that the solution of the paradox suggested by Sims is unacceptable.

macroeconomics must have an equilibrium foundation. Whether this is true or not,[18] we need a dynamic foundation of macroeconomics.

2.8   Conclusions

Recently the emphasis of macroeconomics has progressively shifted towards an exclusive analysis of equilibrium positions, and has increasingly neglected disequilibrium dynamics. Notwithstanding this fact (or, rather, because of it), the meaning of equilibrium and the methodological presuppositions and implications of equilibrium analysis are not sufficiently spelled out.

I have tried to show that a syntactic definition, though increasingly popular in recent literature (in particular among new classical economists), is not acceptable as by itself it cannot discriminate between equilibrium and disequilibrium. We must therefore resort to a semantic definition. The multiplying family of semantic definitions have in common an underlying dynamic definition of equilibrium (and disequilibrium), which should be taken as common ground in the economic debate. Then it is possible to clarify what are the requirements for a meaningful equilibrium analysis.

The above general considerations enable us to clarify and compare the ideas of equilibrium held by Keynes and Lucas. Keynes's conception of equilibrium substantially corresponds to the standard dynamic notion, and thus, contrary to the views of authors like Patinkin and Lucas, poses no particular problems. But Lucas's conception, insofar as it is compatible with the dynamic meaning, is nothing but a particular semantic meaning implied by his theoretical assumptions; it does not apply to other theoretical assumptions, in particular those of Keynes's theory. On the other hand Lucas's concept of equilibrium inevitably comes into conflict with the standard dynamic concept. This raises legitimate doubts as to its self-alleged superiority over alternative conceptions.

These are not only matters of definition, for equilibrium is a powerful but possibly misleading simplifying assumption.

Appendix 2A Semantic interpretation of the solution procedure of dynamic functional equations

In this appendix I aim to clarify the assertions argued in the text from a more precisely analytical point of view. To do this I shall examine a system characterized

---

[18] This will be discussed later on in chapters 8, 9 and 10.

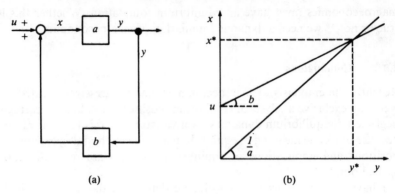

(a) (b)

Figure 1 Static feedback

by a feedback which is influenced by the environment through an input variable. This system, despite its elementary character, will help to clarify some of the matters discussed in the text. I shall represent this system in different languages. While they are equivalent from the formal point of view, and hence it is possible to translate from one to the other of these languages, they have different heuristic functions. The languages I shall use are:

(a) linear algebra (in its analytic representation, and also in its geometric representation where this is allowed by the dimensions of the algebraic space), which serves as a link with modern mathematics;

(b) the algebra of block diagrams, which is much inferior to linear algebra for purposes of manipulation and calculation but which is more intuitively intelligible.

The use of both these mutually translatable languages provides a valuable link between syntactic and semantic aspects of the dynamics of economic systems.

Let us assume that x and y are variables that characterize the state of the system. They constitute the two poles of a feedback, i.e. of a pair of functional relations which are not inversely related:[19]

$$y = ax$$
$$x = by + u \qquad a \neq 1/b, \, a > 0, \, b > 0, \, u > 0 \qquad \qquad (2A.1)$$

This elementary system of equations can easily be represented in the language of block diagrams (see figure 1). The input variable u represents the influence exerted by the environment on the system. Within the block is indicated the transformation which, given the value of the input variable of the block, enables one to obtain the value of the output variable. The small circle represents the 'summation node' which calculates the algebraic sum of the input variables with the specified sign, and the

---

[19] If the two relations were inversely related the system would be singular and would be indeterminate, or without solutions.

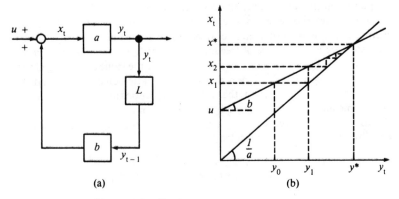

Figure 2   Dynamic feedback

dot represents a branching point after which the same variable is represented by different branches of the circuit.

Generally in a system of simultaneous linear equations, any set of values different from those that 'solve' the system implies a contradiction. This is intuitively obvious if we look at figure 1(b). Assuming that the first function of (2A.1) can be inverted, we can obtain the value of x from both the first and the second equation. But the values are different, except when they correspond to the point of intersection of the two functions, which represents precisely the 'solution' of the system. The two functions cannot be 'true' at the same time except for the solution values.

Thus in statics the solution value is the only admissible value for each state variable, because it is the only one which does not violate the principle of non-contradiction. If we define the set of solution values as equilibrium, any other value, which could be called a disequilibrium, would be unintelligible.[20] Things change radically, however, when we go from statics to dynamics.

The simplest way of making the system (2A.1) dynamic is to introduce a lag into one of the two functions. We obtain, for example, the following system:

$$y_t = ax_t$$
$$x_t = by_{t-1} + u \qquad a \neq 1/b, a > 0, b > 0, u > 0 \tag{2A.2}$$

The new system can be represented in the language of block diagrams by introducing a new block with a lag operator L whose function is precisely to back-date the time index (see figure 2(a)).

It is easy to see that in this case the divergence between the two functions does not imply any logical contradiction, because the values of the same variable obtained from the two equations refer to different dates (see figure 2(b)). A situation like this simply implies the existence of an endogenous process, and hence implies a

---

[20] This is a possible source of the Lucasian idea of non-intelligibility of disequilibrium (see chapters 8 and 9).

disequilibrium in the dynamic sense suggested in the text. Introducing the lag, however, makes the system indeterminate at each instant. The order of the lag determines the number of degrees of freedom (in our example the lag is of the first order so there is one degree of freedom). It is possible to eliminate the degree of freedom and make the system determinate by fixing the value of the lagged variable (or of the n lagged variables if the order is nth). The latter, on the other hand, may be considered as determinate in another system of equations identical to the first except for the time index, which is lagged by one period for all the variables.

Thus we obtain a succession of systems of simultaneous equations from the initial period to the period under consideration:

$$y_0 \rightarrow \begin{cases} y_1 = ax_1 \\ x_1 = by_0 + u \end{cases} \rightarrow \begin{cases} y_2 = ax_2 \\ x_2 = by_1 + u \end{cases} \cdots \rightarrow \begin{cases} y_t = ax_t \\ x_t = by_{t-1} + u \end{cases} \tag{2A.3}$$

Each of the systems of simultaneous equations of (2A.3) is in itself indeterminate, but the whole succession of simultaneous systems can be rendered determinate simply by fixing the value y_0, i.e. the value of the unknown function for the initial period. Each of these systems thus has a solution which cannot correctly be defined as an 'equilibrium' since each period is characterized by an endogenous dynamic process. Indeed we may say that in general the solution, from this point of view, represents a disequilibrium value, unless the initial conditions place the system in equilibrium from the first instant on, and there are no later disturbances to shift the system from the equilibrium path.

This can be further clarified by referring to the theory of dynamic functional equations (see for example Gandolfo, 1983). The succession (2A.3) can be expressed in reduced form by a finite-difference equation (linear, first-order, and with constant coefficients):

$$y_t - aby_{t-1} = au \tag{2A.4}$$

As is well known, the general solution of a linear dynamic functional equation is given by the sum of the particular solution and the general solution of the homogeneous form. The particular solution, which from the semantic point of view can be interpreted as an equilibrium, is found immediately in all cases, such as ours, where the known terms (exogenous or 'input' variables) are constant. It is assumed that the particular solution (equilibrium) is stationary, and this, by equalizing the values of the unknown function with different time indices, allows us immediately to obtain the solution desired. In our case:

$$y^* = au/(1 - ab) \tag{2A.5}$$

If the known term is a function of time, the mathematical textbooks suggest that one should 'try' as a solution a function with the same qualitative characteristics as the known term. This is no surprise in the light of the semantic interpretation suggested in section 2.3: the dynamic behaviour of a system in equilibrium depends exclusively on the exogenous dynamic impulse.

The general solution of the homogeneous form is easily found by getting rid of the known terms (exogenous or input variables), that is to say the influence exerted by the environment on the system. The dynamic behaviour described by the general solution of the homogeneous form thus is purely endogenous and refers to the deviation from equilibrium ($y'_t = y_t - y^*$). The general solution of the homogeneous form is easily found through the iterative method. In fact from (2A.4) we obtain:

$$y'_1 = aby'_0$$
$$y'_2 = aby'_1 = (ab)^2 y'_0$$

. . .

. . .

. . .

$$y'_t = (ab)^t y'_0 \qquad (2A.6)$$

The general solution of the homogeneous form makes it possible to study the system's properties of stability. It is easy to see, in the case we are looking at, that the system is stable if $|ab| < 1$, unstable if $|ab| > 1$, and neutral if $|ab| = 1$ (the trajectory in disequilibrium is 'oscillatory'[21] if $ab < 0$, and 'monotonic' if $ab > 0$).

The general solution of our functional dynamic equation is thus given by the sum of the particular solution and the general solution of the homogeneous form:

$$y^*_t = au/(1 - ab) + (ab)^t y'_0 \qquad (2A.7)$$

The semantic interpretation of (2A.7) is clear. The dynamic behaviour of a system like the one described by equation (2A.2) and by figure 2 is given by the sum of the equilibrium path relative to external coordinates and the disequilibrium path described with respect to coordinates centred on the equilibrium value.

Appendix 2B The concept of Nash equilibrium: a case study

The concept of 'Nash equilibrium' is a particularly interesting case study because it is becoming increasingly popular in macroeconomics and is considered by some authors as the paradigmatic concept of economic equilibrium.[22]

According to an intuitive definition, a Nash equilibrium for a game is a strategy profile such that each player's strategy choice is an optimal response to the strategy choices of other players (see e.g. Binmore, 1986, p. 15).

The prevailing interpretation of Nash equilibrium is in syntactic terms. A Nash equilibrium is considered as the only position of the game in which all the actions of the players are mutually *consistent*[23] given the assumption that all the decisions are

---

[21] In this case it would be more correct to speak of 'improper oscillations', reserving the term 'oscillation' itself for those of the sinusoidal type which can appear only for second-order or higher-order equations (see Gandolfo, 1983, p. 18).

[22] This is the case of Lucas, 1987. See comments in chapter 9.

[23] This does not imply that the players' beliefs about the world are to be consistent: the players may agree to disagree (see Aumann, 1976 and Binmore and Dasgupta, 1987, p. 2).

rational. The syntactic nature of the concept is also revealed by the fact that the numerous refinements of the Nash equilibrium are often called 'solution concepts'.

Notwithstanding its increasing popularity, the concept of Nash equilibrium has been increasingly criticized in recent years. In particular, the concept of rationality that underlies a Nash equilibrium has been found very narrow. Rationality, as understood in game theory, requires that each agent will *perforce* select an equilibrium strategy when choosing independently and privately (see Binmore and Dasgupta, 1987, p. 8). Nash equilibrium rationality is thus consistent with substantive rationality but it completely neglects procedural rationality,[24] not to speak of broader meanings of rationality (see chapter 6).[25] Moreover, in the mainstream tradition of game theory only the existence of a Nash equilibrium has been traditionally explored, while the complex problems of its stability have been almost completely neglected.

The existence of a Nash equilibrium for a wide variety of games has been proved under weak assumptions. Nash himself was able to prove long ago (1950 and 1951) that all finite games have at least one Nash equilibrium in mixed strategies. The emphasis of the analysts has thus been almost completely concentrated on the attempt to generalize the existence proofs and – even more – on the attempt to establish a unique Nash equilibrium, or at least reduce the number of possible Nash equilibria. It turned out in fact that in many cases the solution of a problem (model) in terms of Nash equilibria is undetermined. In order to solve or at least attenuate this problem, a process of refinement of Nash equilibrium started from the very beginning. This gave birth to a proliferating family of equilibrium concepts. Selten (1975) suggests subgame perfect equilibria and trembling-hand perfect equilibria; Myerson (1978) speaks of proper equilibria; Kreps and Wilson (1982) define sequential equilibria; Banks and Sobel (1985) introduce 'divine equilibria', etc.

Very little work has been done, however, with regard to the stability of Nash equilibria. What is worse, recent results are not very encouraging. It has been proven, for example, that for almost all finite games with discrete or continuous time-generalized gradient processes, mixed-strategy Nash equilibria are unstable (Stahl, 1988). Unfortunately most authors agree that unstable Nash equilibria are of no use for economic analysis (Binmore and Dasgupta, 1987, p. 6). In addition, even if an equilibrating process exists and is carried out in the minds of the players, as in the theory of rational agents, or in real time, as in evolutionary game theory, it

---

[24] There are a few isolated exceptions such as the tracing procedure of Harsanyi and Selten (Harsanyi, 1975) and the rationalizing algorithm of Bernheim (1984) and Pearce (1984). See Binmore, 1986, p. 3, n. 5.

[25] Sometimes rationality considerations can sensibly be invoked in defence of choices different from equilibrium in game-like situations, but only by postulating an underlying concealed game (usually a repeated game or a super-game) which the agents are 'really playing' (Binmore and Dasgupta, 1987, p. 8). This statement proves that in game theory only equilibria are actually analysed and rationality is ultimately of a substantialist type. However, it also opens a window on a fascinating, though almost unexplored, world. Since any disequilibrium may be interpreted as equilibrium in the frame of a hierarchy of nested equilibria, game theory could aim to accommodate the analysis of disequilibria and of the implications of procedural rationality. Unfortunately this attempt implies a degree of complexity which is beyond the current technical capabilities of model-builders.

still does not follow that the current version of game theory, founded on Nash equilibria, is an appropriate tool, if the underlying environment is changing too rapidly for things to settle down (see chapters 5, 6 and 9).

The lively debate on the legitimacy of the concept of Nash equilibrium confirms that it is necessary to switch from an interpretation of economic equilibria in syntactic terms to one in dynamic terms.

3

Dynamic instability and economic models

> Positions of unstable equilibrium, even if they exist, are transient, non-persistent states, and hence on the crudest probability calculation would be observed less frequently than stable states. How many times has the reader seen an egg standing upon its end? (Samuelson, 1947, p. 5)

> [Filippo Brunelleschi] suggested to the other masters, both the foreigners and the Florentines, that whoever could make an egg stand on end on a flat piece of marble should build the cupola, since this would show how intelligent each man was. So an egg was procured and the artists in turn tried to make it stand on end; but they were all unsuccessful. Then Filippo was asked to do so, and taking the egg graciously he cracked its bottom on the marble and made it stay upright. (Vasari, 1568, p. 146)

3.1   Introduction

There is a long-standing conviction that a model which describes a dynamically[1] unstable equilibrium cannot be used to describe, explain or forecast economic reality. The motivation for this is well expressed by Samuelson's famous comment reported in the first epigraph above.

Similar assertions were repeated in even cruder versions by Samuelson in other parts of the *Foundations* (and elsewhere). He contended that unstable equilibria are not only less likely to be observed than stable ones,[2] but that they are 'infinitely improbable' in the real world. It is precisely in this

---

[1] In what follows we have to keep in mind the distinction between *dynamic* stability and *structural* stability. Roughly speaking, dynamic stability refers to the convergence of a process towards equilibrium and structural stability refers to the persistence of qualitative behaviour. Structural stability will be discussed in the next chapter while dynamic stability will be analysed in this chapter.

To keep the argument as general as possible, in this chapter and in the rest of the book I will not distinguish among different concepts of dynamic stability (asymptotic, orbital, global, local, etc.). In appendix 3A (this chapter) a very general concept of dynamic instability will be introduced as a common reference for this book.

[2] This is true only under a strict *ceteris paribus* condition. An example would be a comparison among equilibria within the same dynamic system.

30

'strong' version that 'Samuelson's dogma' became accepted. Fisher reports the following statement expressed by an 'extremely prominent economist': 'The study of stability of general equilibrium is unimportant, first, because it is obvious that the economy is stable and second, because if it isn't stable we are all wasting our time' (1983, p. 4).

Unfortunately this opinion is very popular among economists. Disequilibrium and instability are often treated as embarrassing taboos to be mentioned as seldom as possible. This attitude turns out to be a sort of ostrich policy encouraging a dangerous evasion of very serious problems.

In section 3.2 I want to remind the reader that a necessary prerequisite of comparative statics is a thorough analysis of the stability properties of the relevant equilibria. I will then argue in section 3.3 that the same is basically true also for the comparisons between different stationary stochastic processes. Although these comparisons are at the root of the policy evaluation exercises advocated by the new classical economists, this requirement is systematically neglected.[3] I will then argue in section 3.4 that, contrary to some misinterpreted casual observations and influential received wisdom, it is not obvious that market equilibria in actual economies are stable. There is a sort of observational equivalence between market stability and market instability constrained by objective bounds (ceilings and floors in the behaviour of economic variables) and/or policy interventions, which makes the interpretation of empirical evidence much more difficult than is generally assumed. Unfortunately the two hypotheses, though observationally equivalent, are not at all equivalent from the point of view of economic policy. Conclusions will follow in section 3.5.

In the first appendix (3A) I will briefly set out the concept of dynamic stability which will be used later in the book. In the second appendix (3B) I will summarize a few elementary concepts of ergodic theory which can offer a good deal of help for the much-needed, but almost non-existent, study of the 'dynamic stability' of (stationary) stochastic processes.

3.2 The dynamic behaviour of an economic system in disequilibrium

We have seen in the preceding chapter that there are good reasons to pay particular attention to the equilibrium positions of an economic system. But this does not imply that its dynamic behaviour in disequilibrium can be disregarded.[4]

---

[3] One of the rare exceptions is Sargent (1984) who recognizes the necessity of postulating the ergodicity of the compared stationary processes (see section 3.3 and appendix 3B). However, the ergodicity of the relevant processes cannot be simply postulated in empirical applications: an explicit proof should be provided and this, to the best of my knowledge, is never done.

[4] In this section I will draw heavily on the first part of the excellent book by Fisher (1983).

First of all, in many cases the analysis of disequilibrium dynamics is indispensable in order to legitimize the use of equilibrium configurations. This is true in particular if we are interested in exercises of comparative statics. As Samuelson (1947) showed long ago, comparative statics makes no sense unless we assume that the equilibrium positions we intend to compare are dynamically stable. If the equilibria were not stable, the dynamic behaviour in disequilibrium could no longer be considered as transitory, and hence would have to become the main object of the analysis and in particular of any comparisons used in economic policy choices. Even if the equilibrium were stable, comparative statics would have little meaning if the convergence towards equilibrium, after a change in one or more parameters, were not fast enough to justify the assumption that the system would be sufficiently near equilibrium before there was another change in the parameters.

Stability and rapidity of convergence, however, are necessary but not sufficient conditions for a correct use of comparative statics. Further conditions are required to exclude the following circumstances:

(a)   *path dependence*: in general, the equilibrium towards which the system converges depends not only on the initial conditions but also on the path of adjustment. Disequilibrium dynamics often modifies the structure of the parameters (for example agents' endowment of productive resources), and hence it modifies the characteristics of the set of possible equilibria;

(b)   *indeterminacy*: in the case of a plurality of equilibria, even in the absence of the above effects, only the analysis of dynamic behaviour in disequilibrium makes it possible to see towards what equilibrium the system is converging. Unfortunately the existence of a plurality of equilibria is not the exception but the rule (see Arrow and Hahn, 1971).

In each of these cases, comparisons between different systems should be based on a method of comparative dynamics in which the dynamic behaviour occurring in disequilibrium is not excluded from the analysis. As yet no satisfactory methods of this type have been fully developed, but we cannot meanwhile just assume that the two complicating factors mentioned above are absent. We must provide a convincing argument that in the particular case under examination such effects either do not exist or have a negligible impact for the specific purposes of the analysis. As we shall see later (chapters 8 and 9), Lucas and most other new classical economists seem generally satisfied to assume that such complicating factors are absent. In addition, since they consider disequilibrium as unintelligible (Lucas, 1981) they do not even seek for a method capable of assessing their importance. On the contrary Keynes prefers to maintain a continual awareness of these problems even if he is not in a position to solve them by analytic methods.[5] This is considered necessary for working out qualitative indications of a probabilistic type regarding the behaviour of the system, and also for avoiding errors of judgment into which we would otherwise inevitably fall.

A full awareness of the importance of disequilibrium positions and of dynamic behaviour in disequilibrium must be attributed to economic agents themselves. Since a disequilibrium position generates profitable opportunities for arbitrage, there is no reason to deny that rational economic agents are capable of discovering and exploiting such opportunities in their personal interest. Under these hypotheses, however, there is no *a priori* guarantee of convergence to a Walrasian equilibrium. The economy may converge towards a quantity-constrained equilibrium, such as Keynes's under-employment equilibrium.

Recently it has been rigorously shown that on such a hypothesis the dynamic stability of a Walrasian equilibrium is assured only if the number and magnitude of favourable surprises remain below a certain threshold.[6] In this view, the stability of general equilibrium depends above all on unforeseeable favourable objective factors, especially technological innovations.[7] The validity of Schumpeter's intuitions (1911, 1939) may thus be vindicated and rigorously argued. A swarm of unforeseen innovations of the kind described by the great Austrian economist could hardly fail to destroy the stability of the circular flow. However, it should be underlined that instability depends on the agents' perception of the existence of favourable surprises. If this perception varies discontinuously according to conventional criteria, as Keynes has suggested, the stability of the equilibrium cannot be taken for granted even in the absence of sizeable objective favourable surprises.

The hypothesis of perfect foresight, typical of the traditional formulation of general equilibrium, as well as the hypothesis of rational expectations,[8]

---

[5] It may be observed in passing that before the *General Theory* Keynes's attention was concentrated on disequilibrium behaviour and its implications (including path-dependence or hysteresis), while in the *General Theory* his attention was essentially shifted to the second problem (indeterminacy connected with the existence of a continuum of under-employment equilibria).

[6] This may be considered as the most general condition of dynamic stability of a Walrasian economic equilibrium. This result has recently been demonstrated by Fisher (1983) who has extended and generalized the so-called 'Hahn process' (see Hahn and Negishi, 1962).

[7] The same effect may be provoked by other types of objective surprises: unexpected variations in taste, availability of raw materials, change in the environment (including the political, institutional and ecological contexts). Stability may further depend on disequilibrium behaviour itself which could alter the set of favourable opportunities.

[8] Strictly speaking this is true only in the substantialist interpretation of the rational-expectations hypothesis (see chapter 6).

typical of new classical macroeconomics, implicitly exclude the possibility that favourable surprises of a systematic nature will be perceived. The problem of instability is thus eliminated by definition within these families of models, but it is not eliminated in reality. The problem is actually only shifted and reappears in the form of a severe limitation in the range of applicability of the model.

3.3   Dynamic instability in a stochastic framework

The conceptual problems which we have underlined in reference to deterministic systems cannot be overcome by just switching to stochastic systems. The language is different, and this has partly concealed the analogies, but the problems are substantially the same as far as the conceptual content is concerned.

As we have seen in section 2.4 a stationary stochastic process is seen by new classical economists as the stochastic analogue of a deterministic equilibrium. In both cases a certain degree of time invariance is postulated, which is not possessed by alternative states or processes.[9] But one cannot share the opinion expressed by a few new classical economists that by using this 'new' concept of equilibrium the shortcomings of the 'old' concept of equilibrium could be overcome. In particular, it is stressed that while the old deterministic concept is static in the sense that it implies that 'nothing changes in the system', the new stochastic concept is dynamic in the sense that it is consistent with a wide variety of dynamic motions within the system (Lucas, 1981). This point of view is unacceptable: first because it is not true that in the old concept nothing changes in the system (see above, section 2.4), and second because in the new concept the systematic part does not change endogenously through time, so it should be taken as the analogue of a stationary equilibrium. The only conceptual difference is that in the stochastic framework the ongoing equilibrium of the systematic part is consistent with a wide variety of possible dynamic behaviours on the part of the realizations of the stochastic process.

In any case a stochastic equilibrium still needs a dynamic foundation just as a deterministic equilibrium does. This involves, first of all, a thorough analysis of its 'dynamic stability' properties. We need to know to what extent a stationary stochastic process will converge to the original probability distribution if perturbed in its systematic part. Knowing the properties of the Gaussian distribution would be of limited practical use if we didn't know, from the central-limit theorems, that under quite general circumstances it is likely to be the limiting distribution of a stochastic

---

[9] In the case of strict stationary processes all the statistics are time-invariant. In the case of wide-sense stationary processes the mean is constant while the autocorrelation depends only on the time interval. See e.g. Papoulis, 1984, or Sargent, 1979.

process. Similarly we need to know the stability properties of a stationary stochastic process in order to assess its robustness and to appraise its implications for economic analysis and policy.

For the purposes of both economic theory and applications we need to know how robust is a stationary stochastic process with regard to perturbations in its structural characteristics. This is true in particular if we want to make comparisons among different stationary stochastic processes. The heuristic model of the new classical economists, as specified by Lucas and Sargent (see chapter 9), is designed precisely for comparing the characteristics of the systematic features of different stochastic processes for purposes of policy evaluation. This sort of exercise might be called 'stochastic comparative statics', as it is closely analogous to a comparison of the features of different stationary equilibria. As in the deterministic counterpart we need to know whether the compared stationary processes have sufficiently similar degrees of robustness. This requires an explicit proof that the disturbed moments of the probability distribution will converge fast enough towards the original stationary values. In addition, if we can discover a stochastic process different from the one we live in, which is better in terms of welfare and no less robust, then before trying a transition through policy intervention we should also study whether the transition is possible in a sufficiently short time and whether the welfare costs of the transition process justify the attempted switch. But this can be done only by very thoroughly studying the dynamic behaviour of a stochastic process 'out of equilibrium'. This requirement is almost always disregarded,[10] although an analysis of the point is not completely beyond existing technical knowledge. Stochastic convergence has been systematically studied in particular by ergodic theory, which has found extensive applications in natural sciences (see appendix 3B). It is curious but revealing that this rapidly developing branch of mathematics has been so rarely applied in economics (*ibid.*). This might be just another sign of the incautious use of equilibrium in economics.

The switch towards a systematic use of stochastic models in macroeconomics is a welcome development, but should never become an excuse for an improper use of the equilibrium concepts or for neglecting to provide a thorough dynamic foundation of their meaning and their robustness.

3.4 Dynamic instability and structural change

It is certainly unlikely that an egg will stand on its end, as Samuelson reminded us in the first epigraph above, but that is why – one may object –

---

[10] One exception is the interesting recent literature on how the agents learn about a rational-expectations equilibrium. See e.g. Bray and Kreps, 1986.

the egg-cup was invented. The fact that the vertical position is unstable but nevertheless desired can explain the introduction of a stabilizing device such as the egg-cup. An alternative strategy, like the one Brunelleschi suggested in the episode reported by Vasari in the second epigraph, is a transformation of the system in order to stabilize it.

To drop the metaphor, a model which describes an unstable system can help to explain the interventions meant to stabilize it. In particular the structural changes which characterize an evolutionary system can often be interpreted as 'mutations' able to preserve or enhance certain desirable characteristics of the system which are jeopardized by its intrinsic instability.

For example, consider a social system characterized by an unstable equilibrium. All those who hold that the *status quo* is desirable will attempt to modify the system with the aim of stabilizing its equilibrium, while its opponents will try to enhance the degree of instability. The result of the conflict often is a change in the system and therefore in its equilibrium configuration. The new equilibrium may then be unstable and generate conflicting dynamics of the type just described, and so on. In an evolutionary process of this kind, a model characterized by an unstable equilibrium would seem more adequate for describing each of its stages as well as explaining and forecasting the dynamic behaviour of the system and its structural changes.

The fallacy of 'Samuelson's dogma' lies in its implicit assumption that the structure of the real system to which the model refers is linear and invariant. But one does not easily come across such a case in economic systems. On the contrary it is increasingly recognized that – generally speaking – economic systems are nonlinear and cannot be safely approximated by linear models (see e.g. Lorenz, 1989). In addition we often meet situations where structural modifications can be interpreted as interventions intended to stabilize unstable equilibrium configurations. For example this is the case with many corrective interventions of economic policy which aim to counteract a rising monetary disequilibrium and to stabilize the system by modifying some of its structural features.[11] On the other hand a disequilibrium which tends to persist may actually stimulate structural interventions designed to stabilize the equilibrium value of one or more key variables. A typical example in economic literature is that of the so-called 'financial innovations' which intervene to increase the quantity of money or its velocity of circulation in situations of persistent excess money demand, thus restoring the equilibrium. In Keynes's words, 'when money is rela-

---

[11] This may be true not only of structural interventions but also of conjunctural ones if, as often happens, they leave structural traces.

tively scarce, some means of increasing the effective quantity of money are found' (GT, p. 273). According to some authors, the development of credit and financial intermediaries can be interpreted on these lines.[12] The balance between money demand and money supply could, in the long run, turn out to be sufficiently stable without implying the dynamic stability of the financial structure in all its stages.

Thus there might be valid justifications for the use of an unstable model to describe, explain and forecast the behaviour of a real system which is nonlinear or is subject to structural changes. The empiricist counter-objection is that economic systems tend not to move very far from the equilibrium position, which is taken to prove that they are largely stable. This objection is not valid, however, since a stable linear system may be observationally equivalent to an unstable nonlinear system or to an unstable linear system controlled by stabilizing structural policy interventions. The first case has been thoroughly analysed by Blatt. In a path-breaking paper (1978) he generated a succession of data through an unstable nonlinear business-cycle model similar to that suggested by Hicks (1950) and was able to prove that the data could be very well fitted by a stable linear model with random shocks utilizing standard econometric techniques. The same results could be obtained if the nonlinearity were induced not by objective ceilings and floors, as in the Hicksian model, but by countercyclical discretionary interventions triggered by a disequilibrium exceeding a certain threshold. A third interesting case would be a sequence of structures which are unstable in themselves but such that the state variables do not tend to diverge, beyond certain limits, from the equilibrium path due to stabilizing structural interventions.

Unfortunately, the equivalence between stability and instability in the above circumstances holds as far as observation by means of standard econometric techniques is concerned, but it does not hold at all for economic analysis. In particular the implications for economic policy are radically different. A stable system can regulate itself, while in an unstable one stabilizing policy interventions are necessary. The problem thus has to be faced through more sophisticated econometric techniques which can discriminate between the different stability hypotheses (Blatt, 1983).

But, how likely should we consider to be the hypothesis that an economic system is dynamically unstable? According to the prevailing opinion, as we have seen, this is 'infinitely' unlikely. On careful examination this assertion implies a few questionable hidden assumptions. First of all the speed of

---

[12] On this subject see Cameron, 1967 and the literature quoted there. According to a famous economic historian the discovery of America itself can be interpreted as an answer to the chronic monetary disequilibrium (deficiency of precious metals) which characterized the second half of the fifteenth century (Vilar, 1971).

divergence from a certain equilibrium can be extremely slow according to a standard relevant for the problem at hand. The physical world is full of interesting instances. The following example is macroscopic in every sense: according to one of the more widely held cosmological theories (the 'big-bang' theory),[13] the universe originated from a great explosion and expanded from then on, progressively diverging from the original critical point. Thus the universe itself could be considered as a system characterized by dynamic instability. Whether this hypothesis is acceptable or not, no one would claim that the unstable behaviour of the universe cannot be observed, since this theory was actually suggested by the accumulation of a series of experimental data (Doppler effect, etc.).[14]

In addition recent studies have ascertained that whenever the complexity of a system increases, so does the probability of its being unstable. This is well known to mathematicians[15] and natural scientists.[16] Since economic systems are very complex, greater attention should be given to the analysis of instability in economics as well.

3.5   Conclusions

The analysis of the dynamic behaviour of a system in disequilibrium is necessary to give a solid foundation to macroeconomics. A researcher should always be aware of its role in determining the outcomes of aggregate economic activity and should attribute this kind of awareness to the agents themselves.

Stability analysis is necessary in order to assess what implications the equilibria considered may have for economic analysis and policy. In particular, for purposes of comparison among equilibria it is wise to stick to the received view that it is necessary to give a proof that the compared equilibria have similar stability properties.

Dynamic instability itself should not be considered as a sort of taboo in economic analysis. It is a possibility which cannot be ruled out in complex systems like modern economies. Dynamic stability and instability may be observationally equivalent whenever we allow for nonlinearities or struc-

---

[13] See e.g. Hawking, 1988.

[14] Unobservable are, paradoxically, the stable subsystems or 'black holes' which capture light rays (*ibid.*).

[15] An important early contribution on this subject was given by May, 1976. For a thorough recent survey on complex dynamics see Lorenz, 1989.

[16] For instance, I. Prigogine remarked that 'the more elements in interaction there are, the higher the degree of the secular equation which determines the actual frequencies of the system. Therefore the probability of having at least a positive root and instability is greater' (Prigogine, 1974, p. viii).

tural changes which might be induced by stabilizing interventions. Unfortunately, these two hypotheses have completely different implications for economic policy, as the first suggests a *laissez-faire* policy while the second suggests the need for stabilizing interventions.

These observations could be considered obvious, but macroeconomists have recently disregarded and even openly challenged them (see chapters 9 and 10). This is in large part due to the switch from a deterministic to a stochastic point of view. I have argued that the traditional view on the role of stability is still valid in the framework of a stochastic point of view. We still need to prove the robustness of the equilibria analysed (stationary stochastic processes) by proving their 'dynamic stability' properties. In addition we cannot avoid a thorough analysis of the 'disequilibrium' behaviour of a stochastic process in order to study the existence and the welfare implications of the transition processes to new policy regimes.

Appendix 3A A general concept of dynamic instability

I need not discuss here the different varieties of dynamic instability concepts suggested so far in economics. I will just recall the basic features of 'strict-set instability', a concept of dynamic instability recently introduced in economic literature. This is a fairly general concept of dynamic instability since it includes as special cases most other concepts of dynamic instability utilized in economics: asymptotic instability, quasi-stability, limit-cycles, etc.

This concept of dynamic stability has been chosen in this book because it is relatively general and because, in my opinion, it is very close to the concept of stability utilized by Keynes in the *General Theory*.

Here I shall only give a definition for autonomous differential equations (see Nishimura, 1982). In intuitive terms one might say that a system of autonomous differential equations has a strictly stable set if all the solutions sooner or later penetrate inside a bounded set and remain there afterwards (see figure 3). Let us examine a system of autonomous differential equations:

$$\dot{x} = f(x) \qquad x(0) = x_0 \qquad f \colon R^n \to R^n \text{ is } C^1 \tag{3A.1}$$

I can thus introduce the following definitions:

(1)   A set in R^n is a bounded set strictly stable of a trajectory $y(t)$ if the set is bounded and a $T \geqslant 0$ exists such that $y(t)$ belongs to the set for $t \geqslant T$.

(2)   The differential equations (3A.1) have a strictly stable set if a strictly stable set exists for all the solutions $x(t)$ of (3A.1).

The concept of strict-set instability was introduced by Yoshizawa (1966) and has been developed by La Salle who has established the sufficient conditions. These are

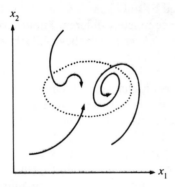

Figure 3   Strict-set stability

reasonable in economics as shown by Nishimura (1982). However, the concept can be considered actually useful only if the strictly stable set is rather 'small' and the velocity of 'penetration' rather high.

Appendix 3B **Ergodic theory and economics**

Ergodic theory studies the 'long-term' average behaviour of systems. By 'long-term' behaviour I mean here the average behaviour of a system as it appears from a large number of successive observations (the time unit may be very short: in statistical mechanics, for example, molecular collisions may occur so often that only 'long-term' averages may be observed).

The basic problems studied by ergodic theory refer to the conditions in which historical time 'doesn't matter'. This of course is meant to simplify the analysis of actual systems by granting their observability and predictability.

The word 'ergodic' is a neologism introduced at the end of last century by the great physicist Boltzmann who formulated what is called the ergodic hypothesis. (The word derives from the Greek for 'energy path'.) The hypothesis amounts to saying that the time average of a stochastic process should coincide with its space average (see below), i.e. that the long-term time average along a single history (or orbit) should equal the average over all possible histories. This allows one, through the observation of a single history, to estimate the statistics of the actual stochastic process and to forecast the average characteristics of possible future histories.

The ergodic hypothesis proved wrong as a general factual hypothesis but stimulated analysis of the conditions under which it is true. The first general statements of these conditions came from Von Neumann and Birkhoff, who in 1931 proved the two basic ergodic theorems. When a system complies with these conditions it is called ergodic. Today much physics applies only to ergodic systems.

40

Dynamic instability and economic models

Samuelson (1968) rightly observed that the same is true also for neoclassical economic theory.

Let X be the state space of a system. The evolution of the system is represented by a transformation $T: X \to X$, where Tx gives the state at time $t+1$ of a system which at time t is in state x. In order to provide a formal analysis of the behaviour of the system one has to specify the mathematical nature of X and T. Three main cases have been analysed by three specialized branches of mathematics:

(i) X is a differentiable manifold and T is a diffeomorphism: the case of differentiable dynamics;

(ii) X is a topological space and T is a homeomorphism: the case of topological dynamics;

(iii) X is a measure space and T is a measure-preserving transformation: the case of ergodic theory.

Needless to say, the three cases raise similar problems. Often they address the same problem from different points of view which may be complementary. Thus it is somewhat surprising that ergodic theory, unlike differentiable dynamics and topological dynamics, has so far not been very much applied in economics (among the few and scattered exceptions are Champernowne (1953), Steindl (1965), Samuelson (1968), Davidson (1982–3) and Sargent (1984)). This is partly due to the fact that economic theory began to be expressed explicitly in probabilistic terms only recently. What is worse, a few streams of thought which have introduced systematic probabilistic modelling in economics have simply assumed, rather than proved and analysed, the ergodicity of their model economies. This is the case in particular of new classical economics and VAR econometrics.

Let (X,β,μ) be a probability space and $T: X \to X$ be a one-to-one onto map such that T and T^{-1} are both measurable: $T^{-1}\beta = T\beta = \beta$. Assume further that $\mu(T^{-1}E) = \mu(E)$ for all $E\epsilon\beta$. A map T satisfying these conditions is called a measure-preserving transformation. The systems (X,β,μ,T) are the fundamental objects studied by ergodic theory.

The orbit $\{T^n x: n\epsilon Z\}$ of a point $x\epsilon X$ represents a single complete history of the system, from the infinite past to the infinite future. We may think of the σ-algebra β as a family of observable events, with the T-invariant measure μ specifying the (time-independent) probability of their occurrence. If a measurable function f: $X \to R$ represents a measurement made on the system, we may think of $f(x)$, $f(Tx)$, $f(T^2 x), \ldots$ as successive observed values of a certain variable y_t. We will now briefly consider the two basic problems of ergodic theory: the problem of stochastic convergence and the problem of recurrence.

A fundamental problem of ergodic theory is whether the long-term time average of a large number of successive observations of the variable $y_t = f(T^k x)$ converges towards a central value $f^*(x)$.

Whenever we have

$$f^*(x) = \lim_{n \to \infty} (1/N) \sum_{k=0}^{N-1} f(T^k x)$$

$f^*(x)$ may be thought of as an equilibrium value of the variable y_t.

A convergence of this sort was proved early on in special cases. Borel proved in 1909 the so-called 'strong law of large numbers', in cases where the fT^k are independent and identically distributed. General convergence theorems, however, were proved only in 1931 by Von Neumann who was able to demonstrate the general convergence in the mean squares sense ('mean ergodic theorem'), and by Birkhoff who was able to demonstrate under what hypotheses convergence existed almost everywhere.

The second basic question considered by ergodic theory is the study of general recurrence properties (or qualitative behaviour) of orbits. In particular, as mentioned before, it is desirable that the time average and the space average coincide. A system (or just the transformation T itself) is called ergodic if the time average of every measurable function coincides almost everywhere with its space average. The study of recurrence properties permits one to establish whether a certain system is ergodic or not. Birkhoff proved that this is true if and only if the orbit of almost every point visits each set of positive measure: this is implied by the property of strong mixing, a very demanding recurrence property.

Ergodic theory would be very useful for studying the robustness of stationary stochastic processes which describe economic equilibria. Let us assume that the stationary stochastic process is characterized by a stationary distribution $f^*(x)$. We should study the characteristics of the set H of perturbations $h_i \epsilon H$ such that $h_i(T^k)$ still converges to the stationary distribution $f^*(x)$, as well as the rapidity of convergence.

In addition, for the sake of comparative statics (of the stochastic variety), if we live in the stochastic process characterized by T_0 and $f_0^*(x)$, preference for an alternative process characterized by T_1 and $f_1^*(x)$ is meaningful only if the compared processes have fairly similar stability properties. In most cases this implies the requirement of ergodicity.

Finally we should prove that there is a possible transformation T' such that $T'T_0$ will assure the convergence of the existing process towards the preferred system T_1. In order to prove that, we have to study whether the system $(X, \beta, \mu, T'T_0)$ is ergodic and converges towards the system (X, β, μ, T_1). This analysis would also permit an accurate study of the transition process and in particular of its welfare implications for purposes of policy evaluation.

4

Structural instability and economic change

No complex system is ever structurally stable. (Prigogine, 1974, p. 246)

4.1 Introduction

The concept of structural stability is quite recent. An explicit and rigorous definition was developed only in the thirties in the language of topology. Since then it has played an increasingly crucial role in the development of qualitative mechanics as a fundamental methodological criterion. More recently, its importance has become increasingly recognized in other disciplines, including economics.

Although the received view in economics has always been that a structurally unstable model is useless for economic analysis and should be rejected, rational-expectations macroeconomics has recently reversed this methodological principle without any convincing attempt to justify such a radical change (see chapter 6). Rational-expectations models characterized by a saddle point seem to be the only ones able to give determined results. They are thus generally adopted although in such models the behaviour of the system is structurally unstable.

The issue of methodological acceptability of rational-expectations models exhibiting saddle-point properties cannot be properly discussed unless the methodological implications of structurally unstable models are properly discussed.

In section 4.2 I first introduce a brief account of the genesis of the concept of structural stability. In section 4.3 I will discuss a few important problems involved in the search for a rigorous definition of structural instability. In section 4.4 my attention will turn to the observability and the plausibility of a system having a certain degree of structural instability. In section 4.5 I will be in a position to discuss some methodological implications of structural instability. Conclusions follow in section 4.6. In the first appendix (4A), I will explore a few simple operational concepts of structural instability. In the second appendix (4B) I will analyse in more detail the philosophical points summarized in section 4.2.

4.2   The concept of structural stability: three views

We may consider the topological concept of structural stability as the rigorous version of a philosophical concept worked out at the end of the last century. This philosophical concept has a history of its own whose roots may be traced back to Greek thought. Both the topological concept and the terminology are quite recent, but this should not obscure the deep affinity with preceding ideas. (Similarly, a rigorous notion of equilibrium has been worked out only by modern mechanics, but the concept may be used to interpret older ideas which we consider sufficiently similar, although somewhat less precise.)

If we look at the history of philosophy and science from this broad perspective, we may distinguish three general points of view on the epistemological role of structural stability (or of related, though vaguer, concepts): the 'classical' view worked out by Greek thinkers in the classical period, which prevailed until the 'scientific revolution' of the late Renaissance; the 'modern' view introduced by philosophers like Francis Bacon and scientists like Galileo Galilei, which was rendered precise and explicit only towards the end of last century; and the heterodox point of view developed by Thom since the early sixties. This may be defined as 'neoclassical' because the concept of structural stability is considered central for scientific research, although for reasons partially different from those of the modern view and admittedly reminiscent of the classical view. (Needless to say, this classification is very abstract and schematic. Each of these basic views has been expressed in many variants which would appear quite different when considered at a less abstract level.)

The classical view is the result of a clash, acutely felt by many Greek thinkers of the classical period, between the ubiquitous experience of change, disequilibrium and instability, and a conception of rationality (*logos*) as harmony, equilibrium and stability. This basic contradiction received an epoch-making solution founded on two far-reaching ideas. First of all, both reality and knowledge were articulated in two hierarchical levels in such a way that the superficial one was characterized by change and the deep one by invariance or stability. Second, the two levels of reality were coordinated through the concepts of equilibrium and stability. Structurally stable forms were thus considered as the essences of things (*logoi*) assuring the basic unity, harmony and stability of the universe (*cosmos*). The structure of knowledge mirrored the hierarchical structure of reality. The superficial level of reality, or appearance, was considered as the domain of perception and opinion, neither of which can aspire to the universal truth.

44

Only in reference to the deep level of essences, or *logoi*, can reason establish a universal consensus among rational men through demonstrative arguments.

The Greek 'solution' to the problem of change had a great impact on the history of western thought, connecting the concept of reason in a crucial way with the concepts of equilibrium and stability. It is still very difficult to emancipate our minds from these umbilical connections.

What has been called the 'modern view' did not really break with the deepest roots of classical tradition. However, two far-reaching changes have taken place since the very beginning. As far as science is concerned, the problem of change was reduced to the problem of description or forecast of quantitative change only, conceived as reducible to mere locomotion (Galileo). Scientific explanation was reduced to the description of efficient (i.e. exogenous) causes. Structural change and formal causality were no longer considered as truly scientific problems, because they lacked a clear empirical reference (Francis Bacon), so that structural stability was implicitly postulated in any scientific investigation. In this view, the only possible objects of science were the empirical regularities to be explained by universal laws, both of which were considered as structurally stable. The striking practical success of Newtonian mechanics, built on these principles, convinced most scientists and philosophers of the unquestionable objectivity of the postulated structural stability of the universe.

Structural stability once more became a *problem*, and thus an object of explicit reflection, as soon as it was discovered that the stability of nature cannot be easily demonstrated. This happened only in the second half of the last century when it was shown by Poincaré that all the existing proofs of the stability of the solar system were invalid and that the problem could not be solved by quantitative methods. This gave birth to the modern qualitative mechanics founded on topological methods. A few years later, Hadamard (1898) argued that the problem of the stability of the solar system is undecidable even with qualitative methods, because of its intrinsic structural instability. Although he did not use the phrase, he can be credited with being the first to give a rigorous definition of the philosophical concept of structural stability in its modern version, as clearly distinguished from that of dynamic stability. His paper has been extensively discussed by many philosophers of science. They made it clear that, in the modern view of science, structural stability is a necessary condition for the observability and predictability of scientific phenomena (Duhem, 1906) and for the applicability of scientific determinism (Popper, 1982b).

A rigorous concept of structural stability was worked out only in the thirties,[1] utilizing the powerful language of topology (see section 4B.3). A

---

[1] The path-breaking contribution was that of Andronov and Pontryagin, 1937.

proper application to economics is even more recent.[2] We may consider the topological concept of structural stability (which I will call – from now on – 's-stability' to distinguish it from the philosophical concepts) as the rigorous definition of the modern view as developed by qualitative dynamics.

Recently Thom has put the topological concept of structural stability at the centre of his epistemological and methodological contributions. His reflections are, in a sense, the outgrowth of the modern concept as developed since the birth of qualitative mechanics. Yet he breaks with the empiricism and instrumentalism of this tradition and goes back, in many respects, to the Greeks and the 'classical' point of view. Structural stability is seen as a necessary condition not for the observability and predictability of scientific phenomena, but rather for their intelligibility. He criticizes the instrumentalism of the modern view both in general, because prediction should not be considered as the main task of science (Thom, 1980, pp. 9 and 84–8) and, more specifically, in reference to structural stability. He rightly emphasizes that the usual concept of structural stability does not guarantee predictability (Thom, 1975, p. 26), and moreover that analytical continuation, the scientific operation which is at the root of any successful prediction, is not necessarily a structurally stable operation (ibid., p. 29). Thom accepts the 'modern' opinion that a certain degree of structural stability is a necessary condition for observability, but this is judged as strictly true only for 'experimental sciences' and deterministic processes (Thom, 1980, pp. 4–5). In his opinion, the main reason for praising structural stability is intelligibility, which is basically conceived as an isomorphism between a stable structure of reality and a stable conceptual structure. The analogy with the classical conception of reason (logos) is evident and fully acknowledged by Thom himself. Structural change is brought back to the centre of scientific attention, but only when its behaviour may be considered as structurally stable. It is the structural stability of the meta-level, describing the law of appearance of structural change, which assures its scientific intelligibility.

4.3 Structural stability: relativity and degree

Structural stability is a complex and problematic concept still in rapid evolution in the very 'exact sciences' for which it was originally invented. Various alternative definitions have been recently proposed, the careful study of which is still in progress (see section 4B.3). Here I shall not attempt

---

[2] The first application of which I am aware may be found in a monograph published by Morishima in Japanese in 1950 but translated into English only in 1980. The concept began to spread in economics only in the second half of the seventies.

a thorough study of these definitions either in their technical details or in their reciprocal connections, but only to understand the common logic underlying them.

The basic idea is clearly expressed by the famous mathematician S. Smale: 'this kind of stability is a property of a dynamic system itself (not of a state or orbit) and asserts that nearby dynamic systems have the same structure. The "same structure" can be defined in several interesting ways, but the basic idea is that two dynamic systems have the "same structure" if they have the same gross behaviour or the same qualitative behaviour' (1980, p. 97).

The importance of the concept appears clearly as soon as we consider a system which is subject to 'perturbations', like most real systems. If the perturbed system is equivalent to the original one, it can be considered 'robust' ('coarse') or 'structurally stable' in the sense that it maintains some basic structural characteristics in spite of possible external shocks.

Structural stability is certainly a desirable property for many purposes. This is true in particular in engineering, because there the main purpose is often to construct or regulate a mechanism in order to obtain a desired performance. The more structurally stable the mechanism is the more reliable it will be. For example it is important that a jumbo-jet should be able to fly even if one engine breaks down. On the other hand it cannot be said that the aims of a scientist are always of this kind. A structurally unstable model may play a valuable role for scientific research in particular instances. In order to clarify this assertion the concept of structural stability must be more closely examined.

The existing definitions of structural instability depend crucially on the significance attributed to the concepts of equivalence and perturbation. These are two vague concepts whose mathematical specification is itself arbitrary.[3]

Equivalence between systems implies that their behaviour has some common property which may vary according to different definitions. But they must also differ in some aspects, otherwise they would be identical. Where to draw a line between common and specific characteristics is an intrinsically arbitrary question.

The concept of perturbation raises analogous problems. Firstly we should draw attention to the basic difference between perturbations that are 'arbitrarily small' and those that are just 'small'. A system may be s-stable for arbitrarily small perturbations and s-unstable for small perturbations beyond a certain threshold. This statement is so obvious as to appear superfluous. But there is a problem in the literature. The current

---

[3] On this topic see Cugno and Montrucchio, 1982, section 2.

topological definitions consider arbitrarily small perturbations only, while the philosophical concept (of which topological concepts may be considered a formalization) is generally stated (even by topologists) in reference to small perturbations. Moreover, small but finite perturbations are very important in applications. We should thus provide a thorough formalization of structural stability in the case of small but finite perturbations.[4]

The second very important distinction is between perturbations that do not alter the 'order' of the system (the dimension of phase-space) and those which may have this embarrassing effect. Standard definitions implicitly exclude this second type of perturbation (only Andronov, Vitt and Khaikin, 1937, explicitly bring out the existence and the scope of this hidden assumption). This makes life much simpler for supporters of structural stability by highly increasing its 'likelihood'.[5] Unfortunately the excluded case may be of the utmost scientific interest. This is the case, for example, of the so-called 'parasitic' parameters which play an important role in many fields of physics and engineering (e.g. electric circuit theory and design). The widespread existence of this sort of disturbance greatly undermines the plausibility of structural stability analysis.[6]

The preceding considerations should by now have made it clear that the question of whether or not a system is structurally unstable cannot be answered with a simple yes or no. The answer depends, not only on the definition of structural stability, but also on the fact that it is more suitable to talk about a degree of structural instability.[7] The degree of structural instability may be conceived as a function of different parameters relative to equivalence and perturbation concepts.[8]

[4] Of course 'small' is not a satisfactory concept for mathematicians because it is relative to some unspecified standard. But we could pragmatically overcome the difficulty, for example by defining as small a perturbation whose order of magnitude is less than that of the change in dynamic behaviour triggered by the perturbation.

[5] In fact, as we have seen, the 'likelihood' of structural stability decreases as the order of the system increases. In particular, even the genericity of structural stability in the compact manifold of dimension 2 would be jeopardized by such perturbations.

[6] In the topological analysis of structural stability 'we cannot help being "naive", for, otherwise, we should have to verify that all possible small parasitic parameters, increasing the order of the equation, shall not disturb the stability of a given state. However, we can never carry out this verification exhaustively, since the number of such parasitic parameters in every system is very large' (Andronov, Vitt and Khaikin, 1937, p. xxx).

[7] The concept of 'degree of structural instability' was introduced by Andronov and Leontovich in 1938. The definition offered by these authors is not, however, the only one possible. On the contrary I would be inclined to believe that it is too rigid as regards the first steps of the ladder.

[8] I will not examine here the third crucial element (the topology selected) which, according to Cugno and Montrucchio (1982), characterizes the definitions of structural instability, because a clarification of this point would require a separate work.

A different, though in part symmetrical, approach is that of defining a hierarchy of s-instability degrees. This is the route followed by Andronov, who introduced in 1938 the concept of degree of s-instability which has been developed by the 'Gorky school'. According to this school:

Structurally unstable systems can be divided into 'less structurally unstable' and 'more structurally unstable'. This leads to a classification according to the degrees of structural instability . . . the least structurally unstable systems in the classification are the systems of the first degree of structural instability: under small changes, these systems either go to a structurally unstable system or retain their topological structure . . . A dynamic system of the first degree of structural instability was found to have one and only one structurally unstable singular path, i.e., it has either a multiple equilibrium state, or a multiple limit cycle, or a saddle-to-saddle separatrix. To establish the bifurcations of a system of the first degree of structural instability, it suffices to consider the changes in its topological structure in the neighborhood of its structurally unstable singular path. (Andronov *et al.*, 1967, p. xiii)

This approach puts the problems in the most promising perspective, with regard to both methodology and application. Structural stability, which may be now properly defined in a strong version as zero-degree s-instability, appears as the limiting case of a spectrum.

Systems with a low degree of s-instability have good stability properties, though these are not strong enough for the systems to be classified as s-stable. Here stability and instability lose any emotional connotations. For the sake of application, we only need to know the characteristics and the specific conditions of application of each degree of s-instability.

4.4 Structural instability: plausibility and observability

The principal argument against structural instability is very similar to that against dynamic instability. According to the received view it would be infinitely improbable to observe the existence of unstable structures because they are transient and unobservable. Moreover it can be argued that structural changes are often aimed at preserving certain characteristics of intrinsically unstable structures. The whole course of biological evolution might be interpreted as directed towards increasing the degree of structural stability of living forms. Natural selection has certainly eliminated the more structurally unstable forms of life but not the structural instability of the existing ones.

It is not difficult to find analogous examples in the economic world. When financial instability (or fragility) is mentioned, something analogous to structural instability is implicitly intended: a small perturbation suffices to drastically alter the behaviour of the system by triggering a process of inflation or devaluation, etc. (see chapter 12).

On the other hand, according to some authors, similar phenomena also exist in other natural sciences. For example, according to Prigogine, 'a strict analogy exists between the "invention" of new techniques and the structural instability which generates new ways of functioning of chemical reactions' (Prigogine, 1974).

The eminent Belgian scientist, Nobel-laureate for chemistry in 1977, has in fact demonstrated that a system sufficiently far from thermodynamic equilibrium can violate the second law of thermodynamics, restructuring itself into new forms characterized by a lower degree of entropy. He does not hesitate to generalize these and other similar results of his research, holding that we are led to 'the idea of indefinitely evolutive systems, the idea that by definition no complex system is ever structurally stable' (1974, p. 246). Such a drastic generalization might be considered hasty. However, even the mathematical sciences, 'the paradise of rigour' as Hilbert said, have recently questioned the traditional use of the concept of structural stability. As we will see better in appendix 4B, it has been ascertained that in a complex system structural stability becomes rare and therefore 'improbable', and structural instability becomes frequent and therefore 'probable'. This has induced a profound revision in the concept of structural stability and its methodological significance, accompanied by an attempt to elaborate much more permissive definitions with more attention to the specific characteristics of the research area.

Samuelson many years ago had a very clear glimpse of the problem. He held that

in a physical system there are grand 'conservation' laws of nature which guarantee that the system must fall on the thin line between dampening and anti-dampening, between stability and instability. But there is nothing in the economic world corresponding to these laws, and so it would seem infinitely improbable that the coefficients and structural relations of the system be just such as to lead to zero dampening. (1972, p. 336)

A conservative system characterized by zero dampening is of course s-unstable. However, this reasoning is not convincing, since modern epistemology has established that brute facts of nature, independent of the theoretical framework, do not exist (see Suppe, ed., 1977).

I can thus conclude that there are no *a priori* reasons for regarding a structurally unstable system as either implausible or difficult to observe, particularly in the case of complex systems or of those characterized by structural changes, and particularly in observational sciences. This conclusion seems especially compelling in the case of economics, which is an observational science dealing with very complex systems characterized by important structural changes.

4.5   Structural stability and the methodology of empirical sciences

We are now in a position to discuss the methodological use made of s-stability in the current practice of model-building. As is well known, on the grounds of the 'modern' notion of s-stability (see section 4B.2), structural instability has been almost universally considered a sufficient reason for rejecting a model as useless, if not misleading (among the very few exceptions, see Andronov *et al.*, 1967). An s-unstable model is generally considered hopeless for both descriptive and forecasting purposes. In the light of the preceding conceptual reconstruction, this methodological prescription cannot be taken for granted. It is simplistic and may even be misleading if its rationale is not rightly understood.

We have first of all to clarify what notion and degree of s-instability we are referring to. A model which is s-unstable according to one definition may turn out to be s-stable under another. This already raises strong doubts about the generality of the prescription. For the sake of argument, let us suppose that we have only one possible definition of s-stability (and consequently of s-instability) and only one possible degree for both concepts. The aforementioned methodological prescription would then be acceptable only on the hypothesis that reality is structurally stable. This obvious condition of validity is almost never made explicit. One rare exception is Thom who admits in passing that 'the *a priori* need for structural stability [is only valid] when dealing with a process that is empirically stable', and that 'qualitatively indeterminate phenomena may be described by structurally unstable dynamical systems' (1975, p. 19). Yet he believes that only s-stable systems, processes and structural changes (catastrophes) are really intelligible (see section 4B.4). S-unstable systems, processes, catastrophes may exist but these are considered as a sort of residue which remains outside the scope of human reason. We may only try, in this view, to reduce the area of s-instability, which is the area of our ignorance. This is possible through a series of devices which are able somehow to subsume s-instability under s-stability. The following is a case in point:

The global stability of the universe depends on the law of compensation: when the catastrophes are frequent and close together, each of them, taken individually, will not have a serious effect, and frequently each is so small that even their totality may be unobservable. When this situation persists in time, the observer is justified in neglecting these very small catastrophes and averaging out only the factors accessible to observation. (1975, p. 43)

Notwithstanding this and other devices, how likely may we consider the hypothesis that systems, processes and catastrophes are in general s-stable?

Unfortunately, it is very unlikely whenever the relevant phase space has dimension 3 or more. We know in fact that in this case the set of catastrophe points is likely to be locally dense, which will force us 'to consider the process in the neighborhood of some points as chaotic and turbulent, when the idea of structural stability loses most of its significance' (*ibid.*, p. 18). Moreover, the interaction between two s-stable systems is likely to generate s-instability, because generally the topological product of two structurally stable dynamical systems is not structurally stable (*ibid.*, p. 130). This offers an important key to understanding why the more complex a system is, the more likely it is that its dynamical behaviour will be s-unstable.

Thom recently admitted that the topological notion of structural stability may be considered adequate only for experimental sciences (physics, chemistry and biology) and not for observational sciences: geology, palaeontology, ethnography, history, psychology, social sciences, etc. (Thom, 1980, pp. 4–5). But even in the so-called experimental sciences, even in physics which has always been considered the queen of hard sciences, there are wide and important areas of stubborn inadequacy. The most obvious case is Hamiltonian mechanics, whose models are typically s-unstable, even according to the weakest definition so far worked out for non-Hamiltonian systems.[9]

Notwithstanding all the preceding considerations which leave little hope for the hypothesis that reality is in general s-stable, let us assume for the sake of argument that it is so. Even in this case, s-stability need not always be considered a necessary condition for a useful scientific effort. It depends on the specific aims of the research. In particular, there may be a trade-off between a higher degree of s-stability of the model and a higher degree of satisfaction of other scientific aims. A case in point is the trade-off between s-stability and computability:

Structural stability and computability are, to a certain extent, contradictory demands, because all quantitative and effectively computable models must necessarily appeal to analytic functions [the structural stability of which is problematic] . . . There seems to be a time scale in all natural processes beyond which structural stability and calculability become incompatible. In planetary mechanics this scale is of such an extent that the incompatibility is not evident, whereas in quantum mechanics it is so short that the incompatibility is immediately felt, and today the physicist sacrifices structural stability for computability. (Thom, 1975, p. 29)

---

[9] There have been many recent attempts at working out a much weaker notion of s-stability suitable for Hamiltonian systems, but they soon proved to be far from genericity. (A very clear account of this particular story may be found in AM, pp. 592–5.) We are led to agree that 'an appropriate notion of structural stability for Hamiltonian dynamics must be extremely vague and fuzzy, if not downright statistical. This is a real obstacle to a reasonable philosophy of stability in the Hamiltonian context, and no relief is visible on the horizon' (AM, p. 595).

It is clear from this example that we may wish to sacrifice s-stability to some extent in order to better satisfy other aims of our scientific inquiry such as computability. Something similar we will find in the rational-expectations models (see chapter 6). Other examples may be found. One is particularly emblematic since it relates to the explanation of structural change itself. An important key for understanding structural change in many fields (and first of all in social sciences like economics) consists in seeing it as a stabilization process meant to preserve certain qualities of the existing structure. We already have an abstract theory of stabilization of s-unstable systems which may be very useful in pursuing this line of thought (Petitot, 1979). The application of this theory to the evolution of biological and social structures would offer a wealth of analytical and methodological insights.[10]

We may conclude this critical analysis of the recent debate on s-stability versus s-instability by observing that the widespread claim that only s-stable models are useful in empirical research must be considered unjustified. The received view claims that only s-stable models may assure the observability and predictability of empirical phenomena. However, s-stability is neither a necessary nor a sufficient condition for either observability or predictability. That it is not a *sufficient condition for observability* is clarified by the classical discussion on observability of the behaviour of dynamical systems offered by system theory (see e.g. Marro, 1979). It is not a *necessary condition for observability*, because 'it is an everyday experience that many common phenomena are [structurally] unstable' (Thom, 1975, p. 126), and because many models successfully employed in science, are, as we have seen, s-unstable. It is not a *sufficient condition for predictability* because the topological notion of s-stability cannot rule out the possibility that 'the perturbed system may have a completely different structure from the original system after sufficient time has passed', since 'it is not required that the homeomorphism h commutes with time' (*ibid.*, p. 26). It is not a *necessary condition for predictability* because, for example, to forecast the results of a stabilization process we must first analyse the characteristics of the s-unstable system which undergoes that stabilization process. Finally, we may agree with Thom that a certain degree of s-stability is a necessary

---

[10] For example, we could better understand the deepest reasons for the irreversibility of evolution and historical time:

> The notion of stabilization (partial or total) defines a preordering among singularities. The asymmetry of these relations, somehow expressing the irreversibility of stabilization processes, may appear slightly paradoxical. It depends on the fact that the property of stability is an open one. Thus, whenever through the 'explosion of a critical point' or through the separation of critical values of f, we stabilize f in f' by infinitesimal deformation, we cannot come back from f' to f unless by finite deformations. By infinitesimal deformations we may only, as soon as we reach f', get f' again, because f' is stable. (Petitot, 1979)

condition for intelligibility. But this, generally speaking, implies a certain degree of s-instability.

In conclusion, there is no reason to doubt that in many cases, *ceteris paribus*, we should try to minimize the degree of s-instability of the model, but this methodological rule should never become a dogma. We should always take account of the specific ends of current research and of the characteristics of empirical evidence.

4.6   Conclusions

In this chapter I have tried to clarify the methodological implications of the structural instability of a model.

I have stressed first that structural instability is a matter of degree and that its degree depends on the definition of perturbation and on that of equivalence between perturbed systems. I have then emphasized that structurally stable and structurally unstable models may be observationally equivalent whenever the possibility of structural intervention is considered, but have different implications for the choice of structural stabilization policies. The plausibility of structural stability depends on the degree of complexity of the system. The more complex is the system, the less likely it is that an economic system be structurally stable.

The traditional methodological prescription that a model should be structurally stable is thus acceptable in its crude version only if the reality described by the model is structurally stable. In applied research this requirement cannot simply be assumed; it has to be thoroughly argued. In general the requirement of structural stability depends on the characteristics of the reality to which the model is applied, the particular definition of structural stability adopted, and the aims of research.

As we will see (chapter 6), new classical economists apply structurally unstable models to a reality postulated as structurally stable. This contradiction seems not easily justifiable in the light of the preceding discussion.

Appendix 4A A few operational concepts of structural instability

---

Let us describe an economic system in terms of block diagrams (for the sake of simplicity I will here consider a discrete-time linear system of the kind considered in appendix 2A). Let us define as the 'flow structure' (or 'connective structure') the structure of oriented arrows connecting the variables of the system. It may be rigorously expressed by a 'connective matrix' or by a digraph, i.e. directed graph (see Siljak, 1978). Let us define the set of coefficients written inside the blocks as the set of 'functional coefficients' since they express, in the linear case, the functional relations among the endogenous variables. Let us define as the 'functional structure' of the system the matrix of functional coefficients written in the order specified by the connective structure (we may in principle change one or more functional coefficients without changing the connective structure or vice versa, although often a structural change affects both).

In principle, a change in the functional coefficients and/or in the connective structure of the system affects its dynamic behaviour. This is obvious for functional coefficients, since they appear with a crucial role in both the particular solution and the general solution of the homogeneous form (see appendix 2A). However, not only the value of these coefficients, but also their connective position is important, as may be easily verified by changing their position without changing their value.

A few useful definitions may now be introduced. A system undergoes a *prima facie* structural change whenever its functional structure and/or its connective structure is modified. Let us define as a '*genuine* structural change' a structural change *prima facie* having the effect of modifying the dynamic behaviour of the system (i.e. its equilibrium and disequilibrium properties). This effect does not necessarily occur, because different functional structures may have the same reduced form and thus the same dynamic behaviour. From now on when I speak of structural change I will mean a *genuine* structural change.

A system is structurally unstable when a *small* perturbation is sufficient to induce a *discontinuous* structural change. A small perturbation may be understood as 'arbitrarily small', as in most topological definitions. But this 'strong' definition is too demanding for economics. The main problem of many economic analyses is to know how the economic system will react to perturbations of finite dimensions (e.g. to alternative economic policies). 'Small', in this 'weak' sense, is a relative concept. It is natural for our purposes to specify the meaning of perturbation in relation to the size of the induced discontinuous structural change. This heuristic criterion may be made operational only by specifying what is meant by 'discontinuous' structural change. According to a first, *strong*, definition, a structural change is discontinuous whenever

(a) the equilibrium properties (not only the equilibrium values) are altered: this happens whenever the number or the type of equilibria change;

(b) the disequilibrium properties are altered in their sign (not only in the speed of convergence or divergence to or from an equilibrium point).

As this definition is very demanding, it is convenient to propose a weaker definition whereby a discontinuous change is taken as any quantitative change exceeding a certain preassigned standard, even without any of the qualitative transformations mentioned above.

The two pairs of definitions of small perturbation and discontinuous structural change can be combined to produce three definitions of structural instability which are of interest for economics:

(i) (strong) structural instability, which derives from the joint utilization of the strong concept of perturbation and of the strong concept of discontinuous structural change;

(ii) ϵ-structural instability, which derives from a joint utilization of the weak concept of small perturbation (exceeding a value ϵ) and the strong concept of discontinuous structural change;

(iii)   weak structural instability, when the perturbation is either weak or strong and the structural change weak.

Only the first definition is traditionally associated to structural stability by topological literature. However, the other two meanings may also be useful for economic analysis. Here I shall not develop a formal analysis of these three concepts and their interrelations, but will just consider a very simple example.

Let us take the usual version of the dynamic multiplier. According to the strong version of structural instability, the system would be structurally unstable only for $c = 1$. In that case, an arbitrarily small perturbation impinging on the marginal propensity to consume would alter the qualitative dynamic behaviour of the system in the strong sense. In fact, with c exactly equal to one (and in absence of autonomous expenditure) the system would be in neutral equilibrium (which would be then undetermined); with $c < 1$, the Keynesian case, the system would have one stable equilibrium; with $c > 1$ the system would have one unstable equilibrium (these three cases may be easily visualized with the well known cross diagram).

Let us assume now that $c < 1$, but with a value very close to one (say 0.95). The system would not be structurally unstable according to the first definition, although it would be considered as such in ordinary language in many practical occurrences. As a matter of fact, a very small perturbation (say $\Delta c = +0.06$) would be enough to induce a discontinuous structural change in the strong sense. The system may be thus considered ϵ-structurally unstable for $\epsilon \geqslant 0.05$.

Let us assume again that the marginal propensity to consume has a value very close to one. Any finite perturbation in the marginal propensity to consume, even a very small one, will induce a much larger percentage change in income and expenditure which may be considered as discontinuous in the weak sense of the word. We may legitimately wonder whether we should apply to this kind of behaviour a concept of structural instability (though in a weak version), or some other concept. Yet there are good reasons for emphasizing, with this terminology, a certain kinship with (strong) structural instability. In ordinary language we would call a system exhibiting such behaviour unstable in a sense different from that of dynamic instability. Moreover, this sort of behaviour is typical for parameter values close to those generating strong structural instability.

Appendix 4B **Structural stability and the epistemology of change**

This appendix may be interpreted as a set of notes meant to give the interested reader more information on the historical and philosophical background of the issues discussed in the main text of this chapter. The topological concept of structural stability (or s-stability) can help us to better understand the related epistemological issues, while these will help us to understand the genesis, the meaning and the methodological implications of the topological concept.

4B.1   Equilibrium, stability and change in ancient Greece

One of the main problems that fuelled philosophical and scientific investigation in ancient Greece was the apparent and puzzling contradiction between the all-pervading experience of change and a concept of rationality deeply rooted in a need for invariance. The history of the suggested solutions to this dilemma is very interesting for understanding the genesis of concepts such as equilibrium and stability and their role in the methodology of systems dynamics. Our brief sketch of this history will be confined to four leading figures of the classical period: Heraclitus (576–480 BC), Pythagoras (c. 580–c. 500 BC), Plato (428–347 BC) and Aristotle (384–322 BC), and will be concerned only with the evolution of the epistemology of change, and more specifically with the genesis of a concept of reason, the Greek *logos*, interpretable in modern terms as a structurally stable form.

Heraclitus

The philosophical 'problem of change' is dramatically emphasized by Heraclitus. Before him, the *cosmos* was conceived as a sort of stable 'container' (like a house or a tent) encompassing all existing things. A process of change could happen only inside the 'container' without seriously undermining its basic stability. Heraclitus questioned this traditional paradigm, maintaining that everything changes (*panta rei*) without exception. However, at the same time he shared the common Greek opinion that any knowledge implies a certain degree of stability, and in particular that a truly rational knowledge implies a sort of absolute stability or invariance. The solution to this dilemma suggested in his fragments may be considered as one of the deepest roots of the received epistemology of change.

First of all, he observed that opposite dynamic tendencies may offset each other. The ensuing principle of 'unity of opposites' conceived as 'harmony of contrasting tensions as in a bow or in a lyre' may be considered as very near to the modern concept of equilibrium.

The second suggestion for solving the dilemma of change is found in the idea of a stable law regulating change. This important contribution is in a way adumbrated in his theory of fire which, always changing, does not change: 'every process in the world, and especially fire itself, develops according to a precise law: its measure'. Reality is thus articulated in two levels: the level of empirical phenomena, which is characterized by change, disequilibrium and instability, and a meta-level describing the invariant laws of change which are characterized by equilibrium (*measure*) and stability.

This 'solution' of the problem of change has been, since Heraclitus, almost universally accepted. Most subsequent research has been concerned with the ontological and epistemological nature of the two levels and of their reciprocal relations.

Methodological foundations of macroeconomics

Pythagoras

Heraclitus contemptuously declared that Pythagoras was a 'master charlatan'; this would prove that 'a wide knowledge does not teach one to think right'. However, his basic ideas on the problem of change were seen as consistent with those of Heraclitus by Plato, who was able to produce a sort of powerful synthesis.

The Pythagorean school was at first not directly concerned with change but with the opposition unity/multiplicity. However, the two problems imply each other. Change implies a multiplicity of states characterizing an object which conserves its basic identity, i.e. an invariant unity often called *essence* by Greek thinkers. The essences of all the objects could be then reduced to a common one, conceived as a sort of all-encompassing unity. The ultimate reduction of all phenomena to a basic substance, often called *monas*, has always been a main preoccupation of Greek thinkers. Heraclitus believed that fire was such a substance, but he was unable to clarify how the reduction of all events to fire could be rationally reconstructed. Pythagoras was the first to show a rigorous procedure of reduction of multiplicity to unity.

His procedure of reduction was grounded on two basic concepts: (a) that of *measure* (or proportion) by which a couple (or multiplicity) of numbers could be reduced to an integer; (b) that of *form* by which geometry could be reduced to arithmetic.

A measure was conceived by Pythagoras as an integer number expressing the essence of two or more numbers and, indirectly, of all things. It was conceived as the equilibrium value of a process of measurement. Any procedure of measurement was thus seen as a typical expression of human reason, which is able to discover unity and equilibrium behind multiplicity and change. This belief was greatly corroborated by an extensive experimental study of the mathematical relations implied by music. It was discovered that the harmonic relations among different sounds can be expressed in terms of ratios between natural numbers. Numbers appeared then even to the senses as harmonic unities of a multiplicity.

A geometrical form was conceived by Pythagoras as a structure of equidistant points. Any basic ratio or proportion was interpreted as the 'germ' of a geometrical figure which could be obtained by a sort of steady-growth method (called the *gnomon*). Moreover, the sum of all the points belonging to a geometric figure was considered as a synthetic expression of their 'essence', which gave origin to square numbers, triangular numbers, cubic numbers, etc. (this terminology still survives for powers).

As we have seen, any geometric figure could be reduced through the *gnomon* to a basic ratio which, in turn, could be expressed by an integer number. This two-stage procedure of reduction of forms to natural numbers had a degree of rigour and precision till then unknown, and soon became the paradigm of rationality for all Greek thinkers. Unfortunately the validity of this procedure rests on the assumption that all the numbers involved are rational, otherwise the reduction would be impossible as the process of measurement would never come to an end, i.e. a position of rest or equilibrium. We may now understand why the discovery of irrational numbers profoundly undermined the Pythagorean research programme and produced, at the same time, a dramatic crisis in the development of Greek thought.

Plato

Plato was fascinated by the crystal-clear notion of rationality developed by the Pythagorean school, but at the same time he was very much concerned with the ubiquity of change so vividly expressed by Heraclitus. He wanted to reconcile these two great traditions. His powerful synthesis is founded on two basic ideas: (a) the primacy of geometry; (b) a radical distinction between reality and appearance, and correspondingly between *episteme*, i.e. scientific knowledge or knowledge of reality, and *doxa*, i.e. opinion or knowledge of appearence.

As we have seen, Pythagoras tried to show that geometry was reducible to arithmetic, but he had to face the formidable problem of irrational numbers arising quite naturally in simple geometry. Plato believed that the crisis of irrationals could be overcome by recognizing that the simplest constituents of the universe are the semi-equilateral triangle and the half-square triangle, which incorporate the two basic irrational numbers $\sqrt{2}$ and $\sqrt{3}$ (Popper, 1969, p. 157). In other words, he believed that all the magnitudes could be reduced to the proportion $1:\sqrt{2}:\sqrt{3}$, while, according to Pythagoras, all were ultimately reducible to unity. Rational intelligibility was then conceived as a reduction, at least in principle, to these elementary geometric figures. The Greek concept of reason – *logos* – finds with Plato a powerful assessment as, to use the perceptive words of Thom, 'structurally stable form'. This concept, which was to have a deep influence on the following development of western science and philosophy, arose first of all from Plato's rejection of the Pythagorean primacy of arithmetic in favour of a sort of primacy of geometry. We may now understand why Plato wrote on the door of the Academy that entry was forbidden to anyone ignorant of geometry. In addition, we should remember here that the great geometric synthesis performed by Euclid was originally conceived as a formal expression of the Platonic cosmology.

The second main ingredient of the Platonic synthesis, the sharp distinction between reality and appearance, was not altogether new. It was adumbrated by Heraclitus and Pythagoras and developed by the Eleatic school (Parmenides and Zeno). In their opinion, only 'what is' is, and 'what is' has to be conceived as an invariant unity. Multiplicity and change are thus a mere appearance. We may have true knowledge, i.e. certain and demonstrable knowledge (*episteme*), only of essences or *logoi*, conceived as structurally stable forms. The knowledge of disequilibria or unstable processes is a matter of opinion (*doxa*). The hierarchical model of both reality and knowledge, as well as the belief in their basic correspondence, was to exert an enormous influence on the history of western thought.

Aristotle

Aristotle did not alter the basic Platonic views on the epistemological problem of change (Popper, 1945). A rational understanding of phenomenic change involves, exactly as in Plato, its deduction from a meta-level characterized by stable structures called essences. These are put in a hierarchical order according to the degree of their stability: the highest level is characterized by the essences which are absolutely stable and are called substances. There are, of course, important differences between Aristotle and Plato, but they are ontological rather than epistemological. (The main one is well known: the essences are conceived not as mere 'copies' of ideas, but as immanent in real things.)

We must mention three main features which develop, rather than alter, the fundamental features of Plato's epistemology:

(a)   any change, and in particular structural change, is interpreted as the actualization of dispositions implicit in the essence of things. This idea can already be found in Plato, but is systematically developed by Aristotle;

(b)   four kinds of change are distinguished: local (translation or locomotion), quantitative (increase or diminution), qualitative (alteration) and substantial (generation or corruption). Although Aristotle himself adumbrates the possibility of an ultimate reduction of all kinds of movements to locomotion, the main role in his analysis is played by qualitative and substantial movements, i.e. 'structural' change;

(c)   rational knowledge of causes. There are four kinds of causes: the material cause or *substratum*, the formal cause or *substance*, the final cause or *entelechy*, and finally the *efficient cause*. The material cause is considered as relatively unimportant for explaining change: the substratum (or matter) is seen as a sort of undetermined power or disposition. The crucial concept is that of formal cause, or *logos*, which provides the rational explanation of change. The final cause is typically the end of an action and is practically identified with the actualization of a formal cause. The efficient cause is the only concept of cause that survived in orthodox modern science: it was interpreted, broadly speaking, as any exogenous impulse which originates or modifies the movement of a thing without altering its essence. With Aristotle the classical view of rationality, change and their reciprocal relations (involving a crucial role for structural stability), may be considered to be fully worked out. It was to dominate, mainly in the Aristotelian version, until the scientific revolution of late Renaissance.

4B.2   The 'modern' view of structural stability

The main authors of the 'scientific revolution' of the late Renaissance wholeheartedly believed in what today could be called the structural stability of nature, which has to be discovered through experience and experiment and expressed by invariant and universal mathematical laws. So, for instance, Kepler referred to the 'mathematical harmony' of the universe as its real essence, and Galileo declared that the book of nature is 'written in the language of mathematics'. The concept of structure was considered as metaphysical, and it survived in science only with the meaning of 'mathematical form' of natural laws (e.g. in Francis Bacon). The invariance of natural laws, then, was at first the only meaning of structural stability to survive in the modern view. Though its validity was only postulated, it was apparently confirmed by the spectacular progress of mechanics and by its practical success. In this view, the postulated correspondence between invariant empirical regularities and invariant universal laws, as well as the quantitative character of both, assures the observability and predictability of scientific phenomena and, at the same time, the applicability of scientific determinism.

This point of view began to be seriously questioned, and at the same time to be explicitly related to stability, only in the second half of the last century – as soon as it was realized that notwithstanding all the spectacular success of mechanics, the stability of the solar system had not yet been demonstrated and could not be demonstrated by the traditional (quantitative) methods. In fact Newton was able to prove the stability only of a two-body system; but the difficulty of proving the stability of a n-body system was for a long time believed to be only a technical problem. Moreover all the great scientists who have developed mechanics since the second half of the eighteenth century (e.g. Laplace, Lagrange, Poisson and Dirichlet) claimed to have proved that the solar system is stable. But the validity of their methods, based on series expansions, was doubtful since they did not succeed in demonstrating that the series converged. On the suggestion of Weierstrass, King Oscar of Sweden offered a prize for the solution of this problem. This was given in 1889 to Poincaré, who did not solve the problem but was able to prove that the series expansions for the preceding proofs were divergent. Almost contemporaneously, it was discovered by Bruns (1887) that no quantitative method other than series expansions could resolve the n-body problem. This produced an acute crisis in mechanics which brought the quantitative period to an end.

The new qualitative point of view worked out by Poincaré led to the birth of the rigorous version of the concept of structural stability. We may clearly see its genesis in a famous paper written by the well known French physicist Hadamard (1898).[11]

In this paper a clear distinction is made between the problem of dynamic stability (for the solar system) and the problem of the structural stability of its behaviour. In fact, Hadamard believes that the first problem cannot be solved because of the structural instability of the model describing the dynamics of the solar system. The methodological inference drawn by Hadamard, and fully worked out by Duhem a few years later (1906), was that a structurally unstable model is useless for applied science. This opinion, which was perfectly in line with the *horror instabilitatis* that characterized classical and modern science, entered as a dogma the received view of scientific theories.

The background for better understanding its role is clearly depicted by Abraham and Marsden in their book *Foundations of Mechanics*:

---

[11] He was able to work out a rigorous example which suggested that
  no finite degree of precision of the initial conditions will allow us to predict whether
  or not a planetary system (of many bodies) will be stable in Laplace's sense. This is
  due to the fact that mathematically exact initial states which determine orbits, and
  others which determine geodesics going to infinity, cannot, as we have seen, be
  disentangled by any physical measurements. (Popper, 1982b, p. 40; Hadamard's
  paper is extensively summarized and discussed also in Duhem, 1906.)

At the turn of this century a simple description of physical theory evolved, especially among continental physicists – Duhem, Poincaré, Mach, Einstein, Hadamard, Hilbert – which may still be quite close to the views of many mathematical physicists. The description, most clearly enunciated by Duhem (1906), consisted of an experimental domain, a mathematical model, and a conventional interpretation. The model, being a mathematical system, embodies the logic, or axiomatization, of the theory. The interpretation is an agreement connecting the parameters and therefore the conclusions of the model and the observables in the domain.

Traditionally, the philosopher-scientists judge the usefulness of a theory by the criterion of adequacy, that is, the verifiability of the predictions, or the quality of the agreement between the interpreted conclusions of the model and the data of the experimental domain. (AM, p. xix)

Duhem made it clear that *adequacy* requires the structural stability of the model, when the model is slightly perturbed. Otherwise, however precise the instruments quantifying the conditions of our experience, we might always deduce from determined experimental conditions an infinite range of different practical results (Duhem, 1906, p. 154). An unstable model would thus be useless for describing empirical evidence.

Although the basic concept of 'structural stability' as expressed by Hadamard and Duhem is quite intuitive, a full understanding of its implications is rather tricky because it involves many complicated epistemological issues. Unfortunately these unsettled questions have been almost completely neglected in this century. This is one of the reasons why, despite an extensive and rapidly growing literature on the topological criterion for structural stability, 'it is safe to say that a clear enunciation of this criterion in the correct generality has not yet been made' (AM, p. xx). We should first of all realize that each formalization of the concept so far worked out refers strictly to 'the model only, the interpretation and domain being fixed. Therefore, it concerns mainly the model, and is primarily a mathematical or logical question' (*ibid.*, pp. xix–xx). Unfortunately, as we have seen, the methodological significance of 'structural stability' also depends on other considerations, interrelated with the logical features of the model but partially independent of them.

4B.3   The topological definition of structural stability

A rigorous and successful formalization of the modern notion of 'structural stability' was offered only in 1937 by Andronov and Pontryagin on the basis of modern differential topology.[12]

The intuitive notion of structural stability underlying this research programme is the following: a system is said to be *structurally stable* if, for any small change

---

[12] A slightly earlier version of the same notion, defined 'stabilité de permanence' and referred primarily to the truth value of mathematical propositions, may be found in the neglected but path-breaking contributions of two French-speaking mathematicians (Bouligand, 1935, and Destouches, 1935). Nevertheless it was the version of Andronov, a well-known Russian engineer, and Pontryagin, the famous Russian mathematician, that actually triggered a fruitful research programme and stimulated an extensive literature.

induced by a perturbation in the vector field, the system thus obtained is equivalent to the initial system (Arnold, 1978, p. 88). The concept was extensively developed first by the 'Gorky school' founded by Andronov (Smale, 1980, p. 147), and, subsequently, outside the Soviet Union, as soon as the classic book by Andronov, Vitt and Khaikin (1937) was translated into English by Lefschetz (1949).

Attention was concentrated at first on the definition of 'equivalence'. The finest classification of a dynamical system should consider as equivalent only diffeomorphic systems, which 'are indistinguishable from the point of view of the geometry of smooth manifolds' (Arnold, 1978, p. 89). However, a classification up to diffeomorphisms is much too fine in the sense that 'too many systems turn out to be inequivalent'. That is why a coarser equivalence has been introduced, the so-called topological equivalence: 'two systems are *topologically equivalent* if there exists a homeomorphism of the phase space of the first system onto the phase space of the second, which converts the phase flow of the first system onto the phase flow of the second' (*ibid.*). Unfortunately, even topological equivalence is too fine. The main reason is that the period of motion of the cycle is a continuously changing *modulus* with respect to topological equivalence as well. To avoid that, a new notion of equivalence has been worked out: 'two systems are said to be topologically orbitally equivalent if there exists a homeomorphism of the phase space of the first system onto the phase space of the second, converting oriented phase curves of the first system into oriented phase curves of the second. No coordination of the motions on corresponding phase curves is required' (*ibid.*, p. 90).

Arnold considers this 'the final definition of structural stability' – a view that, if taken seriously, should be judged as very naive. Even this last definition is very demanding. Moreover, to appraise its validity, we have to consider it in the natural context of the history of differentiable dynamics. The succession of three definitions of structural stability described above may be understood as part, perhaps the prologue, of the so-called 'yin–yang' parable:

At one point in the history of differentiable dynamics, it was hoped that even though an arbitrary phase portrait was too complicated to classify, at least the typical garden variety would be manageable. And so began the search for generic properties of vector fields . . . Since then, most properties proposed eventually fell to a counterexample, and the ever-widening moat between the generic and the classifiable became known as the yin–yang problem . . . we may think of the generic vector fields G as heaven (yin) and the Morse–Smale systems M as earth (yang). Differentiable dynamics attempts to build a tower from earth to heaven, in spite of warnings from Puritan poets and others. (AM, pp. 531, 536)

Genericity is a very important concept. A property is said to be generic when it is possessed by 'almost all' systems of a certain set.[13] According to topologists, only a theory of generic systems may be simple, powerful and manageable. Moreover, the knowledge of the behaviour of generic dynamical systems would be enough to

[13] Smale (1966) made precise the concept of 'almost all' as 'dense open set', or at least as 'Baire set' (a countable intersection of open dense sets). This definition is now almost universally adopted in differential topology.

approximate the behaviour of any dynamic system, since an arbitrarily small deformation would suffice to transform a non-generic case into a generic one (see e.g. Arnold, 1978, chapter 6).

We may well understand why the dream of differential topology in its infancy was the genericity of structural stability. This dream seemed to be about to materialize when Peixoto (1962) was able to prove that structurally stable dynamical systems are generic in a two-dimensional compact manifold (Smale, 1980, p. 88). Steve Smale vividly recollects the enthusiasms of that golden age:

Peixoto told me that he had met Pontryagin; who said that he didn't believe in structural stability in dimensions greater than two, but that only increased the challenge. In fact, I did make one contribution in that time. Peixoto had used the condition on D^2 of Andronov and Pontryagin that 'no solution joins saddles'. This was a necessary condition for structural stability. Having learned about transversality from Thom, I suggested the generalization for higher dimensions: the stable and unstable manifolds of the equilibria . . . intersect transversally . . . my overenthusiasm led me to suggest that these systems were almost all (an open dense set) of ordinary differential equations. If I had been at all familiar with the literature (Poincaré, Birkhoff, Cartwright-Littlewood), I would have seen how crazy the idea was.

On the other hand, these systems, though sharply limited, would find a place in the literature, and were christened Morse–Smale dynamical systems by Thom. (Smale, 1980, p. 148)

Morse–Smale systems are a sort of generalization of 'non-recurrent gradient systems' (Thom, 1975, p. 26) and constitute the basis of the yin–yang towers. They have wonderful properties: a finite number of critical elements, most of the known generic properties, very strong stability properties, etc. (AM, p. 534). Unfortunately, Smale soon discovered that s-stability is not a generic property for compact differential manifolds of dimension 3 or more (Smale, 1966). This theorem acted as an ice-cold shower on the mathematical community.

We may now fully understand the yin–yang parable. In the beginning we had heaven on earth, i.e. both genericity and structural stability, but Smale ate the apple and we have been suddenly driven away from our earthly paradise. A gap opened between earth and heaven and, from then on, mathematicians have been striving to build a tower to reduce the size of this gap, by building up weaker notions of structural stability.[14]

---

[14] Important weaker concepts have been proposed, first of all, by Smale himself: λ-stability and Ω-stability. λ-stability is weaker than Ω-stability, which is weaker than s-stability. Unfortunately, within days of the proposal of these weaker notions of stability, the first counterexample was constructed (Abraham and Smale, 1970), killing hopes that they might be generic properties of vector fields. Smale then tried to build up a parallel tower, the A-tower, based on his 'Axiom A' of 1966: 'although it subsequently turned out to be a little bit shorter than the tower of stability, it has wonderful features . . . reasonable bounds for numbers of critical elements and so forth' (AM, p. 537).

Unfortunately, the construction even of this tower had to stop far from heaven (a very lucid account by the chief architect himself may be found in Smale, 1980, pp. 90–4). Other

4B.4   Structural stability in Thom

It is most unfortunate that Thom's work on structural stability and morphogenesis has attracted a lot of attention only for its inspiring influence on 'applied catastrophe theory' developed by Zeeman and others (see e.g. Zeeman, 1977), rather than for its far-reaching epistemological and methodological insights. Thom's own aim was mainly to contribute to 'a general theory of models', as the subtitle of his famous book declares. He always considered 'catastrophe theory' not actually as a theory in the usual sense but rather as a hermeneutic theory, or, better, 'one methodology, if not a sort of language, which helps organizing the data from experience' (Thom, 1980, p. 53). In addition, on many occasions he has declared his scepticism about the validity of current applications of 'catastrophe theory' to different disciplines (see e.g. Thom, 1980, pp. 68–74 and 88–92). It is time to begin an appraisal of Thom's contribution to epistemology and methodology. I will focus on the concept of structural stability, which as we have seen is considered as the crucial condition for intelligibility in any scientific analysis.

The primacy of geometry

Thom vindicates a sort of epistemological primacy of geometry: 'to understand means, first of all, to geometrize' (Thom, 1980, p. 2). Understanding is basically conceived as a reduction or substitution of a simple invisible for a complicated visible. But why should the simple invisibles be geometric? One of the main reasons seems to be the following: we may consider properly intelligible only those structures of which we can have an intuitive knowledge, and we can have an intuitive knowledge only of geometric structures. In addition 'there is no intelligible language without a geometry, an underlying dynamics whose structurally stable states are formalized by the language' (Thom, 1975, p. 20). Simple invisibles are thus, according to Thom, to be conceived as topological forms. Let us briefly recall here two basic examples of reduction to simple invisibles:

(a)   Thom's morphological analysis is founded on the basic distinction between regular points (having a neighbourhood, close enough, of qualitatively similar points) and catastrophic points. From the ontological point of view, Thom appears inclined to believe that 'each point is catastrophic to sufficiently sensitive observational techniques' (Thom, 1975, p. 38, and 1980, p. 2). But from the epistemological point of view he observes that 'this situation is almost unbearable for the observer: in most cases the observer tries to neglect the details and is satisfied with a coarser description keeping only the "average" features in order to reintroduce regularity almost everywhere' (Thom, 1980, p. 3).

towers have been recently built up (for the tower of absolute stability, see AM, p. 541), but heaven seems farther away than ever. Maybe eventually, as Abraham and Marsden and other mathematicians still hope, a generic notion of stability will be found. If so, it will be certainly much weaker than the weakest of those hitherto worked out.

(b)   A second crucial distinction is that between static forms and metabolic forms. A static form has the following properties: 'the boundary of its support is generally not complicated, being locally polyhedral, and it is comparatively rigid and insensitive to perturbation' (*ibid.*, p. 101). The typical example is a solid body like a stone, but also any system whose dynamics are of the gradient type. A metabolic form, on the contrary, has the following properties: 'the boundary of its support can have a very complicated topology and is generally fluctuating and very sensitive to perturbations'. Typical examples of metabolic forms are 'a jet of water, a wreath of smoke (these forms are defined purely by their kinematics), a flame, and (disregarding their complicated internal morphologies) living beings' (*ibid.*, p. 102). From the ontological point of view, Thom inclines to the belief that 'probably, according to the *panta rei* of Heraclitus, every form is metabolic when the underlying phenomena ensuring its stability are examined in sufficiently fine detail'. Observable reality may be thus *prima facie* conceived as highly complex and unstable. From the epistemological point of view, on the contrary, whenever possible we have to reduce metabolic forms to static forms (and metabolic processes to static processes) in order to make them fully intelligible. This procedure of reduction is the methodological key of the current version of catastrophe theory founded on structural stability and static forms (Thom, 1975, p. 43).

This point of view is very close to that of Plato, as is underlined by Thom himself. In this interpretation, catastrophe theory considers observable phenomena as mere reflections of things, exactly as in the Platonic myth of the cavern. To understand the nature of things we have to 'multiply by an auxiliary space to define in the resulting space the simplest structure giving by projection the observed morphology' (Thom, 1980, p. 78). Each of these structures, which is substantially equivalent – in Thom's opinion – to a Platonic *logos*, may be interpreted in modern terms as a structurally stable configuration of singularities. To better understand the Thomian concept of *logos* we have first of all to understand the epistemological role of singularities.

The role of singularities and of their stable unfoldings

The concept of singularity plays a crucial role in Thom's epistemology. Roughly speaking, we may consider the concept of singularity as a generalization of the concept of equilibrium (a rigorous definition may be found in Thom, 1975, pp. 38–9). A singularity is seen as a sort of 'essence' exactly like equilibrium in Greek thought: 'in a singularity, actually, concentrates a global being which may be reconstructed by unfolding' (Thom, 1980, p. 160). This is fundamental, according to Thom, because 'intelligibility . . . was always understood as requiring a concentration of the non-local in a local structure' (*ibid.*). Explanation as opposed to description is thus, as suggested by the etymology, the inverse process, i.e. the 'unfolding' from the local to the non-local: 'the universal unfolding is nothing but a way of unfolding all the intrinsic information contained in a singularity' (*ibid.*, p.

22). This, according to Thom, rehabilitates the famous Aristotelian opposition between power and act, because the unfolding of a singularity makes explicit all the possible actualizations of the virtual behaviours implicit in the singularity.

The universal unfolding of a singularity is considered by Thom as the key idea of catastrophe theory, and as an important development of the constellation of ideas which was the source of differential calculus: 'It is, in a sense, a return to eighteenth-century mathematics, after all the great analytical and formal construction of the nineteenth century' (*ibid.*, p. 23). The basic procedure is to express all the qualitative information of the Taylor expansion of a germ of differentiable function through a series composed of a finite number of terms. The so-called seven 'elementary catastrophes' are nothing but the list of the seven singularities which have a stable universal unfolding of dimension $\leqslant 4$.

Among the singularities, the crucial role, in Thom's theory, is played by the attractors which we may interpret as a generalization of the concept of stable equilibrium. The attractors are considered by Thom as the main regulative force of observable dynamics: 'every object, or form, can be represented as an *attractor C* of a dynamical system' (1975, p. 320) and 'every morphology is given by the conflict of two (or more) attractors' (1980, p. 66). Analogously Thom maintains that the meaning (signification) of a word 'is precisely that of the global topology of the associated attractor (attractors) and of the catastrophes that it (or they) undergoes' (1975, p. 321). We have here a correspondence between the definition of the meaning of a word and the substance of the thing which the word refers to, which is admittedly reminiscent of Aristotle's theory of definition. In particular, the correspondence between knowledge and reality is founded on arguments which are typical of Greek gnoseology. As is well known, Aristotle maintained that 'science in act is identical to the object'. Analogously, Thom maintains that:

There are simulating structures of all natural external forces at the very heart of the genetic endowment of our species, at the unassailable depth of the Heraclitean logos of our soul, and . . . these structures are ready to go into action whenever necessary. The old idea of Man, the microcosm, mirroring world, the macrocosm, retains all its force: who knows Man, knows the Universe. (*ibid.*, p. 325)

The problem of morphogenesis

The problem of change may now be addressed. Thom concentrates his attention on a particular kind of change, almost completely neglected by official science: morphogenesis. Its characteristics depend on an underlying dynamics which is in general so complex that it cannot be exhibited in precise (quantitative) terms. However, Thom emphasizes that we can develop a qualitative analysis of a morphogenesis without knowing the underlying dynamics and the global evolution of the system (Thom, 1975, pp. 7–8). Then, 'from a macroscopic examination of the morphogenesis of a process and a local and global study of its singularities, we can try to reconstruct the dynamics that generates it' (*ibid.*).

According to Thom, all the basic intuitive ideas of morphogenesis may be found in Heraclitus (*ibid.*, p. 10). First and foremost, the relation between morphogenesis and conflict, which is reinterpreted as a struggle among attractors: 'All creation or destruction of forms, or morphogenesis, can be described by the disappearance of the attractors representing the initial forms, and their replacement by capture by the attractors representing the final forms' (*ibid.*, p. 320).

This process, called catastrophe, may be of two kinds: a conflict catastrophe or a bifurcation catastrophe. In the first case, we have at least two attractors whose catchment basins have a common frontier: 'this is the geometrical interpretation of the Heraclitean maxim that all morphogenesis is the result of a struggle' (*ibid.*, p. 47). We have a bifurcation catastrophe, when 'an attractor enters into competition with itself (after continuous variation)' (*ibid.*). This is reminiscent of Greek dialectics, particularly in the Platonic version.

Although structural change, or morphogenesis, is at the centre of catastrophe theory, we should never forget that only a structurally stable morphogenesis is considered intelligible. In other words, catastrophes are explained as stable discontinuities of a stable and continuous topological configuration of singularities. Thom seems aware that this epistemological attitude could appear somewhat paradoxical: 'it may seem difficult to accept the idea that a sequence of stable transformations of our space-time could be directed or programmed by an organizing center consisting of an algebraic structure outside space-time itself' (*ibid.*, p. 119).

This is an unavoidable implication of the Thomian conception of structural stability, as a necessary condition of intelligibility. We find here a very deep analogy with Greek thought. The phenomenological level, characterized by conflict, disequilibrium and change, may be explained only with reference to a meta-level characterized by harmony, equilibrium and stability. This is the strength but also the weakness of Thom's approach.

Although Thom's methodology may be considered as a useful first step for the study of the structural dynamics of a system, we should be fully aware of its limitations. They become fully apparent in applied catastrophe theory. The basic routine procedure is the following. We describe the morphology of a process in the space of control (exogenous) variables by a geometric surface, which is composed of equilibrium points (stable in the accessible part, and unstable in the inaccessible part). It is then claimed that the motion of the system is described by the 'motion' of a representative point on this surface as a consequence of the change of one or more control variables. When the representative point meets a discontinuity it jumps down (or up) to the lower (or upper) fold or surface. But this jump is not explained; it is only the expression of a convention, the 'Maxwell convention' (Thom, 1980, pp. 65–7). As we see, the motion of the system is somehow 'explained' in terms of a structurally stable configuration of equilibria, which is indeed very close to the spirit of Greek methodology. However, we should actually avoid interpreting the 'movement' of the representative points as the description of the movement of the system, since it is only the result of a method of 'comparative statics' (Smale, 1980, p. 130), which does not say anything at all about the actual trajectory of the system, unless we believe that the dynamic impulses are exclusively exogenous. In particular, in this approach, neither disequilibrium dynamics nor endogenous dynamics can have any role.

Efficient and formal causes

Thom's explanation of structural change involves a theory of causality which is very close to that of Aristotle. First of all, the Greek concept of material cause (or substratum) is very close to that of substrate space (of any process of change), which is interpreted by Thom as undetermined power (*ibid.*, p. 102). This power is 'shaped', i.e. restricted and determined, by the formal cause which plays the crucial role in both Aristotle's and Thom's explanation of change. Any dynamic process is seen as the actualization of dispositions intrinsic to the essence, or formal cause, of the thing undergoing the change. The process is triggered off and somewhat conditioned by exogenous forces, called 'efficient causes', which cannot change the form or essence of things. In other words, the efficient causes can only actualize dispositions implied by the formal cause, and in this sense they are a secondary factor in change. The role of a final cause may be understood simply as the actualization of a formal cause (Popper, 1945; Thom, 1980). The process of change for any object always depends on its structure, either in terms of its internal dispositions (formal cause) or in terms of their actualizations. Modern science reduced the scientific problem of causality to that of finding the efficient causes, completely neglecting formal causes which were considered unobservable. However, it is doubtful whether modern scientists have actually succeeded in remaining faithful to this principle. A case in point is Newton. Only mechanical forces, i.e. efficient causes, are explicitly called 'forces' by him. However, according to Thom and other interpreters (e.g. Kuhn, 1977) a formal cause is not altogether absent, although it is only implicit: the law of gravitation is the mathematical description of an empirical morphology (Thom, 1980, p. 8). This becomes even clearer a century later, in the famous restatement of mechanics by Hamilton. Thom shows that in Hamiltonian mechanics we may give an interpretation of the same dynamical process in terms of efficient causes (forces) as well as in terms of formal causes, and that there is no reason for choosing the first interpretation (Thom, 1980, pp. 102–5). In fact, the common modern opinion that forces have an ontological status deeper than forms is rejected and possibly reversed by Thom: 'I believe, on the contrary, a form to be in general a concept infinitely richer and subtler than the concept of force, which is anthropocentric and practically reduces any being to a vector' (*ibid.*, p. 105). Here is a new reason why he prefers to start the explanation of change with the study of morphologies. This does not imply, in principle at least, a complete neglect of efficient causes. On the contrary, Thom advocates an integration in the spirit of Aristotle. As we have seen, a morphology is founded on an underlying dynamic process although its analysis may be, for the moment, exceedingly difficult in most cases. The analysis of this process would explicitly reintroduce efficient causes into the explanation of change.

This should not be confused, however, with the crucial role played by efficient causes (control variables) in current applied catastrophe theory. Given a certain morphology which restricts the set of possible changes, the actual change depends on the variation of the value of control parameters, which may be interpreted as efficient causes as they are exogenous and cannot influence the morphology itself. This gives a clear but superficial integration between efficient causes and formal causes. Thom does not seem inclined to consider a change in the control parameters as a real *explanation* of change, but only as a *description* of change.

Final remarks

We have seen that Thom's claim to a deep affinity with Greek thought is fundamentally right. We have not by any means mentioned all the analogies between the two approaches, or even all those brought out by Thom himself. However, those we have analysed should be enough to argue this case. The basic conflict, so deeply felt by Greek thinkers as well as by Thom, between the ubiquitous experience of change and a conception of rationality profoundly rooted in stable equilibria and stable structures, is solved in both cases by reducing any intelligible change to a *logos*, i.e. a structurally stable form. This result is obtained by introducing a hierarchical conception of both reality and knowledge.

These analogies should not cloud the differences which concern not only the technical and analytical apparatus, but also aspects of a deeper philosophical nature. I will mention here only one example. The Greek thinkers always felt the need to close the hierarchical system in a sort of global invariant unity (the *monas*). Thom believes, on the contrary, that intelligibility is necessarily connected with local 'meanings' and that non-local concepts and theories are, strictly speaking, not scientific. That is why catastrophe theory aims to individuate a plurality of local archetypal structures without attempting to coordinate them in a global unity.[15]

In conclusion, we must take Thom's references to Greek thought seriously, if not in their philosophical details, at least in their spirit. By reflecting on these analogies, both in their strengths and in their limitations, we may better understand Thom's epistemology. We have to admire the simplicity, elegance and heuristic power of the structurally stable topological forms which inhabit the meta-level of Thomian rationality. We should moreover be grateful to Thom for having rediscovered and efficiently advertised a conception of change broader than the traditional one prevailing in modern science. But we should be fully aware of the risks of a conception of rationality, such as that of the ancient Greeks, which is closed and static in the sense that it does not leave room for really innovative structural change and thus for authentically creative human intervention.

[15] In addition, we could easily question a few philosophical details of Thom's references to Greek thought, for example his interpretation of the Heraclitean *logos* as a stable structure. Although we may find in Heraclitus an approach to the problem of change which is in fact similar to that of Thom, his *logos* is conceived as a stable equilibrium (harmony of opposite tendencies) rather than as a stable form. The concept of *logos* as a structurally stable form is introduced by the Pythagorean school, which, strangely enough, is neglected in Thom's quotations. A fully fledged synthesis of the dynamical and structural aspects may be found only with the Platonic concept of *logos*.

5

Uncertainty, predictability and flexibility

My second maxim was to be as firm and decisive in my actions as I could
... imitating a traveller who, upon finding himself lost in a forest, should
not wander about turning this way and that, and still less stay in one place,
but should keep walking as straight as he can in one direction, never
changing it for slight reasons even if mere chance made him choose it in the
first place; for in this way, even if he does not go exactly where he wishes,
he will at least end up in a place where he is likely to be better off than in the
middle of a forest. (Descartes, 1637, pp. 24–5)

5.1 Introduction

A monetary economy is a very complex system and is thus very likely to be
characterized by structural instability. This implies a certain degree of
irreducible unpredictability, with regard not only to the exact value of the
outcomes of the stochastic process, but also to the characteristics of the
stochastic process itself. Hence the economic agent has to face a disturbing
amount of 'structural uncertainty' over the future evolution of the structure
of the environment ('environmental uncertainty') and of the economic
system ('systemic uncertainty'). Unfortunately, structural uncertainty cannot be reduced to the kind of uncertainty (often called 'risk') which can be
easily dealt with in economic models. The concept of uncertainty, in a
stronger sense, now urgently requires a creative effort of analysis.

In this chapter I shall introduce and clarify the distinction between 'risk'
and 'uncertainty', and outline some of its implications. It is a distinction
used by both Lucas and Keynes, as well as many of their followers. The
issue cannot be neglected if their general perspectives on macroeconomics
are to be clarified. However, it must be recognized that many distinguished
authors (e.g. De Finetti, Savage, Friedman, Stigler) have denied any
validity not only to the definitions suggested so far for risk and uncertainty,
but also to the rationale underlying the distinction itself. Their criticisms
must be dealt with if the distinction is to be used properly.

In section 5.2 the validity of the principal definitions of risk and uncertainty will be briefly discussed and a more acceptable definition, at least for the purposes of this book, will be proposed.

In section 5.3 a first set of implications of the distinction between 'risk' and 'uncertainty' will be considered. According to the mainstream view, as recently clarified by Lucas (1986), it is only in situations characterized by 'risk' that regularities can be detected in human behaviour, whereas in situations characterized by 'uncertainty' the *scientific method* cannot be applied. On the contrary, according to a different tradition of thought recently clarified by Heiner (1983), regularity and predictability in human behaviour arise only in situations characterized by 'uncertainty'. It will be shown that these two polar points of view can be reconciled in a broader framework.

In section 5.4 further contrasting implications of the distinction will be considered. According to the Keynesian tradition an increase in uncertainty induces an increase in flexibility, while according to a different tradition, recently exemplified by Heiner, the opposite should happen. It will be shown that the concepts of flexibility entertained by the two lines of thought are radically different. However, these contrasting points of view may be reconciled in the context of a two-stage intertemporal decision theory; this will be briefly sketched in various passages of the main text of the chapter and compactly summarized in appendix 5A. Brief conclusions are drawn in section 5.5.

5.2   'Uncertainty' versus 'risk'

According to a time-honoured tradition originated by the classical contributions of Knight (1921) and Keynes (TP), a distinction is made between two kinds of uncertainty: a weak variety which Knight calls 'risk' and a strong variety which Knight calls 'uncertainty' proper. Risk refers to probability distributions based on a reliable classification of possible events. Uncertainty refers to events whose probability distribution does not exist or is not soundly definable for lack of reliable classification criteria.

The main criterion of Knight's distinction is that 'risk' is insurable while 'uncertainty' is not, because 'there is *no valid basis of any kind* for classifying instances' (Knight, 1921, p. 225, original italics). In Knight's view uncertainty, induced by unforeseen changes in economic structure, explains the genesis of profits which are considered the mainsprings of entrepreneurship and thus of all economic activity.

Keynes also distinguishes the concept of probability from the concept of uncertainty (or 'weight of argument'), which refers to the degree of *unreliability* of probabilities. However, he rejects the distinction between insurable and uninsurable risks[1] often made by underwriters. The main reason is that observation, in his view, shows the 'willingness of Lloyd's to insure against practically any risk ... underwriters are actually willing ... to name a numerical measure in every case, and to back their opinion with money' (*ibid.*).

On the contrary, according to Keynes, the degree of uncertainty depends exclusively on the reliability of the probability distribution, and in principle is not correlated with other properties of probability (degree, expected error, measurability). In particular

as the relevant evidence at our disposal increases, the magnitude of the probability of the argument may either decrease or increase, according as the new knowledge strengthens the unfavourable or the favourable evidence; but *something* seems to have increased in either case – we have a more substantial basis upon which to rest our conclusion. I express this by saying that an accession of new evidence increases the *weight* of an argument. (Keynes, TP, p. 77)

Although the points of view of Knight and Keynes are both subtle and ambiguous, as is usually the case with pioneers, in the subsequent debate among economists 'uncertainty' as opposed to 'risk' has been generally taken simply to mean uninsurable risk and/or the non-existence of a probability distribution. Both definitions have been rejected by most mainstream economists of later years. As against the first definition it has been observed that the modern theory (and practice) of insurance, as was already hinted by Keynes, does not in principle exclude insurability against any event, however rare or even unique. The second definition, it has been observed, can make sense only from the point of view of a frequency theory of probability; but this has progressively fallen into disrepute among philosophers of science and also, though to a lesser extent, among economists. From a Bayesian point of view a subjective probability can always be formulated as a bet on a certain event. The only requirement is conformity with a few consistency conditions, but this has nothing to do with the 'objective' characteristics of the event (De Finetti, 1980, Savage, 1972).

These criticisms are correct with regard to the crude version of the two definitions. It may be objected that what is really meant by 'uninsurable

---

[1] Keynes addresses this issue not because of Knight's book, which he did not know of when he published the *Treatise on Probability*, but because

underwriters themselves distinguish between risks which are properly insurable, either because their probability can be estimated between comparatively narrow numerical limits or because it is possible to make a 'book' which covers all possibilities, and other risks which cannot be dealt with in this way and which cannot form the basis of a regular business of insurance – although an occasional gamble may be indulged in. (TP, p. 25) risk' is not that an insurance contract cannot be stipulated, or that its value is completely arbitrary, but that any estimate of the price of the insurance is very *unreliable*.[2] Likewise, in the second definition uncertainty should be related not to the absence of a (subjective) probability distribution but only to its *unreliability*. I will not deny that the distinction between 'uncertainty' (weight of argument) and 'risk' (probability), as posited by both Knight and Keynes and many of their followers, is unsatisfactory. But that does not mean the distinction itself is inherently wrong or irremediably useless, as is believed by many subjectivists (like De Finetti and Savage) and many mainstream economists (like Friedman and Stigler). There are strong theoretical and experimental reasons for retaining the distinction once a better version is formulated – one that sets it on firmer foundations and thus overcomes the objections.

From the experimental point of view, an extensive literature originated by the so-called Ellsberg paradox (Ellsberg, 1961) has shown that human agents are sensitive to the degree of reliability of probability distributions (see Gärdenfors and Sahlin, 1982 and 1983; Hogart and Reder, 1987). From the theoretical point of view I refer the reader to Gärdenfors and Sahlin (1982) and Bewley (1986–7), where a few basic arguments in favour of the distinction are spelled out.

I shall propose a rigorous definition of uncertainty in the heuristic sense of Knight and Keynes, which I will call 'k-uncertainty' to avoid confusion with different uses of the term.[3] To do so I have to abandon one fundamental assumption of strict Bayesianism, i.e. that a decision-maker's beliefs can always be represented by a unique probability measure. That assumption is very demanding as it requires that the agents have fully reliable information about a unique probability distribution. This may be considered true only for a very restricted set of probability distributions, encountered almost exclusively in games of chance with cards, coins and dice.

The main argument in favour of the strict Bayesian assumption is the so-called Dutch-book theorem, which states that if it is not possible to construct a bet where the agent will lose money whichever state turns out to be the actual one, then the agent's degrees of belief satisfy Kolmogorov's axioms, i.e., there is a unique probability measure that describes these

---

[2] This is the point of view of Keynes, as is suggested in the passage quoted in n.1 above. It may be argued that it is also the point of view of Knight. See LeRoy and Singell, 1987.

[3] I would emphasize that the counterposition of risk versus uncertainty is terminologically extremely illogical and should thus be avoided. Uncertainty refers to any situation lacking certainty, and thus also to 'risk' situations. Risk usually designates the 'cost' of a wrong decision and it applies to any kind of uncertainty. Even Knight and Keynes speak of the risk deriving from genuine uncertainty.

degrees of belief. However, this theorem is true only under presuppositions which have been questioned from both the theoretical and the empirical point of view. In particular the central axiom itself – the so-called coherence criterion – need not be satisfied. This axiom implies, for example, that if the agent is not willing to bet on the state s at odds of $a:b$, then he should be willing to bet on not-s at odds of $a:b$. However, it may happen that the agent is not willing to accept either of the two bets. This type of behaviour, often observed in experimental studies, need not be considered irrational since it could depend on the unreliability of the probability estimates.

As an example, let us assume, as Keynes did (GT), that many financial decisions refer to the expectation of whether the actual interest rate will be higher or lower than the 'sure' long-run interest rate. Let us compare three different situations:

(A)   The rational agent knows that in the recent past the rate of interest has oscillated randomly around the 'sure' value, and he does not expect any new development for the future.

(B)   The agent is aware of a new development which will affect the interest rate in the future. However, through an informed analysis of the situation, he sees two offsetting tendencies affecting the interest rate and there is no *a priori* reason to believe that one will prevail over the other.

(C)   A new government has just been elected in a situation characterized by high unemployment and risk of accelerating inflation. The rational agent knows that the government won the election on the promise of eliminating unemployment without increasing the inflation rate, but he believes that this programme cannot be implemented. He also believes that the government will drastically change economic policy in order to show a high profile from the very beginning, but he has no way of predicting which of the two policy objectives will be chosen. Thus he expects that the interest rate will either be pushed down to sustain employment or will be raised to curb inflation.

Let us compare these three cases. In each case, if pressed to bet on whether the interest rate will be higher or lower than the sure interest rate, the rational agent will attribute a 50 per cent chance to both events. However it is likely that he will refuse to bet in the second case, and particularly in the third case, because the reliability of probability distributions is too low. Thus Kolmogorov's coherence axioms need not be satisfied and the proof of uniqueness of probability distribution based on them is not compelling.

Thus let us assume that the agent's beliefs about the states of nature are represented by a set Φ of probability distributions. The set Φ comprises all the probability distributions regarding the states of nature considered as epistemically possible, i.e. consistent with the decision-maker's knowledge in the given decision situation. The decision-maker attributes to each of these distributions a given degree of reliability which will influence his choice. In our example the decision-maker will ascribe a higher reliability to the central values in case (A), where he confidently attributes equal chances to the two possible states. Reliability will be much more evenly distributed in case (B), where he does not know the relative strength of the offsetting tendencies; in case (C) he will consider the extreme values particularly reliable, although he cannot decide in favour of one or the other.

A formal representation of these three cases will suggest a generalization. Since there are only two relevant states in this example (for the sake of simplicity I rule out the possibility that the actual rate of interest will be exactly equal to the sure rate), a probability distribution can be described simply in terms of the probability of one of the two states – say, that the actual interest rate will be higher than the sure value: $P(s_1)$. Let us assume that this probability is measured on the axis of the abscissas. The epistemic reliability τ of each probability distribution for each case covered by the example may thus be easily measured on the ordinate axis as in figure 4.

Of course the decision-maker will consider only the probability distributions whose reliability exceeds a given threshold of minimum reliability (shown in figure 4 as a broken horizontal line). The decision will be taken in two steps. In the first step the set Φ is restricted to a subset Φ^* of sufficiently reliable probability distributions.[4] In the second step the decision-maker chooses the preferred alternative, taking account of all the probability distributions which are assumed to be sufficiently reliable. I do not need here to go into the details of the underlying two-step decision theory. (For an exposition see appendix 5A.) However, I want to stress that it is consistent with a generalization of the standard Bayesian theory. In this case the decision-maker would calculate the expected utility of any alternative for each probability distribution of the subset and would then choose the alternative with the greatest minimal expected utility (for further details see Gärdenfors and Sahlin, 1982, pp. 371–81).

I am now in a position to define the distinction between simple uncertainty ('risk') and k-uncertainty (weight of argument). The case of simple uncertainty ('risk') arises when only one probability distribution is epistemically possible and its degree of reliability is the maximum. This is the case with both strict Bayesianism and frequentism, although the foundations

---

[4] The *first step* can be aptly formalized following the procedure suggested by Heiner, 1983, which I will briefly summarize in appendix 5A.

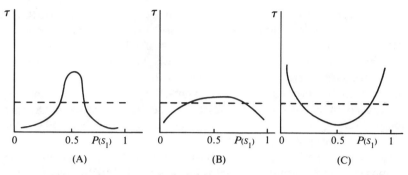

Figure 4   Measures of reliability

and implications of the two points of view are completely different. At the other extreme we have the case in which no probability distribution is considered sufficiently reliable. This case of complete uncertainty or (complete) ignorance has often been emphasized by authors critical of the orthodox view which assumes a unique, wholly reliable probability distribution. Very often quoted, for example, is the following passage of Keynes:

> By 'uncertain' knowledge, let me explain, I do not mean to distinguish what is known for certain from what is only probable. The game of roulette is not subject, in this sense, to uncertainty; nor is the prospect of a Victory Bond being drawn . . . The sense in which I use the term is that in which the prospect of a European war is uncertain . . . or the position of wealth-owners in the social system in 1970. About these matters there is no scientific basis on which to form any capable probability whatever. We simply do not know. (1937, pp. 214–15)

This contributed to the impression that the heterodox point of view was nihilistic (see e.g. Coddington, 1976; Garegnani, 1979), and unduly strengthened the prestige of orthodox theory. But the point of view I am advocating is not at all nihilistic. The presence of k-uncertainty has important analysable consequences for human behaviour.

In order to fully exploit the constructive potential of the distinction here suggested, a measure of the degree of reliability is needed. Many alternatives are possible. Here I shall explore only the simplest one. As a measure of the reliability of first-order probability distributions, defined on states of nature, I will adopt a second-order probability defined on probability distributions.[5] In this case a natural measure of k-uncertainty would be the dispersion of the second-order distributions (in our example the degree of

---

[5]   A more sophisticated measure of reliability is suggested by Heiner, 1983: see appendix 5A.

uncertainty clearly increases from case (A) to case (B) and from (B) to (C)).[6]

The proposed definition, I believe, is very close to the spirit if not the letter of the Keynesian view. The concept of reliability of probability distributions is very close to the concept of weight of argument.[7] The main difference is that I refer this measure to the probability of events and Keynes refers it to the probability of arguments, i.e. (more or less complex) relations between propositions. However, since a proposition in Keynes's sense is very similar to an event in the sense of Kolmogorov (1933), the difference seems not very important.[8]

A strict correlation may be established between the classification here proposed and that recently suggested by Lucas (1981, 1986). According to Lucas it is reasonable to assume simple uncertainty (or 'risk') only when

(a)   the stochastic process faced by the decision-maker is stationary;
(b)   the process has persisted long enough to permit the decision-maker to fully adjust to it.

This is the only case in which it is reasonable to assume that there is a unique fully reliable probability distribution over the states of nature. Whenever the stochastic process is non-stationary, the decision-maker is condemned to confront a plurality of probability distributions, none of which can be considered fully reliable. Lucas's view can thus be seen as an illuminating instance of the distinction suggested above.

One delicate point should be clarified, however. On closer examination the definition of simple uncertainty ('risk') needs a third qualification: ergodicity.[9] Only in this case will the stochastic process converge towards a stationary steady state, assuring the success of learning and convergence towards a fully reliable probability distribution. When the stochastic

[6] This raises a possible objection. The definition of a second-order probability could trigger an infinite regress. Why should we stop at second-order probabilities and neglect higher-order measures? I believe that this argument would be compelling only if the myth of ultimate foundations were accepted. In that case to stop at the second-order probabilities would rightly sound arbitrary. But this argument loses all its strength in a different epistemological perspective, such as that adopted in this book, according to which scientific foundations are always imperfect and local and thus should always be extended as far as possible. In this perspective it is better, in principle, to push back the foundations of the argument one step further: there is no point in stopping at first-order probabilities if we are able to retrogress to second-order probabilities. In addition we know from logic and mathematics that since two is the simplest case of plurality, a lot can be learned from this simple case about the properties on an indeterminate plurality of objects, relations or operations.

[7] Among the early contributors to the concept of 'weight of argument' Keynes mentions Nitsche, who 'regards the weight as being the measure of the reliability (*Sicherheit*) of the probability' (Keynes, TP, p. 85).

[8] This issue will be discussed in more detail in chapter 7.

[9] The concept of ergodicity has been discussed in more detail in appendix 3B.

process is stationary but not ergodic we are already in the realm of k-uncertainty.

Another correspondence may be established between my suggested definition and that of Heiner (1983). In his opinion traditional optimization theory implicitly assumes that the competence of an agent is perfectly adequate to the difficulty of the problem. Even when uncertainty is introduced no gap between competence and difficulty (hereafter called a 'C-D gap') is allowed for. This is clearly unrealistic. According to Heiner, the existence of a C-D gap involves what he calls 'genuine' uncertainty because agents are unable to decipher all of the complexities of the environment and thus to choose the right behaviour. When the environment is stationary and ergodic there is no reason to assume a systematic long-run presence of a C-D gap, while in case of k-uncertainty a systematic C-D gap is unavoidable. Heiner's distinction is thus basically co-extensive with the one I have suggested, although the foundations are somewhat different.

5.3   The sources of regularity in human behaviour

No doubt, the 'scientific method' can be applied to the study of human behaviour only if there is some element of regularity. This requirement should be relaxed as far as possible but cannot be altogether eliminated. Even chaos, as an object of scientific analysis, is defined in such a way as to include an element of regularity.[10] It is thus very important to identify the sources of regularity in economic behaviour. This issue is often discussed in economics from the point of view of predictability (Lucas, 1981, Heiner, 1983). Although regularity is a necessary but not sufficient condition for predictability,[11] the distinction may be disregarded in this chapter.

On this issue two polar positions have recently been formulated by Lucas

---

[10] Consider the following definition of 'chaos':

Let V be a set. $f: V \rightarrow V$ is said to be chaotic on V if

(1) f has sensitive dependence on initial conditions
(2) f is topologically transitive
(3)   periodic points are dense in V

To summarize, a chaotic map possesses three ingredients: unpredictability, indecomposability, and an element of regularity. (Devaney, 1987, p. 50)

In this definition it is clearly stressed that in the midst of the 'random' behaviour characterizing the so-called chaos an element of regularity is needed, namely the density of periodic orbits.

[11] The case of chaos illustrates this point. The first requirement of the definition, sensitivity to initial conditions, implies non-predictability while the third one, as we have seen, implies a certain amount of regularity.

and Heiner (*ibid.*). They have very clearly expressed the two traditional attitudes which have inspired economic research in the past.

According to the 'classical' or 'rationalist' point of view as restated by Lucas, regularity in economic behaviour can be detected only when the stochastic processes analysed are stationary or amenable to stationarity, and economic agents are perfectly competent to deal with the difficulty of the problem in the sense that they know the systematic features of the processes involved in the decisional situation. This, in his opinion, is the only case in which what he calls the 'economic method' applies.[12] This implies that the kind of uncertainty involved in the stochastic processes faced by the agent is merely 'risk'. Whenever there is uncertainty in the strong sense of Knight (and Keynes) the economic method is considered useless (Lucas's point of view on this subject will be further analysed in chapter 8 in the context of his research programme).

According to the 'behaviourist' point of view as restated by Heiner, on the contrary, the behaviour of a perfectly rational agent not affected by a C-D gap in a situation of simple uncertainty ('risk') would be extremely irregular, and thus unpredictable, because he would immediately respond to any perturbation in order to maintain or recover the optimum state. k-uncertainty is therefore the only possible origin of regularity and thus of predictable behaviour whenever – as is unavoidable – the rational agent is affected by a C-D gap. In this case he would stick to rules which would be the more rigid the higher the degree of uncertainty.[13]

I want to show in this section that both points of view, though rather extreme, can be included as special cases in a more general framework.

Heiner is right in denying that regularity of behaviour can emerge only in a situation of 'risk'. And thus Lucas is wrong in asserting that the scientific

---

[12] This statement will be discussed in more detail in chapters 8 and 9.

[13] It is worth summarizing the essence of Heiner's argument, which is based on the concept of reliability. The reliability of an action to be selected is measured by the ratio r/w, which represents the chance of 'correctly' selecting the action relative to the chance of 'mistakenly' selecting it. The agent chooses among the actions included in the set – called the repertoire – of sufficiently reliable actions. In the repertoire are included only the actions whose reliability exceeds a given threshold called the 'tolerance limit' $T = (l/g)[(1 - \pi)/\pi]$, where g represents the expected gains from selecting the action correctly, l the expected loss for selecting it incorrectly, π the probability of right conditions and $(1 - \pi)$ the probability of wrong conditions for choosing the relevant action. This tolerance limit is derived from the following inequality: $gr\pi > lw(1 - \pi)$ which assures that expected gains exceed expected losses. Although Heiner (1983) does not mention the problem, the tolerance limit may be shifted by different attitudes towards risk, which themselves can be 'endogenous' (see appendix 5B).

Since greater genuine uncertainty both reduces the chance of a correct selection and increases the chance of a mistaken selection, the reliability ratio r/w drops and the repertoire shrinks with an increase in uncertainty. Therefore, according to Heiner, 'greater uncertainty will cause rule-governed behaviour to exhibit increasingly predictable regularities, so that uncertainty becomes the basic source of predictable behaviour' (1983, p. 570).

Table 1. *Conditions of predictability*

	Stationary processes ('risk')	Non-stationary processes ('k-uncertainty')
C-D gap = 0	predictability	unpredictability
C-D gap > 0	unpredictability	predictability

method in economics can be applied only in such a situation, although this may be true of his own method. Heiner provides convincing arguments against Lucas's position on this point.

Heiner is wrong in denying that Lucas's point of view has any internal consistency, at least *in principle*.[14] However, as Lucas rightly maintains, a rational agent will not necessarily modify his behaviour in response to any possible perturbation: on the contrary any mistake consistent with the agent's subjective distribution of the relevant stochastic variables will not affect his behaviour. Stable rational expectations, for example, are consistent with *ex post* mistakes induced by unpredictable shocks. This is exactly the case of stationary stochastic processes to which rational agents have adjusted. On this point Lucas's view is sufficiently coherent (the weak points will be discussed in chapters 8–10).

As shown in Table 1, from this perspective the two points of view are not necessarily inconsistent because they refer to different factual hypotheses. In a situation of 'risk', predictability implies a complete absence of systematic mistakes and thus a C-D gap equal to zero. In a situation of 'uncertainty', objective processes are unpredictable and thus a zero C-D gap would make economic behaviour at least as unpredictable as the environment of the decision-maker. However, if a C-D gap exists the economic behaviour may be much more regular (and thus predictable) than the environment (this might be called 'Heiner's principle').

Heiner's and Lucas's points of view may thus be reconciled within a broader framework. However, one point should be further clarified.

Lucas, in contrast to Heiner, does not completely rule out the possibility of a C-D gap in a situation of 'risk'. But in his opinion this gap is not systematic: it is temporary, and explains the fluctuations around long-run equilibrium trends without affecting them. This does not necessarily produce first-order regularities[15] of behaviour in a fluctuating milieu. The

---

[14] The applications of Lucas's point of view are not flawless. I have already mentioned that a further requirement is necessary: ergodicity. Other pitfalls will be pointed out in the following chapters. However, problems also arise with the applications of Heiner's point of view. What I am discussing here is only the legitimacy in principle of the two points of view.

[15] First-order regularities are those that can be directly observed and described. Higher-order regularities require non-trivial statistical and/or theoretical manipulations.

period and amplitude of the fluctuations are highly irregular. However, higher-order regularities may be detected which are based on stable decision rules adopted by agents. In the case of business cycles, for example, it is possible to detect a few regular co-movements between economic time series (see chapter 8).

The regularities induced by Heiner's mechanisms are likely to be first-order regularities since most 'innovations' in the statistical sense are disregarded in a k-uncertain milieu as not sufficiently reliable. Lucas observes that this sort of first-order regularities – in the absence of a proper theoretical foundation – can be detected only through the experimental method, and that this cannot be done in economics (see Lucas and Sargent, eds., 1981, Lucas, 1981 and more detailed comments in chapters 8 and 9). To this one may reply that the scope of the experimental method in economics is probably much wider than was believed until recently (see e.g. Hogart and Reder, eds., 1987). In addition Heiner's theory suggests that it is possible in principle to derive first-order behavioural rules from a rigorous theory of decision-making in an uncertain environment. So there is no reason to exclude k-uncertainty from the realm of scientific economics. In particular Keynes's argument should be taken seriously also from this point of view.

By contrast, Heiner is wrong in considering seriously only first-order behavioural regularities, and in denying any internal consistency to the typical attitude of mainstream economists towards uncertainty (in the sense of 'risk'). A fruitful debate on these issues should go beyond the discussion of the methodological legitimacy of these two points of view and extend to the definition of their empirical scope.

5.4   Uncertainty and flexibility

k-uncertainty is not just a 'black hole' in our scientific knowledge, as is believed by orthodox economists like Lucas, and also by heterodox economists like a few neo-Austrian economists (e.g. Kirzner, 1973) and a few neo-Keynesians (e.g. Shackle, 1972). On the contrary, the degree of k-uncertainty can – and in many cases should – appear as an element involved in scientific relationships, a few of which can actually be formalized.

A particularly interesting case study is that of 'structural flexibility', a property which can be defined as the 'propensity of the system to undergo a change in the structure of parameters in consequence of a perturbation'. It is thus a particular case of structural instability (see above, chapter 4, and, for a further analysis, appendix 12A). Generally speaking, structural flexibility implies non-stationarity, and thus is not analysable through Lucas's method. By contrast, this property is at the centre of Heiner's approach. Many economists agree, moreover, that changes in the degree of k-uncertainty affect the (structural) flexibility of the actions and/or decision rules of economic agents. This nexus is crucial in many contexts, for example in the Keynesian concept of liquidity preference (see chapters 11 and 12).

There are two contrasting currents of thought on the subject. According to a well established tradition, going back at least to Keynes and subsequently developed by authors such as Marshack, Nelson, Hicks, and recently formalized by Jones and Ostroy (1984), an increase in k-uncertainty induces increased structural flexibility. According to a different line of argument, the 'rule-of-thumb' tradition recently developed and formalized by Heiner, an increase in k-uncertainty tends to reduce structural flexibility.

Which view is right? In my opinion both. Once their rationale is thoroughly understood they do not appear inconsistent. To explain why I will briefly summarize the essence of both theories.

Heiner interprets the reduction in the scope of repertoires induced by an increase in k-uncertainty as a reduction in (structural) flexibility (see above, n.13). In particular, 'to satisfy the Reliability Condition an agent must ignore actions which are appropriate only for "rare" or "unusual" situations. Conversely, an agent's repertoire must be limited to actions which are adapted only to relatively likely or "recurrent" situations' (1983, p. 567). This also implies, according to Heiner, that less flexible rules will be chosen.[16]

The 'Keynesian tradition' may be formalized along the lines suggested by Jones and Ostroy (1984). Flexibility is defined in the framework of a sequential decision problem coupled with an information structure. The larger the set of actions which remain feasible in the following period, the greater will be the degree of flexibility of a given action. Flexibility in this sense is a 'deposit of options', and offers the agent the chance to acquire and utilize new information which can increase the reliability of his knowledge (see appendix 5A). Jones and Ostroy are able to prove that an increase in the degree of k-uncertainty perceived by the agent induces an increase in flexibility in the above sense. The same reasoning may be applied to behavioural rules, proving that an increase in uncertainty will increase their flexibility.

---

[16] This proposition is not thoroughly argued by Heiner. He shows that an increase in k-uncertainty reduces the probability of a deviation from the rule followed until then. But he does not make it clear whether this rule is flexible or rigid, and thus whether a deviation would imply more flexibility or more rigidity. The correct way to analyse this problem would be in terms of the choice of a rule from a set of reliable rules (repertoire of rules) which is a subset of all possible rules.

If we now compare the two theories, the reasons for the apparent contradiction between them become clear. The 'Keynesian tradition', as exemplified by Jones and Ostroy, adopts an intertemporal concept of flexibility. An action or rule is chosen which will leave the agent's hands free for a change in the future when new information may convince him of its desirability. On the contrary the 'rule-of-thumb' tradition, as exemplified by Heiner, involves a concept of flexibility which is static or atemporal. The choice of a repertoire of reliable actions (or rules) in a given period is considered as temporally self-contained. The choice is then made within the set of reliable actions or rules.

Both points of view may be included in a single broader intertemporal decision theory. The decision process of a rational agent should be conceived as a two-stage process, as outlined in figure 5. In the first stage he will define the repertoire of actions (or rules) which are sufficiently reliable to be considered for a choice. Here he may apply Heiner's rule: if the degree of perceived uncertainty increases, the repertoire will shrink and *in this sense* flexibility is reduced. In that case it is likely, though here Heiner's relevant arguments are unsatisfactory, that the rules included in the repertoire will be simpler and less flexible (in the static sense).

In the second stage the rational agent will make his choice within the repertoire, taking account also of the requirement for intertemporal flexibility. Thus if the degree of perceived uncertainty increases, *ceteris paribus* he will choose a more intertemporally flexible action in the sense that the set of future possible actions will contain the set of actions which would follow a less flexible action. In other words, if the degree of perceived uncertainty increases, a rational agent will choose an action (or a rule) that will leave open for the future a wider set of possible options and thus a wider set of possible repertoires; the future option will be chosen in the light of newly available information and of the perceived degree of uncertainty.

The nexus between k-uncertainty and static flexibility explains a possible source of behavioural regularities. The nexus between k-uncertainty and intertemporal flexibility explains many interesting phenomena, including the shifts in the liquidity preference schedule in Keynes's theory (see chapters 11 and 12).

5.5   Conclusions

In this chapter it has been argued that a rigorous decision theory in an environment characterized by 'strong' uncertainty is possible. This sweeps away a powerful objection to the analysis of structural change. A rigorous analysis of structural change is possible even when it has to be considered as endogenous, which implies an irreducible non-stationarity of the stochastic process.

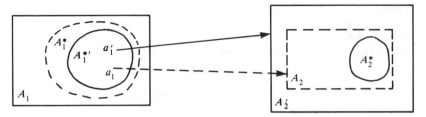

Figure 5   Outline of an intertemporal two-stage decision theory

Endogenous structural change plays a crucial role in the comparison between Lucas's and Keynes's heuristic models. In particular a careful analysis of structural instability in a money economy is important for a thorough appraisal of Keynes's contribution and of the 'Lucas critique' of Keynesian models (these issues will be discussed in the second part of the book, in particular in chapters 8 and 12).

Appendix 5A Decision theory and k-uncertainty

This appendix suggests the outlines of a decision theory sufficiently general to allow the analysis of the impact of k-uncertainty on economic behaviour. The aim is twofold:

(i)   to clarify in a compact way the model of decision theory underlying the arguments of this chapter;

(ii)   to show that a few basic heterodox concepts – neglected by the received wisdom in economics, probability theory and decision theory – have to be taken seriously. This is true in particular for

(a)   the concept of k-uncertainty which involves a plurality of probability distributions, as opposed to simple uncertainty (or 'risk') which is expressed by a unique probability distribution;

(b)   the concept of reliability of probability distributions;

(c)   the concept of structural flexibility.

Needless to say, in many respects the decision theory sketched here is unsatisfactory and should be extended and amended. However, the purpose of this appendix is not to suggest a satisfactory general theory of decision, but only to stress a few neglected requisites.

What follows draws heavily from Gärdenfors and Sahlin (1982), Heiner (1983), and Jones and Ostroy (1984). Whenever possible I have retained their symbols to facilitate cross-reference.

Let us define a decision as a choice of one of the alternatives (options) available in a given situation, defined by a vector of states s_i. Let us assume that in any decision situation there is a finite set $A = \{a_1, a_2 \ldots a_n\}$ of viable alternatives. The outcome of choosing alternative a_i, when the state of nature is s_j, will be denoted u_{ij}; this summarizes the decision-maker's evaluation, given his beliefs about which of the possible states of nature is the true state.

The decision-maker's beliefs about the states of nature are represented by a set Φ of probability distributions, which comprises all probability distributions over the states of nature which are epistemically possible, i.e. consistent with the agent's knowledge. Thus to each state s_j is associated a set of probability values $P(s_j)$ where $P \in \Phi$.

The set Φ of probability distributions is not sufficient to describe the agent's beliefs about the states of nature relevant to a decision situation. In addition we have to introduce a (real-valued) measure τ of the epistemic reliability of the probability distributions in Φ. Although in a given decision situation several probability distributions are epistemically possible, some distributions are judged by the decision-maker as more reliable than other distributions, and this is bound to influence his choice. Let r represent the conditional probability of selecting a certain probability distribution when it is correct, and let g represent the expected gain associated with this choice. Analogously, let w stand for the conditional probability of selecting a probability distribution in the wrong conditions, and l for the associated expected loss. The reliability of the choice of a certain probability distribution can thus be defined as $\tau = r/w$, which measures the ratio between the probability of making the correct choice and the probability of making a wrong choice.

The agent will consider only the probability distributions having a reliability ratio greater than a certain tolerance threshold T. In order to determine this threshold we need further information. Let us assume that the right conditions occur with a probability π. Since we know that the right conditions are recognized with a probability r, the gains expected from the choice of a certain probability distribution are measured by $gr\pi$ and the losses expected from the same choice are measured by $lw(1 - \pi)$. The tolerance threshold is thus given by the inequality $gr\pi - lw(1 - \pi) > k$, where k depends on the aversion to epistemic risk. If the agent is fully averse to epistemic risk, $k = 0$. In this case the threshold T of minimum reliability tolerated by the agent is given by the right-hand side of the following inequality:

$$r/w > (l/g)[(1 - \pi)/\pi]$$

which expresses the 'reliability condition' of Heiner (1983). According to Heiner, T depends only on the environment, whereas I believe it should be made to depend also on subjective variables such as the degree of aversion towards the epistemic risk which is implied by k-uncertainty.

This measure of reliability can be applied to any kind of choice, including the choice of an action or a rule.

The theory of decision here suggested follows a two-stage procedure. In the first stage the agent restricts the set Φ of epistemically possible probability distributions to a subset Φ^* of sufficiently reliable probability distributions which will be called the 'epistemic repertoire'. If the agent is sufficiently disposed to accept the epistemic risk it is always possible to reduce the epistemic repertoire to just one distribution. The strict Bayesian assumption is thus restored, although for different reasons. At the opposite extreme, whenever the degree of k-uncertainty is very high, it is possible that no probability distribution will exceed the tolerance threshold. We may call this a state of (complete) ignorance.

In the meantime the agent restricts the set A of possible actions to a subset A^* of sufficiently reliable actions, which will be called the 'pragmatic repertoire'. The procedure of reduction to a pragmatic repertoire can be conceived in exactly the same terms as the procedure of reduction to the 'epistemic repertoire' analysed in the preceding paragraph. These two procedures are in fact two sides of the same coin. All probability distributions involving events considered insufficiently reliable will be discarded, and at the same time all the events contemplated only in unreliable probability distributions will also be discarded (see Gärdenfors and Sahlin, 1982, p. 370).

In the second stage the decision-maker chooses from within the pragmatic repertoire the action that best suits his objectives according to expectations based on the epistemic repertoire.

Let us assume that expected utility is computed in the usual way for each alternative a_i of the pragmatic repertoire and for each probability distribution of the epistemic repertoire. The minimal expected utility of an alternative, relative to the epistemic repertoire, is then computed in order to implement a maximin criterion for expected utility (MMEU): the alternative with the greatest minimal expected utility should be chosen.

A limiting case is a decision situation characterized by no information at all. This implies that all probability distributions over the states are epistemically possible and that they have equal epistemic reliability. Gärdenfors and Sahlin argue that 'in such a case, the minimal expected utility of an alternative is obtained from the distribution which assigns the probability 1 to the worst outcome of the alternatives' (1982, p. 373). Thus the classical maximin rule for the so-called 'decision-making under uncertainty' turns out to be a special case of the MMEU criterion.

At the other extreme, having full information about the states of nature implies that only one probability distribution is epistemically possible. In this case the MMEU criterion collapses into the ordinary rule of maximizing expected utility applied by strict Bayesianism to 'decision-making under risk'. The theory of decision sketched here is thus consistent with a generalization of Bayesianism whereby the two classical theories of decision under 'risk' and under 'uncertainty' can be encompassed as extreme cases.

The theory of decision considered up to now is atemporal in that it completely disregards the intertemporal links between successive decisions. Now we need a further extension to an intertemporal framework in order to clarify the concept of structural flexibility and its nexus with k-uncertainty.

Let us assume that the agent faces a sequential decision problem. In the first period he chooses an alternative a_1. In the second period, after having observed y_2, he chooses an alternative a_2. In the third period state s_3 is revealed and the outcomes of the two preceding choices are evaluated. The outcome of the choices can be described through the following function:

Methodological foundations of macroeconomics

$$f(a_1,a_2,s_3) = z(a_1,s_3) + u(a_2,s_3) - c(a_1,a_2,s_3)$$

where $z(a_1,s_3)$ is the gain directly deriving from the action of the first period, $u(a_2,s_3)$ is the gain deriving from the action in the second period, and $c(a_1,a_2,s_3)$ is the cost incurred in the transfer from a_1 to a_2. The transfer function is given by

$$G(a_1,s_3,a) \equiv \{a_2 \to c(a_1,a_2,s_3) \leqslant a\}$$

where $A_2 = G(a_1,s_3,a)$ defines the set of alternatives which may be reached in the second period starting from alternative a_1 in the first period without exceeding a transfer cost a in the state s_3.

In the intertemporal framework the set of possible options becomes partially endogenous. Economic behaviour is influenced in an essential way by past decisions.

This is only a very preliminary step towards a satisfactory intertemporal theory of decision. It would be necessary to take into account the fact that the outcomes of a certain choice may be evaluated according to different time horizons, and that it might interact with the outcome of other choices, either contemporaneous or successive. However, the foregoing sketch of an intertemporal decision theory may be enough to clarify a few basic aspects of the nexus between k-uncertainty and flexibility.

Flexibility is a protean concept and the word is often used with completely different meanings. This is a major source of misunderstanding and confusion. To avoid that, it is important to provide a reasoned classification of the most useful meanings.

A first crucial distinction should be made between microeconomic and macroeconomic flexibility. This distinction is necessary because an increase in microeconomic flexibility does not imply an increase in macroeconomic flexibility and vice versa. For instance, an increase in exchange flexibility ('liquidity') of micro units does not necessarily imply an increased liquidity of the economy as a whole. This was already recognized by Keynes (GT, p. 155). Recently a possible conflict between micro and macro flexibility has been recognized by many authors (see e.g. Bruno, 1987, Vercelli, 1988).

From the microeconomic point of view a basic distinction must be introduced between functional flexibility and structural flexibility. Functional flexibility is measured by the elasticity of the function which describes the reaction of the agent to changes in the environment, while structural flexibility refers to the structural characteristics of the decisional situation, i.e. the characteristics of the sets which describe the pragmatic and epistemic possibilities (A and Φ) and the subsets which describe the pragmatic and epistemic repertoires (A^* and Φ^*).

Analogously, from the macroeconomic point of view, a crucial distinction must be introduced between functional flexibility and structural flexibility. Functional flexibility refers to the elasticity of an aggregate behavioural function relative to a variable belonging to the argument of the function. For instance, the widely used expression 'flexibility of wages' is taken to mean the elasticity of an index of wages relative to aggregate employment, to an index of prices or to whatever variable is considered instrumental to a change of wages. Structural flexibility refers to a change in the functional structure of the system (see appendix 3A) and/or in the sectoral composition of the state variables. Within this general classification it is necessary to introduce a few further specialized meanings. For present purposes we need only introduce a further distinction within the category of microeconomic structural flexibility.

The first meaning is that of atemporal (micro-structural) flexibility introduced by Heiner (1983), which concerns the extension of the pragmatic repertoire. In this sense economic behaviour is more flexible the wider the set of reliable possible actions.

The second meaning is that of intertemporal (micro-structural) flexibility recently formalized by Jones and Ostroy (1984), which concerns the extension of the set of choices left open in the future after a certain choice in the present. Whenever there is k-uncertainty, the agent chooses within the repertoire, *ceteris paribus*, taking account of the need to keep a wide range of possibilities open for the future. Hence let us define intertemporal (micro-structural) flexibility in the following way: choice a_1 is more flexible than choice a_1' when, for every transfer cost $a \geqslant 0$, $A_2 \supset A_2'$, i.e.:

$$G(a_1, s_3, a) \supset G(a_1', s_3, a)$$

In other words one choice is more flexible than another when for the same transfer costs a wider range of choices is left open for the future.

In the interpretation suggested here these two concepts of (micro-structural) flexibility need not be considered as mutually inconsistent, as was shown in section 5.4. Thus atemporal rigidity may explain one source of regularity and predictability in economic behaviour. Intertemporal rigidity provides a proper foundation for the analysis of the degree of irreversibility in the decisional process and thus in economic behaviour.

In this perspective irreversibility is rightly seen as an endogenous property of the decision process. This provides a foundation for the concept of *historical time*, as opposed to *logical time*. This distinction has been considered important by many authors, particularly in the Keynesian tradition, but it has so far eluded any attempt at rigorous definition. In this light the time element in a model may be defined as historical whenever it is associated with a process of endogenous change in the sets describing the viable options and the repertoires. Thus, unless complete flexibility can be assumed, we cannot confine the analysis to logical time, which completely excludes intertemporal rigidities. A fundamental weakness of classical theory (in Keynes's sense) lies in its hidden assumption of perfect intertemporal flexibility, and thus in its conception of time as merely logical.

An increase in k-uncertainty has different implications for structural flexibility according to the definition of (micro-structural) flexibility.

An increase in the degree of k-uncertainty diminishes the reliability of current alternatives, as it reduces the probability of a choice in the right conditions and increases the probability of a choice in the wrong conditions. This implies that many alternatives which before were considered reliable enough to be retained in the repertoire now fall below the tolerance threshold. Thus in the first stage of the decision process the pragmatic repertoire shrinks and so the flexibility of the decision-maker's behaviour is also likely to be reduced. In the second stage of the

89

decision process the effect of an increase in the degree of k-uncertainty is completely different. The agent has to choose within the reduced repertoire A^* according to his objectives, which include a desired degree of intertemporal flexibility. Jones and Ostroy (1984) were able to show that an increase in k-uncertainty, measured by an index of dispersion of the second-order probability distributions, increases the degree of intertemporal flexibility desired by the agent. Thus he will choose, *ceteris paribus*, an alternative a' which leaves open for the future a larger set of alternatives, A'.

The apparent contradiction between the behaviourist tradition, as formalized by Heiner, and the Keynesian tradition, as formalized by Jones and Ostroy, is thus resolved in the broader framework offered by a two-stage intertemporal theory of decision. This shows that the nexus between k-uncertainty and structural flexibility is very complex, even when the analysis is restricted to the microeconomic point of view. This nexus would become even more complex if the missing macroeconomic dimension were added to the analysis. As we have already observed, an increase in micro-structural flexibility does not necessarily imply an increase in macro-structural flexibility. Moreover, different dimensions of macrostructural intertemporal flexibility should be distinguished (exchange flexibility or liquidity, financial flexibility or fragility, technological flexibility, public policy flexibility, etc.). These issues will be further developed in appendix 12A.

6

Rationality and expectations

It is demonstrable, said Master Pangloss, that things cannot be otherwise than they are; for as all things have been created for some end, they must necessarily be created for the best end. Observe, for instance, the nose is formed to bear spectacles, therefore we wear spectacles. The legs are visibly designed for stockings, accordingly we wear stockings . . . swine were created to be eaten, therefore we eat pork all the year round. It is not enough therefore to say that every thing is right, we should say every thing is in the best state it possibly could be. (Voltaire, *Candide*, 1759, p. 3)

6.1   Introduction

Besides equilibrium and stability there is a third crucial property which helps to confer some order on the vagaries of economic phenomena: rationality. No one denies that economic behaviour may be irrational, although there are different opinions on the actual impact of irrational drives on economic behaviour. But most economists agree that, at this stage of our knowledge, economic analysis should focus primarily on rational behaviour. This is in any case a necessary benchmark for understanding economic behaviour, even when it deviates from rationality. From this point of view, there is not such a big chasm dividing Keynesian economics from classical economics (old and new). Though Keynesian economists are more prone to allow for irrational elements (like money illusion, animal spirits, shifts in long-term expectations, etc.), most of them prefer to restrict the analysis to rational behaviour. For the sake of comparison, I will thus limit my analysis in both cases to patterns of behaviour which are rational or amenable to some concept of rationality. In any case, as the preceding chapter suggests, much can be done to broaden the coverage of rationality by extending and articulating its meanings.

Economists are still very far from understanding rational economic behaviour. In addition they strongly disagree as to what rationality should mean in economic analysis. One of the main conflicts is over expectations formation. Rational expectations stress the importance of a consistent application of the hypothesis of rationality in gathering, processing and utilizing economic information. Still, this hypothesis may be interpreted according to different conceptions of rationality.

In order to clarify these issues I will first, in section 6.2, discuss different meanings of rationality in relation to the features of dynamic behaviour and the constraints faced by economic agents. In section 6.3 the hypothesis of rational expectations is seen as an equilibrium of the cognitive-decisional process; this interpretation has profoundly different implications corresponding to different conceptions of equilibrium. In section 6.4 I will briefly survey some of the arguments which have been advanced to justify this hypothesis. I will then point out in section 6.5 a few serious difficulties arising from the standard solution procedures of rational-expectations models. Then, in section 6.6, I will stress that in all existing interpretations the concept of rationality involved in the rational-expectations hypothesis is a very limited one, as it completely neglects what might be called creative rationality. Conclusions follow in section 6.7.

6.2   Rationality, dynamics and constraints

The hypothesis of rational expectations is an excellent proving ground for testing the validity of the concepts and arguments developed in the preceding chapters. This, however, cannot be done without some further preliminary considerations on the concept of rationality.

The subject of rationality is extremely broad and complex. Fortunately, for our purposes we need discuss only one very circumscribed aspect of this vast theme: the link between various concepts of rationality and certain crucial aspects of the dynamic behaviour of an economic system.

Generally speaking, the dynamic behaviour of the system depends on the dynamic behaviour of the individual agents and that of the environment. The agents' behaviour depends, *ceteris paribus*, on their option sets which are shaped and constrained by the structure of the economic system and the structure of the system's environment. It is routinely assumed that an agent cannot modify his option set either directly or indirectly by affecting the structure of the system or its environment.[1] The agent may be defined in this case as 'option-taker'; rationality is restricted to the problem of the optimal choice out of a given option set in order to adapt to a given environment. This kind of rationality, which I will call *adaptive*, has been considered either exclusively in the light of equilibrium (*substantive* rationality) or from

---

[1] The structure of the economic system and the structure of the system's environment jointly constitute the environment of the individual agent.

the point of view of the global dynamic behaviour of the agent (*procedural rationality*).

Substantive rationality refers to attributes of the equilibrium configuration of the system,[2] while *procedural rationality* refers to attributes of the dynamic process seen in all its dimensions (including disequilibrium).[3] The equilibria analysed by these two forms of rationality do not necessarily coincide. This is true, in particular, when the equilibrium identified by the criteria of substantive rationality is not unique, or is not stable (from the dynamic and/or structural point of view), or is not meaningful for describing, explaining, predicting or controlling reality. In that case the 'procedural' equilibrium, i.e. the equilibrium identified by criteria of procedural rationality, does not necessarily coincide with the 'substantive' equilibrium. To see whether these circumstances are relevant or not one must adopt the point of view of procedural rationality. The problem is to establish whether, in given circumstances, the rational procedure converges with sufficient rapidity towards the substantive equilibrium. Thus from the point of view of procedural rationality one can argue for the importance and meaningfulness of an economic equilibrium, while from the point of view of substantive rationality the importance and meaningfulness of the equilibrium are simply assumed.

Having said that, a rigorous characterization of the two concepts is extremely difficult because they are often confused almost inextricably within the conception of a single author, and often within a single text. I consider a process to be *rational from the procedural point of view* when it can be interpreted as an adequate procedure, given the circumstances, for solving a certain problem. When the problem is formalized in a model describing a dynamic system, the 'solution' can be interpreted as an optimal equilibrium, though only in relation to the constraints. However, one must always be aware of the gap that exists, except in particular cases which are very rare in economics, between the procedural optimum of the model and the 'objective' optimum of the real problem. Hence the solution is generally

---

[2] According to Simon,

> behaviour is substantively rational when it is appropriate to the achievement of given goals within the limits imposed by given conditions and constraints. Notice that, by this definition, the rationality of behaviour depends upon the actor in only a single respect – his goals. Given these goals, the rational behaviour is determined entirely by the characteristics of the environment in which it takes place. (1982, pp. 425–6)

In this case, 'appropriateness' to the achievement of given goals is generally identified with optimization and equilibrium.

[3] According to Simon, 'behaviour is procedurally rational when it is the outcome of appropriate deliberation. Its procedural rationality depends on the process that generated it' (1982, p. 426). This process is often interpreted as a 'process of learning', or 'movement towards equilibrium' (*ibid.*, p. 219).

to be considered as a simple approximation of the objective optimum. The equilibrium of the model, whether of short, medium or long period in the standard theoretical economic sense, is thus by definition 'transitory' because it is always subject to revision once it becomes possible to find a better approximation, or once the characteristics of the real problem change.

The point of view of procedural rationality in the interpretation suggested here does not necessarily reject the optimizing procedure of 'classical' economics (old and new), nor does it necessarily refuse to give attention to equilibrium configurations, which are often interpretable as optimum configurations given all the constraints.[4] However, this methodology must be seen in a perspective radically different from the prevailing one, which is strongly influenced by the 'substantivist' conception.[5] In the present case there is no implicit or explicit presumption that the optimal equilibrium of the model must coincide with the optimal equilibrium of reality. Indeed one cannot sensibly avoid the contrary conjecture that the optimum of the model cannot in general coincide with the objective optimum, especially in a complex context involving uncertainty, such as the economic context. Hence there is the crucial problem of evaluating the significance of the equilibrium as the optimum solution of a real problem. That significance depends, among other things, on the uniqueness and stability of the equilibrium, as well as on the 'distance' between model and reality (see section 3.2).

I shall now give a definition of substantive rationality in its *strong* version. The equilibrium described by a model may be considered *rational from the point of view of substantive rationality* when it coincides with the equilibrium that characterizes the objective optimum (henceforth denoted by the word Equilibrium with a capital E). Here the point of view of procedural rationality is completely reversed. It is *assumed*, more or less explicitly, that the reality under examination is characterized by an optimal equilibrium (state, path or configuration), given certain aims and circumstances, and it is *assumed* that only this equilibrium is scientifically relevant. One possible justification, often proposed, is that any other equilibrium would be only transitory as it would imply the existence of overlooked

---

[4] Simon makes clear that 'we can *formally* view [the efficient computational procedures typical of procedural rationality] as optimising procedures by introducing, for example, a cost of computation and a marginal return from computation, and using these quantities to compute the optimal stopping-point for the computation' (1982, p. 435). However, the equivalence is not complete *semantically* for the reasons already discussed in section 2.6.

[5] According to Simon, 'The shift from theories of substantive rationality to theories of procedural rationality requires a basic shift in scientific style, from an emphasis in deductive reasoning within a tight system of axioms to an emphasis on detailed empirical exploration of complex algorithms of thought' (1982, p. 442).

opportunities that would sooner or later be discovered and exploited by agents acting in their own interest. Hence in this view the exact procedure by which Equilibrium is reached has no scientific importance, at least *prima facie*. Moreover this path depends on many accidental contingencies which are very difficult, if not impossible, to take account of in a precise analysis. Unfortunately these justifications are not convincing for the reasons which forbid the use of a pure-equilibrium approach already spelled out in chapters 2 and 3.

The above definition of substantive rationality is certainly 'extremist', and I would not wish to attribute it to any modern economist. But its influence can be traced in all the arguments which ignore the existence of bounds to human rationality. Its influence can be discerned whenever an equilibrium model is used without being accompanied by an adequate analysis of its meaning and importance. This attitude has drastic consequences, for example, in the 'pure equilibrium' method proposed by Lucas and adopted by the new classical economists (see chapter 2 above and chapter 9). Such a method in which ignoring disequilibrium movements is considered possible, indeed opportune, is incompatible with the dictates of procedural rationality; it can be based only on a substantivist conception of rationality.

I propose to distinguish from the above *strong* substantive rationality a less demanding version which I will call *weak* substantive rationality. Although, even in this case, rationality is indissolubly linked to equilibrium states, these are considered temporary states, as the cognitive and operative bounds of human rationality are recognized. In other words, strong substantive rationality assumes unbounded rationality, while weak substantive rationality assumes bounded rationality.[6] Weak substantive rationality is much less vulnerable to criticisms and paradoxes, as we will see in reference to the rational-expectations hypothesis. However, having accepted bounded rationality, I see no reason for maintaining an exclusive link between rationality and equilibrium.

The forms of rationality considered up to here all refer to a given structure of the agent's environment, and in this sense can be interpreted as variants of adaptive rationality.[7] Until now we have ignored the specific

---

[6] The distinction between bounded and unbounded rationality is often assumed to overlap with the distinction between substantive and procedural rationality. However, the substantivist approach, which strictly links rationality to equilibrium, does not always completely disregard the limits of human rationality. Rational-expectations literature, for example, generally assumes that agents have a limited information set, which is already a partial acknowledgment of the limits of human rationality.

[7] Simon distinguishes between 'adaptation', a rational process characterized by a 'movement toward a "better"', and optimization, a rational process characterized by the 'choice of a "best"' (see Simon, 1982, p. 219). However, as Lucas (1986) makes clear, even

aspect of human rationality, that which distinguishes it from animal rationality. All living beings are endowed with a certain degree of adaptive rationality; in this respect the difference between them is more quantitative than qualitative. The real qualitative difference lies in the human capacity to consciously modify the environment. This requires the exercise of a form of rationality which transcends the adaptive form we have described – a rationality aiming to select and realize adequate conditions for action. I call this form of rationality *creative*, as it aims to modify the structure of the economic system or the environmental conditions that affect it. In this case the agent must be seen as 'option-maker', having the ability to shape his own environment and even the set of options he faces. Also, creative rationality can be analysed from the point of view of equilibrium (*utopic* rationality) or from the point of view of global dynamics (*designing* rationality). *Utopic* rationality may be defined as the proposition of an ideal economic structure, different from the existing one, corresponding to some sort of intrinsic and invariant optimum. *Designing* rationality may be defined as the search for adequate procedures by which, for given ends and under given circumstances, the structure of the economic system (and as far as possible the environment itself) may be modified in the desired direction.[8] In Table 2 I give a synoptic representation of the main forms of rationality considered above.

Creative rationality is almost entirely absent from the 'hard core' of economic theory, but it is present – though often only implicitly – in the heuristic model and in the vision of individual economists. Thus, for example, the final aim of Keynes's theoretical and practical work is a reform of capitalism based on the rejection of *laissez-faire*, while the monetarists (old and new) are seeking a reform of capitalism such as to create a perfectly competitive market and restore an ideal state of *laissez-faire*. This form of rationality is not generally attributed to economic agents, except for the authorities who make economic policy. They and they alone are granted the ability to modify the structure of the economic system and/or of the environment. That faculty must be restored to economic

optimization can be interpreted as the terminal state of a process of adaptation. For this reason I find it appropriate to use the word 'adaptive' in both instances. What is common to both hypotheses is the effort of the decision-maker to adapt to a given environment. It could be objected that Simon's concept of procedural rationality is probably not meant to be applied only to a given environment. However, applications of procedural rationality in economics generally have so far accepted such a restriction. I prefer thus a new term ('designing rationality') for denoting option-making rationality in a global dynamic context.
[8] In an adaptive context the environment is defined as the set of variables which are not controllable by economic agents. In the broader context advocated here the environment itself can and must be conceived as modifiable (see chapter 9).

Table 2. *Varieties of rationality concepts*

	Adaptive rationality (agent is 'option-taker')	Creative rationality (agent is 'option-maker')
Equilibrium	substantive	utopic
Dynamic	procedural	designing

agents if we are to avoid reducing the science of economics to the status of an 'imperfect ethology'.[9]

6.3 Rational expectations and equilibrium

To understand the significance and limits of the hypothesis of rational expectations we must focus on the cognitive-decisional process, that is to say on the interaction between the cognitive process and the decision process of economic agents. Any change in the agents' knowledge modifies their conduct, which in turn generates information that modifies their knowledge. Like any interactive process, the cognitive-decisional process generally has in principle one or more equilibrium configurations.

A rational-expectations equilibrium is nothing but a particular case of equilibrium of the cognitive-decisional process. Thus it has all the advantages of any other equilibrium concept, and must be used with the same caution (see above, chapters 2 and 3). Existing interpretations and applications concentrate exclusively on the properties of rational-expectations equilibria without bothering to give them an adequate dynamic foundation.[10] These equilibria are generally seen as expressions of substantive rationality, but often it is not clear whether the strong or the weak form is involved.

Muth's original definition is conveniently ambiguous; it can be interpreted either way: 'expectations of firms (or, more generally, the subjective probability distribution of outcomes) tend to be distributed, for the same

[9] The comparison between ethology and economics is developed in several places by Lucas (1981). From the methodological point of view economics is said to be inferior to ethology because in economics experimental techniques are of limited use.

[10] There have been interesting attempts in this direction which have studied the process whereby economic agents learn the characteristics of a rational-expectations equilibrium (for a survey, see e.g. Bray and Kreps, 1986). However, these seminal contributions can be considered only as preliminary steps towards a satisfactory dynamic foundation of rational-expectations equilibria.

information set, about the prediction of the theory (or the "objective" probability distribution of outcomes)' (Muth, 1961, pp. 319–20). This definition is interpretable in strong or weak substantive terms depending on whether or not the theory is assumed to be 'true'.[11]

According to the most lucid and general definition in terms of substantive rationality, rational expectations imply that the distribution of subjective probability of economic agents coincides with the objective distribution that generated the data (see for example Lucas, 1981; Lucas and Sargent, eds., 1981). This definition implies (and is implied by) an alternative definition according to which economic agents do not commit systematic *ex post*[12] errors in predicting the future (Begg, 1982, p. xi).

Lucas and other rational-expectations theorists recognize that rational expectations are applicable only on the assumption that the stochastic processes involved are stationary. This assumption, together with the preceding definition, implies that the cognitive-decisional equilibrium is *permanent*. This is absurd because it would imply that both the history of facts and the history of ideas are completely irrelevant. Lucas himself implicitly rejects this extreme thesis (Lucas, 1981, p. 276). In any case, such a definition is plainly unacceptable because it implies the perfect predictabi-lity (of the systematic part) of the future, which leads to insuperable epistemological problems (see above, section 2.7 and below, section 9.3).[13]

The impracticability of defining rational expectations in terms of strong substantive rationality explains why Lucas and the other new classical economists often, intentionally or not, slip into an alternative interpre-tation in terms of *weak substantial rationality*. One need only discard the assumption that the distribution assumed by the model is a truthful representation of reality. In this case the cognitive-decisional equilibrium

[11] In the present context it is not necessary to give a precise explanation of what is meant by 'true' (see e.g. Popper, 1972). I shall only note that the use of the concept of truth does not necessarily imply the adoption of a realist epistemology, which many new classical economists certainly would not accept.

[12] If we limit ourselves to excluding systematic *ex ante* errors, this affirmation would be compatible with an interpretation in terms of weak substantive rationality, but the equilibrium would generally have to be considered as purely transitory.

[13] Popper maintained that '*for strictly logical reasons, it is impossible for us to predict the future course of history*' (1957, p.v). The crucial part of the argument goes as follows:
  '(1) The course of human history is strongly influenced by the growth of human knowledge . . .
  '(2) We cannot predict, by rational or scientific methods, the future growth of our scientific knowledge . . .
  '(3) We cannot, therefore, predict the future course of human history' (*ibid.*, pp.v and vi).
The argument is founded on the proof that, for logical reasons, '*no scientific predictor –* whether a human scientist or a calculating machine – *can possibly predict, by scientific methods, its own future results*' (*ibid.*, p.vi).

must be considered as a simple 'approximation' of the true equilibrium. Its validity is thus in principle purely temporary, as it is sure to be falsified very soon by a structural change in the process under analysis and/or in the model used (perhaps through the development of more powerful techniques, as Lucas likes to think). An interpretation of rational expectations in terms of weak substantive rationality is much less subject to criticism, but it implies the renunciation of all the 'strong' results on which the new classical economists have founded their anti-Keynesian counter-revolution.

6.4   Justifications of the hypothesis of rational expectations

The significance and importance of the hypothesis of rational expectations may be better understood if we examine some of the arguments which have been advanced to justify it.

The hypothesis can be justified *ex post* as is suggested by Friedman's methodology of positive economics, and/or *ex ante* by arguing that it is reasonable. I shall not comment here on the *ex post* justifications.[14] I will only observe that the results of empirical tests are anything but conclusive (see, for example, Lovell, 1986), and that in any case a definitive refutation of the economic hypotheses appears impossible. The *ex post* justifications can thus be considered only as more or less persuasive arguments, not as fully demonstrative proofs. Their logic is that of procedural rather than substantial rationality: 'while not literally correct, the paradigm may offer a more useful rule of thumb to working economists than any approach yet elaborated' (Begg, 1982, p. 69).

However, most proponents of rational expectations have not given up the idea of an *a priori* justification. This can be clearly seen from the very adjective 'rational', which refers to a principle considered cogent by most economists. These justifications appeal in an inconsistent way sometimes to weak substantive rationality and sometimes to strong substantive rationality. The first point of view is acceptable but incompatible with Lucas's heuristic model (see chapter 9), while the second is compatible with the latter but proves unacceptable.

Perhaps the most widespread justification of rational expectations is that it is the only hypothesis of expectations formation which is compatible with the principles of general economic equilibrium, as it aspires to be rigorously

---

[14] A particularly lucid version of this type of justification is the following: 'the rational expectations paradigm may be considered in the same spirit as the maximizing assumption, once the subject of much debate in economics but now considered to be fundamental . . . Like utility, expectations are not observed . . . one can only test if some theory, whether it incorporates rational expectations or, for that matter, irrational expectations, is or is not consistent with observations' (Prescott, 1977, p. 30).

based on the maximization of utility and profits. Indeed in this context it proves indispensable to extend these principles to the process of expectation formation, assuming that information, which is a scarce resource, is used in an efficient way. The argument works, but in no way does it imply that economic agents manage to avoid systematic *ex post* errors. That depends on the quality and quantity of the existing information, and on the procedures for handling that information (Frydman and Phelps, eds., 1983). All we can say is that economic agents will not consciously commit *ex ante* errors of prediction. Similarly, it is undoubtedly correct to assert that if economic agents realize *ex post* that they have committed errors of prediction they will try to correct them, but it is by no means certain that the learning process must rapidly converge towards an equilibrium, especially a 'permanent' equilibrium.

The cognitive-decisional equilibrium identified by the hypothesis of rational expectations must therefore be considered as a transitory equilibrium which is not necessarily meaningful. But this point of view is incompatible with the pure-equilibrium method so dear to Lucas and the other new classical economists. According to Sheffrin, for example, no acceptable justification could be proposed for rational expectations (as an objective optimum) based on the maximization of utility or profit. In fact, since information is scarce and can be acquired only at a cost, it would be indispensable to know the specific nature of the cost function in order to see whether Muthian rationality emerges as the solution of a problem of constrained maximization. This result should be considered very unlikely (see e.g. Sheffrin, 1983, p. 17).

6.5 The solution procedure of models with rational expectations: indeterminacy and instability

The study of the solution procedures of rational-expectations models raises, in a different form, the same problems we have already discussed. The difficulty is to avoid both dynamic and/or structural instability and indeterminacy. For the new classical economists these are two horns of a dilemma. Each of them conflicts with the hypothesis of *strict regularity* of the phenomena studied by economic science, which involves perfect predictability of the systematic part of economic processes (conceived as stationary and ergodic stochastic processes). This result is obtained only by introducing a succession of *ad hoc* assumptions:

(a)   a unique equilibrium exists;
(b)   this unique equilibrium is a saddle point;
(c)   the stable variety of the saddle point is of unitary dimension, or in

any case not greater than the number of control variables ('free to be set': see Burmeister, 1980, p. 804);

(d)   there are reasonable auxiliary assumptions that justify the restriction of admissible values to the stable variety;

(e)   there are 'providential' variables subject to discontinuous leaps (*jump variables*) which guarantee the immediate and perfect compensation of stochastic shocks.

Each link of this chain of assumptions is open to grave objections. Since the strength of a chain cannot exceed that of its weakest link, this chain of assumptions cannot be considered robust enough to be acceptable in a scientific context.

The first link in the chain is certainly very weak. Many economists (including Taylor, 1977; Shiller, 1978; Futia, 1981; Gourieroux, Laffont and Monfort, 1982; Farmer and Woodford, 1984) have observed that linear rational-expectations models may have a *continuum* of stationary equilibria. The hope expressed by the new classical economists that this happens because these models are not rigorously derived from the optimizing behaviour of economic agents (see for example Taylor, 1977; Gourieroux, Laffont and Monfort, 1982, p. 424) has not so far been confirmed. In particular it has been ascertained that this form of indeterminacy can be found in overlapping-generations models (see Calvo, 1978; Wallace, 1980; Grandmont, 1985; Azariadis and Guesnerie, 1982). On the other hand it can be shown that the result obtained by Hansen and Sargent (1980), according to which the equilibrium with rational expectations is unique for a class of economies in which one sole agent solves a linear-quadratic problem of optimization, depends crucially on the assumption that the agent has an infinitely long life (Farmer and Woodford, 1984).

The second link in the chain is not less fraught with perplexity. Equilibrium with rational expectations is formalized as a saddle point in order to determine a unique converging path (Begg, 1982; Burmeister, 1980). A model characterized by a saddle point is structurally unstable, in the sense that a small disturbance that moves the economy off the converging path radically modifies the behaviour of the system and makes it unstable. This type of model has always been rejected by the regularist scientific tradition (in economics by the classical school). The new classical economists reverse that traditional view: what was formerly considered a vice they take as a virtue (or make a virtue of necessity?), and introduce a *deus ex machina*, arbitrarily restricting the range of admissible values to the converging path alone. This procedure is puzzling because all the admissible paths are compatible with the assumptions of the model and hence also with rational expectations.

The third link in the chain (see point (c) above) is clearly arbitrary. As for the fourth link (point (d)), additional *ad hoc* assumptions are brought in which are completely independent of rational expectations. These assumptions play a decisive role, because if they were well founded they would assure the determinacy of the solution and at the same time its structural stability. The following auxiliary assumptions have been suggested:

(1)   Economic agents solve an intertemporal problem of optimization. Convergence is assured by a condition of transversality (Burmeister, 1980).
(2)   It is demonstrated that all non-convergent paths sooner or later conflict with the assumption of perfect competition, and hence are 'dynamically inefficient' in Samuelson's sense (*ibid.*).
(3)   Economic policy chooses the initial conditions in such a way as to place the economy on the stable path (Begg, 1982).

None of these auxiliary assumptions is convincing. With regard to the first, it must be observed that this condition does not work when the temporal horizon is finite. In this case the stable branch of the saddle point does not satisfy the condition of transversality necessary for an optimum, and hence cannot be chosen as the optimal path. In the case of an infinite horizon, it is well known that transversality is not in general a necessary condition for optimality.[15]

The second assumption, like any other which presupposes an infinite horizon, is not particularly robust. In fact, as is well known, some paths that are Pareto-inefficient in an infinite horizon are Pareto-efficient in a finite horizon.[16] However, in a model with agents who have finite lifetimes perfect competition and maximization of utility and profits can generate inefficient paths (see Diamond, 1984).

As for the third assumption, this clearly conflicts with the ideas of the classical economists (old and new). The authorities responsible for economic policy are asked to intervene in a discretionary way to compensate for single stochastic shocks whose size and nature, by definition, cannot be foreseen. At times even the existence of a metaphysical 'collective rationality' is invoked, contradicting the methodological individualism dear to the classical school.[17]

In connection with the fifth link in the chain (see point (e)) we must first of

[15] As has been demonstrated by numerous examples, and confirmed by arguments like those of Burmeister (1980, p. 807).
[16] As a familiar example Burmeister mentions a steady-state-equilibrium path with capital stocks exceeding their 'golden-age' value.
[17] It has been observed that arguments of this type reproduce, though unconsciously, teleological arguments of the Aristotelian type.

all point out that even if the choice of initial conditions were a happy one and placed the economy on the unique stable path, the stochastic errors permitted and even implied by the hypothesis of rational expectations would suffice to place the economy on a diverging path. The same thing could happen if rational agents used the 'right' model in the 'right' way, but were led by the available data to commit even infinitesimal errors of measurement. This type of difficulty is 'solved' with dubious nonchalance by postulating the existence of 'jump variables'. The latter are elements of the state variables which are capable of compensating instantaneously and discontinuously for any errors of measurement or calculation on the part of economic agents. Their arbitrary character is clearly brought out by the formal requirement that their number must equal the dimensions of the unstable variety. Otherwise the required compensatory leap might not exist. Here I do not wish to deny that some jump variables may suggest the existence of effective compensatory mechanisms. However, the persuasive force of these arguments cannot be considered great until such mechanisms are completely integrated into the model. If that were possible the global topology of the model would become structurally stable, but then it would be hard to escape indeterminacy.[18]

Thus the new classical economists do not manage simultaneously to avoid indeterminacy and instability (dynamic and structural). Despite the great abundance of *ad hoc* arguments, indeterminacy can be avoided only if some sort of instability is accepted.

These criticisms are not meant to be purely destructive. There are at least two possible ways out, though these move away from the direction indicated by Lucas. One way out can be sought by accepting the instability and/or indeterminacy of the model as a characteristic which in some way represents the features of real economies. A second, more traditional way out could be to hold on to the dynamic and structural stability of the model and at the same time to accept a certain margin of indeterminacy.

Each of these strategies is consistent in itself; one or the other may be preferred depending on the object and purpose of the analysis. In both cases one would have to give up the postulate, dear to new classical economists, of quantitative and 'permanent' regularity of the economic phenomena

---

[18] The same arguments which are applied to the stable branch of a saddle point can be applied to a globally unstable equilibrium interpretable as a 'degenerate' saddle point whose convergent variety is of null dimension. The mechanisms already reviewed should guarantee that this equilibrium, though globally unstable, is always satisfied. The only difference would be that the convergence assured in this case would be towards a stationary value instead of towards a convergent path. Finally, even if we accept the elimination of instability (dynamic and structural) and disregard all paths which are not convergent, it cannot be denied that the convergent path is dynamically unstable: a typical 'razor's edge' of the Harrod type that has scandalized generations of 'classical' economists.

under investigation, and content oneself with a postulate of essentially qualitative and transitory regularity. Moreover, we could no longer avoid giving serious consideration to uncertainty and historic time. Economics would lose its illusory appearance of an 'exact science', and would regain the humbler but basically more human status of an argumentative discipline.

6.6 Rational expectations and adaptive rationality

Rational expectations, in the substantive version of new classical econ-omists, apply only to stochastic 'equilibrium' processes which are stable, or in other words stationary and ergodic. Nonetheless, their alleged superior-ity emerges especially in their use as a tool for dealing with the only admitted example of structural instability, which derives from the exercise of creative rationality by the authorities that make economic policy. In fact a model with rational expectations by definition cannot explain or foresee a change in the environment, i.e. in the rules of economic policy. It can only perform an exercise in 'comparative statics' involving different stationary equilibria which are assumed to be stable and permanent. Nothing can be said about the processes of transition from the existing equilibrium to a new equilibrium, and hence about whether or not there can be a rapid convergence to a certain equilibrium, or about the possible interaction between the 'traverse' process and the new equilibrium. The study of these processes may be extremely important in evaluating their implications for social welfare. So there is a problem of transition to the new regime, which cannot be ignored and cannot be dealt with through a model with rational expectations interpreted according to the substantive version.

Without prejudging the problem of which hypothesis on expectations is best for dealing with problems of transition or structural change, I would observe that rational-expectations equilibria emerging as temporary states analysed in terms of procedural rationality would not necessarily be incompatible with the study of such processes. The possible existence of disequilibria (in the semantic sense) is not excluded in this case. Nor is the permanence of suboptimal situations like those studied by models of bounded rationality. In this case, however, I do not see any reason to restrict the analysis exclusively to equilibrium paths (see above, section 2.7).

6.7 Conclusions

Muthian expectations are rational in a very restrictive sense of the term, at least in the hitherto prevalent interpretation suggested by the new classical economists. As we have seen, this view focusses on the property of optimality of economic equilibria, while virtually ignoring the other dimensions of economic activity which are manifested only outside an equilibrium situation, and which call for a broader meaning of rationality. Rational expectations in this narrow, strictly adaptive, sense imply forms of behaviour that should be considered irrational, because they violate the dictates of the highest, specifically human form of rationality: creative rationality. The latter, in fact, aims at transforming the environment into more satisfactory forms, necessarily violating the conditions of stationarity which the new classical economists consider indispensable for the applicability of rational expectations. On the other hand the Panglossian attitude that often accompanies a purely or mainly substantive conception of rationality (according to which 'we live in the best of all possible worlds') leads to profoundly irrational behaviour because it tends to atrophy our imagination, and hence our capacity for conscious control of the institutional and natural environment. In particular the emphasis on an extremely restricted category of information, focussing exclusively on 'market fundamentals', induces a dangerous inattention to other types of information which might be extremely valuable for a full and correct exercise of human rationality. We arrive at a paradox whereby a theory based on the efficient use of economic information favours a narrow and distorted use of it, because it is limited to a very restricted subset of the existing information (based on the erroneous notion that all other information is irrelevant).

The hypothesis of rational expectations completely loses these negative implications as soon as one ceases to interpret a cognitive-decisional equilibrium as objective and permanent. In this case the hypothesis of rational expectations would become compatible with the exercise of rationality in all the dimensions described here, but it would completely lose the extreme theoretical implications on which the new classical economists have built their reputation.

7

Probabilistic causality and economic analysis: Suppes, Keynes, Granger

> As our knowledge is partial, there is constantly, in our use of the term cause, some reference implied or expressed to a limited body of knowledge. (Keynes, TP, p. 306)

7.1 Introduction

At the root of the modern notions of causality in economics we find authors like Keynes, who often used causal concepts in developing his economic arguments, and Tinbergen, who gave a version of 'process analysis' particularly suitable for a causal analysis. A crucial step for working out a notion of causality rigorous and general enough for economic analysis was taken in the late forties and early fifties when causality was redefined in the language of matrix algebra which was to find a widespread application in economics. A seminal contribution in this direction came from Goodwin (1947), who was able to clarify the relation between 'unilateral coupling', as he preferred to call what would later be called a 'causal relation', and the formal properties of matrices necessary to express it.[1] This contribution inspired the papers written in the early fifties by Simon (1952, 1953, 1954),[2] who adopted an explicitly causal language referring openly to the philosophical literature on causality. Simon's conception of causality rapidly became the most influential notion of causality in economics, and remained so until very recently. Its dominance was challenged only much later by the conception worked out by Granger (1963, 1969, 1980) and developed by Sims (1972, 1977). This conception has been found congenial by many new classical economists trying to undo the Keynesian revolution, while that of Simon has often been favoured by Keynesian economists.[3] Concepts of

---

[1] The importance of this contribution for the modern development of causal analysis in economics is pointed out by Velupillai, 1982, p. 79.
[2] This is explicitly recognized by Simon himself (1953, fn. 5). We should recall that a similar conception of causality was independently worked out in the same years by Wold (1949, 1954).　　　[3] See e.g. Pasinetti, 1974.

106

causality are thus crucially involved in the current lively debate on the foundations of macroeconomics.

In order to clarify certain aspects of this debate I shall use the rigorous conception of probabilistic causality recently worked out by the well known epistemologist Suppes (1970, 1984) with the aim of explicating[4] the causality concepts of Keynes and Granger. I will argue in particular that:

(a)   Keynes's conception of causality is probabilistic and in many respects anticipates that of Suppes;

(b)   Granger's conception of causality is *prima facie* philosophically legitimate (which was denied by Zellner, 1979, among others), since it may be interpreted in its turn as a version of Suppes's probabilistic causality, but its application to economic models is philosophically questionable;

(c)   there are no grounds for believing that in economic analysis Granger causality should in general be preferred to alternative conceptions of causality.

The structure of this chapter is as follows. I will briefly set out (in section 7.2) and discuss (in section 7.3) Suppes's theory of probabilistic causality. I will then utilize this theory for interpreting Keynes's conception of causality (section 7.4). Likewise, I will briefly set out (in section 7.5) and discuss (in section 7.6) Granger's theory of probabilistic causality. Conclusions follow in section 7.7.

7.2   Suppes's probabilistic causality

Probabilistic causality has occupied a central place in the philosophic debate on causality since the publication in 1970 of a monograph by Suppes that rapidly became a classic of epistemological literature. Probabilistic causality therefore has a very short history, though we could mention a few earlier seminal contributions which remained almost completely neglected (Reichenbach, 1956; Good, 1961–2; and, as we shall see, Keynes, TP). At first sight this might appear quite surprising because both ingredients of the concept have been on the stage of philosophical debate for a very long time (more than two millennia for causality and more than two centuries for probability). This may be ascribed to the fact that causality and determinism were considered mutually inseparable until very recently, when the quantum physics revolution (which began in the twenties) had had time to percolate through into common wisdom, and probabilistic language (after Kolmogorov's axiomatization in 1933) began to acquire the sophistication needed to fit the subtleties of causal language.

---

[4] On the concept of explication see e.g. Carnap, 1950, chapter 1.

It is rather early to attempt a full appraisal of the scope of probabilistic causality in disciplines such as economics. No doubt much work is needed to develop and adapt it to the specific requirements of economic analysis. Suppes's conception is particularly fruitful for this purpose, because its point of view is taxonomic rather than prescriptive. The starting point of his analysis is not, as was typical in earlier literature, a stipulative definition of causality proposed as the paradigm for a correct use of the concept. All attempts in this direction proved rather unsuccessful because the range of application of each of these concepts was shown to be very narrow compared to the wide variety of meanings that may be found in scientific languages.

Suppes thus prefers to start from a 'weak' definition of causality which may be considered the 'least common denominator' of a wide variety of causal concepts. This is seen as a necessary premise for articulating the basic definition so that the ensuing causal analysis may evolve in diverse directions to fit the different characteristics of many subjects and languages. This approach agrees very well with a discipline like economics, where causal intuitions are particularly varied and heterogeneous.

The starting point is the concept of '*prima facie* cause' which may be roughly defined in the following way: 'An event B is a *prima facie* cause of an event A if and only if (i) B occurs earlier than A, (ii) the conditional probability of A occurring when B occurs is greater than the unconditional probability of A occurring' (Suppes, 1984, p. 48). In other words, the occurrence of event B increases the probability of the occurrence of event A. *Prima facie* causality is thus a necessary, though not sufficient, condition for identifying a peculiar causal relation. Such a weak concept is unable to discriminate between 'genuine' and 'spurious' causes because even 'spurious' causes appear to increase the probability that the effect will occur.

In order to discuss this and the following problems, we must now introduce a slightly more precise definition of *prima facie* causality. Let us assume that A_t and $B_{t'}$ are events defined as 'subsets of all the possible outcomes', i.e. in the sense, introduced by Kolmogorov (1933), of the mathematical theory of probability. In addition, let us assume that the events are referred to a well defined instant of time. We may thus introduce the following definition:

> B_t is a *prima facie* (potential) cause of $A_{t'}$, relative to the background information Z_t, iff
> (i) $P(B_t \cap Z_t) > 0$ and $t < t'$
> (ii) $P(A_{t'}/B_t \cap Z_t) > P(A_{t'}/Z_t)$ (7.1)

This definition is identical to that put forward by Suppes (1970) except for two specifications, implicit in Suppes, which are particularly relevant for what follows.

First of all I have stated explicitly that *prima facie* causality does not necessarily presuppose the actual occurrence of events. This allows a consistent utilization of Suppes causality within an explicit theoretical context, because the concept becomes applicable not only to single events but also to *types of events* and not only to directly observable magnitudes but also to *dispositions*. As is generally agreed, types of events and dispositions are essential ingredients in any theoretical argument.[5] I also stated explicitly from the very outset that in Suppes's approach any causal statement or inference is always relative to a *corpus* of information, organized by theoretical hypotheses, which may be defined as 'background information'. This should be kept firmly in mind in order to understand the nexus linking the conceptions of causality of Suppes, Keynes and Granger.

We are now in a position to analyse the distinction between genuine and spurious causes. Let us begin by examining a couple of examples. One of the favourite examples of a spurious cause, at least since Laplace, has been that of the barometer. The sudden shift of the barometer pointer is a *prima facie* cause of the storm which breaks out shortly afterwards, because the first event induces an upward revision of the probability of the second event. But the barometer shift is not a genuine cause of the storm, for both events are effects of a third cause, the drop in the atmospheric pressure. In other words, as soon as we take account of the common cause, the effect becomes stochastically independent of the spurious cause. In Reichenbach's terminology, the common cause *screens off* the *prima facie* stochastic influence of the spurious cause (Reichenbach, 1956). This suggests the following definition:

B_t is a *spurious* cause of $A_{t'}$ iff
(i) B_t is a *prima facie* cause of $A_{t'}$,
(ii) there is a $t'' < t$ and an event $C_{t''}$ such that
$$P(B_{t'} \cap C_{t''}) > 0$$
$$P(A_{t'}/B_t \cap C_{t''}) = P(A_{t'}/C_{t''})$$
$$P(A_{t'}/B_t \cap C_{t''}) \geqslant P(A_{t'}/B_t) \tag{7.2}$$

The barometer example might, because of its theoretical obviousness, obscure the crucial role played by the conceptual framework in any argument aimed at discriminating between spurious and genuine causes. An example drawn from economics may better illustrate this point. Both Keynes and classical economists would readily have admitted that an increase in real wages above the full employment level could be considered as a *prima facie* cause of a reduction in employment. However, Keynes would have considered such a cause to be spurious, since both events would have been interpreted as joint effects of a reduction in effective

[5] See e.g. Suppe, ed., 1977.

109

demand. On the other hand a classical economist, who rejected the principle of effective demand and accepted Say's Law, would have considered such a cause to be genuine.

Suppes's approach refers back to the prestigious Humean tradition, aiming to extend its range of validity to the analysis of probabilistic phenomena. In addition he goes 'beyond Hume' in two points that have a great epistemological importance.

First, as we have already emphasized, any causal statement has meaning only in relation to a given theoretical framework. Suppes is here influenced by the contributions of post-positivist philosophers (such as Kuhn, Lakatos, Fayerabend), which he integrates into his version of critical empiricism.

The second point gives a stimulating perspective on the vexed question of 'causal production', which many authors consider an essential characteristic of any satisfactory causal concept, but which Hume and his followers considered as a bit of metaphysical baggage to be carefully avoided. Suppes finds a way to analyse the problem without violating Humean anti-metaphysical principles. There is no point in denying the existence of 'causal mechanisms' that describe and explain how the causal influence is produced or transmitted from cause to effect, provided we are aware that these mechanisms may vary in different phenomena and may be interpreted in multifarious ways by different theories. In the history of thought we find diverse paradigms of the typical, or 'ultimate', causal mechanism. For instance in Descartes's philosophy the paradigmatic causal mechanism was based on the impact of physical bodies, whereas for Kant it was based on the reciprocal influence of attractive and repulsive forces. In economics too we can easily detect a contrast between authors who base the intelligibility of phenomena on individual reactions to external stimuli, and authors who base it upon an equilibrium configuration of interdependent relations.

Suppes's own point of view, reflecting his epistemological pluralism, rejects the existence of an 'ultimate' causal mechanism. Different causal mechanisms may co-exist in different empirical and/or theoretical contexts. Moreover, even within the same empirical and theoretical contexts, the paradigmatic causal mechanism accepted by one generation of scholars is further analysed and explained by a subsequent generation of scholars in terms of simpler and more basic mechanisms. Suppes is led by these arguments to consider causal mechanisms as 'black boxes', the role of which in causal 'production' may be analysed without contravening Humean anti-metaphysical principles.[6]

On these premises Suppes was able to work out a very flexible concept of

---

[6] Bunge (1982) and other authors criticized Suppes's theory of causality because in their opinion it completely neglects causal production.

causality that may be applied in different empirical and theoretical contexts. We cannot survey here the interesting articulations, specifications and developments of the concept explored by Suppes and his followers. We shall only briefly recall two aspects which are particularly useful for the following analysis.

First of all, Suppes defines deterministic causality as a particular instance of probabilistic causality:

B_t is a sufficient cause of $A_{t'}$ iff
(i) B_t is a *prima facie* cause of $A_{t'}$,
(ii) $P(A_{t'}/B_t) = 1$ (7.3)

Suppes causality may thus be applied also to deterministic causality.

In addition, Suppes causality applies also whenever probability is not measurable on a cardinal scale. This is particularly important in disciplines like economics where this uneasy circumstance often prevails, as Keynes and many other economists have recognized. As Hicks recently maintained, in economics probabilities are in most cases only ordinable, and then often not even in a complete way (Hicks, 1979, p. 115). Suppes's theory may be easily adapted to these cases by translating his quantitative theory into a qualitative one, following the suggestions put forward by Keynes (TP) and developed by Koopman (1940). According to Keynes and Suppes the qualitative conception of probability is essentially comparative and is founded on the following primitive relation:

B given A is at least as probable as D given C (7.4)

As Keynes wittily observed: 'no proposition is in itself either probable or improbable, just as no place can be intrinsically distant' (Keynes, TP, p. 7).

7.3   Suppes's theory of probabilistic causality: open questions and glimpses beyond

As Suppes recognized, his theory of probabilistic causality raises more problems than it is able to solve. That, however, may well be considered as the hallmark of a progressive research programme. Suppes himself points out and discusses many of these open questions with a very constructive and anti-dogmatic attitude. Let us examine a couple of them which are particularly relevant for applications in the field of economics.

First of all, Suppes's definition of cause applies only to events. Suppes admits that this assumption is potentially restrictive because 'many causes are not conceived as events' (Suppes, 1970, p. 71). This limitation is common to many theories of causality, but is particularly awkward for that of Suppes which is meant to explain the current use of the term rather than to stipulate 'the right one'. Moreover, the concept of 'event' chosen by Suppes appears, at first sight, very different from the usual ones. In ordinary language, by 'event' we mean a change of state rather than a state described in terms of set theory. However, nothing prevents a definition of a change of state in set-theoretic terms, so that in this sense ordinary events are Suppes events, although the opposite is not always true. Moreover in ordinary language events are *actual* events, while in Suppes events are *possible* events which may or may not be actualized. Thus Suppes's meaning includes the ordinary meaning but is much broader, and ultimately overlaps with the philosophers' definition of 'state of affairs' or 'proposition'.[7] In short, any object definable in set-theoretic terms may be considered as a Suppes event.[8] This is true in particular for economic variables, which are often defined in set-theoretic terms and are indeed easily definable that way. We may conclude that Suppes's probabilistic causality may be widely applied in economics.

The second difficulty is more serious. Suppes's probabilistic causality in the existing version applies only to instantaneous events. This is a grave limitation for a discipline like economics which often deals with events having a significant temporal extension ('chunk events', in Suppes's terminology). This is true in particular of the stock variables (such as wealth, capital, inventories, etc.); as for flow variables (such as income, saving, investment, etc.), they are almost never measured at an instant of time. Moreover this problem is particularly serious whenever, as in macroeconomics, aggregation is likely to introduce a temporal extension into the variables involved.

We may, however, entertain a reasonable hope that Suppes causality can be extended to chunk events. The theory of probabilistic causality recently worked out by Salmon,[9] which is in many respects complementary to that of Suppes, concentrates precisely on the causal analysis of chunk events (called 'processes'). An integration of both theories seems not impossible and would be invaluable for working out a theory of probabilistic causality suitable for economic analysis.

The second set of problems is no less serious. The assumption introduced by Suppes, in the spirit of Hume, that the cause must precede the effect, excludes contemporaneous causation, although we may find many

---

[7] See on this line Spohn, 1983. The same opinion has recently been expressed by Suppes himself (1981, p. 25).

[8] The conviction that the traditional meaning of event, defined as a change of state, is too restrictive for most uses of the term, has recently become widespread among philosophers and methodologists. On this subject see e.g. Kim, 1973.

[9] Since the early sixties Salmon, following Reichenbach, has been developing a very interesting theory of probabilistic causality. An excellent synthesis has recently been given by Salmon himself in an important monograph (1984).

instances of the latter in ordinary language as well as in various scientific languages. This assumption is thus inconsistent with the explicative rather than stipulative point of view adopted by Suppes's theory. This difficulty cannot be overcome within the current version of Suppes causality because, if we drop the requisite of strict temporal inequality, it is possible to prove that any cause is spurious (Suppes, 1970, p. 22). Suppes justifies this assumption by appealing, for the physical world, to the principle of 'retarded action'; and, for social sciences, to a time-consuming process of communication necessarily mediating individual decisions. Both arguments can be accepted only from a well defined theoretical and methodological point of view. For example in social sciences this presupposes methodological individualism, which is not accepted by all macroeconomists. A serious attempt to extend Suppes's theory in such a way as to include contemporaneous causation would be more consistent with the spirit of his contribution. Here I wish to suggest the outline of an extension which could achieve this result.

The basic idea, following a time-honoured tradition in economic theory, is to distinguish between 'historical' (or 'ontological') time t and 'epistemic' time θ (often called by economists 'logical').[10] By historical time I mean the time characterizing natural and social history, which is fully independent of any kind of human activity; by epistemic time I mean any irreversible order of succession, independent of the historical sequence, attributed by the epistemic subject to the elements of a process. A good example of epistemic time can be seen in the irreversible order of computation implied by a recursive function (this kind of order of succession gives the formal foundation for both Goodwin's unilateral coupling and the causal relation in Simon and Wold).

I am now in a position to reformulate Suppes's first definition in the following way:

> $B_{t\theta}$ is a (potential) *prima facie* cause of $A_{t'\theta'}$, relative to the background information Z_t, iff
> (i) $P(B_{t\theta} \cap Z_t) > 0$
> (ii) $t < t'$ and $\theta \leqslant \theta'$, or $t = t'$ and $\theta < \theta'$
> (iii) $P(A_{t'\theta'}/B_{t\theta} \cap Z_t) > P(A_{t'\theta'}/Z_t)$ (7.5)

This definition overcomes the difficulties encountered by Suppes in defining a concept of contemporaneous causation consistent with his theory. We may define a relation of contemporaneous causation whenever (7.5) is specified in the following way: $t = t'$ and $\theta < \theta'$. In other words, the order of succession between cause and effect is in this case merely epistemic

---

[10] This distinction appears, though with somewhat different meanings, in authors such as Robinson, Hicks, Shackle and Georgescu-Roegen.

Methodological foundations of macroeconomics

and does not imply a temporal succession in the historical sense. The relation between investment and income in Keynes's static multiplier is an example of contemporaneous causation. In this case we have an epistemic succession based on the exogeneity of investment relative to the income-expenditure circuit, but we do not have a succession in historical time.

Suppes causality is a special case of (7.5) whenever $t < t'$. I will call this kind of causality 'sequential', using the terminology suggested by Hicks (1979). We may distinguish two different kinds of sequential causality: e-sequential whenever $t < t'$ and $\theta < \theta'$, i.e. when the order of succession is both historical and epistemic, and h-sequential when $t < t'$ and $\theta = \theta'$, i.e. when the order of succession is historic but not epistemic. An example of e-sequential causality may be given by a lagged recursive function (e.g. the dynamic multiplier of Keynes where the autonomous investment, being exogenous, cannot be an effect), while an example of h-sequential causality may be given by a lagged reversible function (e.g. Keynes's equality between aggregate expenditure and lagged aggregate income; here both variables are considered as endogenous: the only reason to individuate a causal order lies in the historical temporal lag).

7.4 Keynes and Suppes

In his economic contributions Keynes often employs a causal language, but in these writings he never clarifies the precise meaning of the causal concepts used. However, the issue is discussed in some detail in the *Treatise on Probability* (1921), where he worked out the foundations of his epistemological point of view. We find there a very interesting outline of a theory of probabilistic causality which in many respects anticipates the more mature and sophisticated theory of Suppes. Interpreters of Keynesian thought have neglected this link[11] partly because they could not be acquainted with a fully fledged theory of probabilistic causality, which is very recent. Keynesian causality has thus been interpreted as a version of deterministic causality close to that of Simon and Wold. The trouble is that Keynes explicitly judges deterministic causality to be not very useful, especially for 'Moral Sciences':[12] 'One is led, almost inevitably, to use "cause" more widely than "sufficient cause" or than "necessary cause", because, the necessary causation of particulars by particulars being rarely apparent to us, the strict sense of the term has little utility' (Keynes, TP, p. 306).

Keynes feels the need of a concept of causality much more comprehen-

[11] An important exception may be found in Carabelli, 1984 and 1988, where Keynesian causality is correctly interpreted as probabilistic causality.
[12] Keynes classifies economics among 'moral sciences', whose method is contrasted to that of the natural sciences. See e.g. Keynes, CW, Vol. 14, p. 300. This topic is analysed in more detail in chapter 13.

114

sive than the traditional one. What is required is a concept of '*probable cause*, where there is no implication of necessity and where the antecedents will sometimes lead to particular consequents and sometimes will not' (*ibid.*, p. 306). He is fully aware of the novelty and difficulties of this task, because 'a partial or possible cause involves ideas which are still obscure' (*ibid.*, p. 182). The main problems arise from the conviction, then universally shared, that physical determinism could not be questioned.[13] Keynes manages to get round the obstacle by introducing a crucial distinction between the *causa essendi*, i.e. the ontological cause which in the physical world must be conceived as deterministic, and the *causa cognoscendi*, i.e. the epistemic cause which may be conceived as probabilistic. He puts the main emphasis on the second, because 'we wish to know whether knowledge of one fact throws light *of any kind* upon the likelihood of another. The theory of causality is only important because it is thought that by means of its assumptions light *can* be thrown by the experience of one phenomenon upon the expectation of another' (*ibid.*, p. 308).

Ontological causality (*causa essendi*) is interpreted as a limiting case of epistemic causality, whenever we have accurate enough knowledge of a certain set of phenomena to be able to determine a necessary or sufficient cause. This is possible only if we are able to determine the nomic conditions K, both formal and theoretic, and the existential conditions, both general L_t and hypothetical H_t, which make the causal influence of one event on another sufficient or necessary.

The nexus between ontologic and epistemic causality is clarified by Keynes through a succession of formal definitions of causality, which constitutes a sort of descent from the paradise of certainty to the hell of uncertainty. The starting point is given by the definition of *causa essendi*:

Event B is a sufficient cause of event A in conditions kl, iff
(i) proposition b describes an event B prior to event A, described by proposition a
(ii) $a/bkl = 1$ and $a/kl \neq 1$ (7.6)

This definition may be easily translated into Suppes's language, setting $a = A_t$, $b = B_t$, $kl = K \cap L_t = Z_t$. This is possible because, as we have seen, Suppes's events are strictly analogous to Keynes's propositions. Definition (7.6) is translated in the following way:

B_t is a sufficient cause of $A_{t'}$ relative to $Z_t = K \cap L_t$, iff
(i) $P(B_t \cap Z_t) > 0$ and $t < t'$
(ii) $P(A_{t'}/B_t \cap Z_t) = 1$ and $P(A_{t'}/Z_t) \neq 1$ (7.7)

---

[13] As is rightly observed by Weatherford (1982, p. 106), this depends very much on the fact that Keynes was writing in that happy epoch that preceded the quantum mechanics revolution.

Notice that B_t is a (potential) *prima facie* cause of $A_{t'}$ because condition (ii) implies that $P(A_{t'}/B_t \cap Z_t) > P(A_{t'}/Z_t)$. Keynes's formulation (7.7) is thus strictly equivalent to Suppes's definition (7.3).

Keynes then progressively weakens definition (7.7) by relaxing the conditions under which a concept of ontological causality may be defined. An intermediate step, for example, is the definition of a 'possible sufficient cause', when the background information Z_t includes a set H_t of existential hypotheses. The last step in this chain of definitions is that of the *causa cognoscendi*:

> B_t is a *causa cognoscendi* of $A_{t'}$ relative to Z_t iff
> (i) $P(B_t \cap Z_t) > 0$
> (ii) $P(A_{t'}/B_t \cap Z_t) \neq P(A_{t'}/Z_t)$ (7.8)

It may be easily verified that a *causa cognoscendi*, which does not imply a necessary or sufficient nexus between cause and effect, corresponds to a (potential) *prima facie* cause as stated by Suppes in definition (7.1), apart from the two following differences:

(a)   The temporal lag is not required. Keynes does not exclude the possibility of an epistemic cause contemporaneous with its effect. It is no wonder that contemporaneous causation may be found in his economic contributions.

(b)   The positive statistical relevance of the cause for the effect is not required. In other words a cause might also reduce the probability of the occurrence of the effect (in which case the cause is 'negative' or inhibitory).[14]

Keynes stops here in the *Treatise* because the theory of epistemic causality ends up by overlapping with his theory of probability. Still, I believe it is not improper to consider Keynes as a forerunner of the theory of probabilistic causality, especially in Suppes's version.

7.5   Granger's probabilistic causality

The causality concept worked out by Granger in the sixties (1963 and 1969), following a suggestion by Wiener (1958), has been and still is at the centre of a lively debate over its range of validity and its implications for economic theory. A few economists and econometricians have even questioned its epistemological legitimacy on the ground that it was inconsistent with an alleged philosophical tradition (see in particular Zellner, 1979). Even so, Granger causality rapidly became the prevailing conception of causality in

---

[14] This possibility is admitted by Suppes himself, though it is not made explicit in the definitions cited here.

economics and econometrics, partly because at the beginning it was found particularly congenial to the monetarist tendencies which became so popular in the seventies.

Its fortune may be dated back to the publication of an influential article by Sims (1972), who used Granger causality to argue that the money stock exerts a strong causal influence on nominal income and not vice versa. Granger causality rapidly became very popular with the new classical economists, partly because it was found to fit in well with the rational-expectations hypothesis.[15] This conception also became an important source of inspiration for the 'new econometrics' founded on time-series analysis 'without pretending to have too much *a priori* economic theory' (Sargent and Sims, 1977 and Sims, 1980a). An appraisal of its epistemological legitimacy and its range of validity is thus very important. The analysis developed in the last few pages turns out to be useful also for this task.

Granger develops his conception of causality through a succession of definitions which, not unlike that of Keynes, follows a downward path towards 'the hell of uncertainty'. It is justified in this case by the need to reach a definition of causality which is fully 'operative', i.e. amenable to empirical verification.

Let us assume that Y_n and X_{n+1} are two stochastic variables and Ω_n is a complete set of information available at time n and F is the function describing the conditional distribution of X. The starting point is the following definition:

- Y_n is cause of X_{n+1} iff
$$F(X_{n+1}/\Omega_n) \neq F(X_{n+1}/\Omega_n - Y_n) \tag{7.9}$$

In other words, 'for causation to occur, the variable Y_n needs to have some unique information about what value X_{n+1} will take in the immediate future' (Granger, 1980, p. 330). In order to make this definition operative, Granger has to substitute for the complete information set Ω the incomplete information sets J_n, an information set actually available at time n, and J'_n, comprising information set J_n plus the past and present values of Y_n. We obtain the following definition:

Y_n is a *prima facie* cause of X_{n+1} relative to the information set J'_n iff
$$F(X_{n+1}/J'_n) \neq F(X_{n+1}/J_n) \tag{7.10}$$

The use of incomplete information sets makes it necessary to introduce two qualifications which bring Granger's definition closer to that of Suppes:

[15] Lucas and Sargent explain why 'Granger causality is of natural interest for scholars of rational expectations' in the 'Introduction' to Lucas and Sargent, eds., 1981, pp. xxii–xxiv.

(a)   the causal statement must be interpreted in relation to a given set of background information;

(b) Y_n is thus only a *prima facie* cause since we cannot exclude the possibility that adding new information might cause it to become spurious.

The definition is not yet operative because up to this point an empirical test refers to population attributes of X_{n+1}, which we cannot know. Granger is thus compelled to be content with the first moment of the distribution, introducing the following definition:

Y_n is a *prima facie* cause in mean of X_{n+1} relative to the information set J'_n iff

$$E(X_{n+1}/J'_n) \neq E(X_{n+1}/J_n) \tag{7.11}$$

In addition Granger limits himself to point forecasts of X_{n+1} using a least-squares criterion. We may eventually express an operative definition of Granger causality, assuming that $\sigma^2(X_{n+1}/J_n)$ is the variance of the one-step forecast error of X_{n+1} given J_n:

Y_n is a *prima facie* cause in mean of X_{n+1} relative to the information set J'_n iff

$$\sigma^2(X_{n+1}/J'_n) < \sigma^2(X_{n+1}/J_n) \tag{7.12}$$

In other words, the knowledge of Y_n increases one's ability to forecast X_{n+1} in a least-squares sense, because it reduces the variance of forecast errors. Since much current economic and econometric practice is prediction-oriented, we may well understand why this definition, although very restrictive, has appealed to many. However, the definition actually tested is further restricted to linear predictors (Granger, 1969, p. 429; and 1980, p. 338), owing to the limitations of the available modelling and forecasting techniques:

Y_n is a linear *prima facie* cause in mean of X_{n+1} relative to the information set J'_n iff definition (7.12) is applied to a class of linear predictors. (7.13)

From now on the term 'Granger causality' will stand for the concept stipulated in this last definition.

Before discussing this concept's range of validity, we must recall that its operational implementation is subject to further limitations. The principal ones are made explicit by Granger himself through the following axioms:

Axiom A. 'The past and present may cause the future, but the future cannot cause the past' (Granger, 1980, p. 330). This axiom excludes not only backward causation, whose relevance is questionable, but also 'contemporaneous causation' which – as we have seen – is considered important by many economists.

Axiom B. The information sets contain no redundant information (*ibid.*, p. 330). This axiom is much more restrictive than it may appear at first. Redundant information could generate the erroneous conviction that a certain *prima facie* cause is spurious. This difficulty is particularly serious with economics, whose time series often follow very similar fluctuating patterns.

Axiom C. All causal relationships remain constant in direction through time (*ibid.*, p. 335). This axiom has been considered very stringent by a few critics (see e.g. Zellner, 1982, p. 314). However, Granger is right in pointing out that this assumption, though not literally true, is usual in causal inference and, indeed, in scientific inference in general. The related hypothesis that the series are jointly covariance stationary should be considered much more disturbingly restrictive. This assumption, according to Granger, is not strictly necessary for the definition of causality but is required for practical implementation. He admits that economic time series are often non-stationary, but he believes that they can be made stationary by transformations such as those suggested by Box and Jenkins (1970). Unfortunately it may be shown that these transformations do not preserve the causal properties of the original time series (cf. Conway, Swamy and Yanagida, 1983, pp. 17–23).

In addition we have to emphasize that, as Granger himself stressed (1980), his definition of causality does not apply to single events, to deterministic processes, or to data not measurable on a cardinal scale.

7.6   Granger and Suppes

As we have seen, the range of applicability of Granger causality is much narrower than that of Suppes causality. We may further clarify the issue by translating into Suppes's language Granger's definition (7.10), which is the most general definition that postulates incomplete information, as in Suppes. Let us assume that $A_{t'} = X_{n+1}$, $B_t = Y_n$, $Z_t = J_n$, $B_t \cap Z_t = J'_n$, and that both $A_{t'}$ and B_t occur. Granger's definition (7.10) may thus be expressed in the following way:

> B_t is a *prima facie* Granger cause of $A_{t'}$ relative to the background information Z_t iff
> (i) $A_{t'}$ and B_t occur and $t < t'$
> (ii) $F(A_{t'}/B_t \cap Z_t) \neq F(A_{t'}/Z_t)$ (7.14)

As we may verify by comparing (7.14) with (7.1), Granger causality appears as a particular case of Suppes causality which is at the centre of the modern philosophical debate on causality.[16] This suffices to confer upon Granger causality a *prima facie* philosophical legitimacy which Zellner denies. Moreover, it seems possible that the conception of causality adopted by Keynes and that adopted by the new classical economists, though the latter are uncompromisingly anti-Keynesian, both belong to the same philosophical family.

However, the formal analogy conceals a profound difference. In both Keynes and Suppes background information encompasses a theoretical framework, while in Granger it includes only the past and present values of the relevant stochastic variables. The other peculiarities of Granger causality, such as the exclusive reference to events which have actually occurred, and hence not to types of events and to dispositional magnitudes, all derive from this inductivist point of view. The supporters of Granger causality see this as vindicating its superiority over competing notions of causality. In their opinion Granger causality is the only conception of causality which is actually operative, in the sense that the results of empirical tests are 'non-conditional', i.e. independent of *a priori* theoretical assumptions. This alleged superiority is argued in particular *vis-à-vis* Goodwin-Simon-Wold causality, which was the main existing alternative for economic analysis. It is shown that, from the formal point of view, these two conceptions are strictly analogous, and that the only significant difference is that Goodwin, Simon and Wold always explicitly refer their causal statements to a theoretical framework. Moreover it is admitted that the range of applicability is broader in this second case. If we could prove that the unconditionality claim is wrong, the claim of superiority would in general be refuted. This is what will be argued next.

Many empirical tests of Granger causality have been devised, with different advantages and disadvantages. They all have in common a two-stage procedure of implementation. In the first stage a few statistical tests are applied to empirical data, and in the second stage the results of these tests are interpreted. In the first stage the theoretical hypotheses are not clearly defined. It could be objected that any procedure of selection and manipulation of data already presupposes a theoretical point of view, even if this is only implicit.[17] Whatever one may think of this objection, in the second stage serious difficulties emerge which I consider insuperable. The

---

[16] A thesis in many respects analogous is maintained by Spohn, 1983. He rightly emphasizes, moreover, a few notational problems with Granger's definitions. However, Spohn's analysis does not perceive the crucial point: the profoundly different role that background information plays in the causal theory of the two authors.

[17] See e.g. Blaug, 1980, p.14.

crucial problem is to discriminate between genuine and spurious causes. This cannot be done without an *explicit* intervention of theoretical hypotheses. Granger and Sims believe it is possible to get round this obstacle. They discuss a list of circumstances under which a *prima facie* cause is likely to be spurious, in order to prove that all these circumstances are extremely unlikely in the case of Granger causality. Unfortunately this strategy cannot succeed.

In particular, in order to exclude the possibility of finding a third variable that would make a *prima facie* cause spurious, it is suggested that certain empirical tests be applied to all the variables that might have such an effect. This procedure is clearly unacceptable, unless we make a sufficient number of *a priori* theoretical assumptions regarding the behaviour of the economic system. Otherwise the list of third variables which could induce spuriousness would be virtually infinite.

More generally, we may observe that one cannot demonstrate the exhaustiveness of any list of circumstances which might induce spuriousness. An *a priori* discussion on the likelihood of certain spuriousness-inducing circumstances cannot substantially increase confidence regarding the 'genuineness' of a certain *prima facie* cause, unless one explicitly declares his theoretical background. Thus even Granger causality refers implicitly to a certain conceptual framework. The only real difference in this respect is that the theoretical hypotheses are made explicit by Goodwin, Simon and Wold, while they remain implicit in the arguments of Granger and Sims. The charge of presupposition against the use of Simon and Wold causality may thus be turned against an uncritical use of Granger and Sims causality. What one really cannot do is to assert the truth of a causal statement, 'pretending' that it is 'unconditional' to any theoretical framework.

The supporters of Granger causality seem occasionally unaware of the well known limits of inductive methods, which have been clarified by a prestigious philosophical tradition going from Hume to Popper and beyond. They apparently accept one or more of the following mistaken axioms:

> measurement is possible without theory,
> correlation implies causation,
> *post hoc ergo propter hoc.*

Each of these theses is at times provocatively introduced by the supporters of Granger causality[18] – perhaps in order to flaunt the novelty of

---

[18] An example is given by the following passage of Sims: 'the method of identifying causal direction employed here does rest on a sophisticated version of the *post hoc ergo propter hoc* principle' (Sims, 1972, p. 543).

their conception, as if the new techniques of time series could by themselves overcome these well established methodological principles. In so doing they slip into the pitfalls of 'operationism' and of 'inductivism', long since rejected by the philosophy of science.

However, there is a second line of defence for Granger causality which is less pretentious and more convincing. Granger causality is considered particularly relevant for certain specific scientific aims. We may recall in particular the following claims (see e.g. Sims 1972 and 1977):

(a)   Granger causality is a necessary and sufficient condition for exogeneity, which is a necessary condition for efficient estimation;
(b)   Granger causality is a necessary and sufficient condition for optimal forecasts;
(c)   Granger causality is a necessary, though not sufficient, condition for economic policy (forecast and control).

Unfortunately, even these claims are exaggerated. Granger causality is a necessary but not sufficient condition for predicting the outcomes of processes which are not influenced by policy, or are in any case structurally stable. But it is neither a necessary nor a sufficient condition for correct estimation, nor for prediction and control of processes which are influenced by policy interventions, or which are in any way structurally unstable (Engle, Hendry and Richard, 1983).

We may thus conclude that Granger causality is not useless for a few well defined scientific aims. But the claim of its general superiority over alternative conceptions of causality, in particular that of Goodwin, Simon and Wold, is totally groundless.

7.7   Conclusions

The conception of probabilistic causality in the version given by Suppes has proved to be very useful for clarifying two conceptions of causality which are particularly important for economic analysis: that of Keynes and that of Granger.

In particular I have argued that Keynes causality is probabilistic and in many ways anticipates the more recent and mature theory of Suppes. Granger's conception can in turn be interpreted as a particular version of Suppes causality. However, we have seen that, behind the formal analogies, profound philosophical divergences between Keynes and Granger are detectable. While Keynes, as well as the supporters of the main alternative conception (Goodwin, Simon and Wold), insists that it is necessary to relate any causal statement to a well defined theoretical background, the supporters of Granger causality claim that their conception is superior precisely because of its alleged independence of theoretical hypotheses. This presupposition proves completely groundless. So does then that of Granger causality's general superiority over alternative conceptions, although this does not exclude its utility for well defined and circumscribed scientific purposes. In particular we have seen that it is a necessary, though not sufficient, condition for efficient predictions of the outcomes of processes which are not influenced by policy interventions, or which are in any case structurally stable.

The preceding considerations are not without implications for the lively debate between new classical economists and Keynesian economists. In particular the claims of superiority based on the results of Granger causality tests must be considered as open to question, because they depend on *a priori* theoretical hypotheses which are not explicitly discussed in these contributions.

Part II

Keynes after Lucas

Lucas's scientific paradigm

It almost looks as if [they] were trying to compensate themselves for the loss of an unchanging world by clinging to the faith that change can be foreseen because it is ruled by an unchanging law. (Popper, 1957, p. 161)

8.1   Introduction

In this chapter I will briefly describe the outlines of Lucas's research programme (or 'paradigm') as it was worked out and expressed in the seventies. Needless to say, this research programme had a tremendous impact on macroeconomics, particularly in the English-speaking world. The version of the seventies is now historically dated and has been superseded in many crucial points by Lucas himself and other new classical economists. This is not at all surprising as any lively research programme undergoes an evolution due to internal and external impulses. Therefore the criticisms I shall raise in this chapter should not be mechanically transferred to other new classical economists, or to Lucas's contributions published before or afterwards. In the sixties[1] Lucas was still attempting to contribute to Keynesian literature (see Lucas, 1981, p. 2), while in the eighties[2] he has tried, together with other new classical economists, to go beyond the limitations of his previous work.[3]

---

[1] Lucas's joint paper of 1969, written with Rapping, is clearly the watershed between the Keynesian period and the new classical period.

[2] We can interpret the 'Introduction' written in 1981 with Sargent to their famous book on rational expectations as a sort of reasoned synthesis of the aims and scope of the research done in the seventies. The interview published by Klamer in 1984 but recorded in May 1982 still basically belongs to that period.

[3] Lucas has recently declared (1987, p. 1) that research in macroeconomics
has undergone rapid change in the past 15 years. One way of describing some of these changes is in terms of ideological contests between rival schools of thought: the 'Keynesian revolution', the 'monetarist counter-revolution', and so on. There is no doubt something to be learned by tracing the main ideological currents in macroeconomic research, but I myself find most of this discussion of crises,

Lucas's research programme of the seventies is very important not only for historical reasons, but also because it was the source of his heuristic model (discussed in chapter 9), which is still at the centre of the research carried on by Lucas and the other new classical economists. So, for example, the real-business-cycle literature dramatically departs from the monetarism of Lucas's research programme in the seventies, but explicitly accepts the basic tenets of Lucas's heuristic model (see chapter 10).

In section 8.2 I will summarize the main features of the research programme suggested by Lucas in the seventies. Then in section 8.3 I will discuss the definition of the business cycle proposed by Lucas which plays a crucial role in his contributions to macroeconomics. In section 8.4 I will criticize Lucas's purely monetary theory of the business cycle. I will then scrutinize the celebrated 'Lucas critique' of large Keynesian econometric models (section 8.5) and the so-called 'Lucas's principle' forbidding the use of free parameters (section 8.6). Lucas's research programme cannot be grasped without understanding his conception of economics as an exact science (section 8.7). Conclusions follow in section 8.8.

8.2   Lucas's economic vision

Lucas sees Keynesianism as a temporary deviation from the mainstream of scientific progress in economics – a pathological phenomenon for which he offers both an explanation and a remedy.

In his view the success of Keynesianism arose from the fact that the theory of general economic equilibrium, in the versions available in the thirties, was unable to account for the empirical evidence regarding the business cycle. The economic crisis raised serious problems which demanded a theoretical and practical response, and Keynesianism was developed as a short-cut to meet this urgent need. By now, Lucas believes, that short-cut has become useless if not actually harmful, and the Keynesian deviation from the main road can be dismissed. In his opinion recent advances in theory and modelling techniques have made possible a rigorous foundation, solidly based on general economic equilibrium, for the theory of economic cycles and macroeconomic policy.

Lucas's research programme is meant to implement in practice a sort of anti-Keynesian counter-revolution. His main aim is to re-establish classical theory in a more advanced and satisfactory version which can take account

revolutions and so on, unintelligible, and almost wholly unconnected with the most interesting current research.
This seems almost a retreat from the seventies version of his research programme which heavily relied on the above-mentioned ideological counterpositions (see e.g. Lucas 1981, and Lucas and Sargent, eds., 1981).

of macroeconomic phenomena and provide firm criteria for choosing between alternative economic policies.[4]

The negative argument behind the 'counter-revolution' is that Keynesian macroeconomics, lacking a rigorous foundation in terms of general economic equilibrium, cannot predict how the economy will react to changes in economic policy, and hence cannot provide reliable criteria for choosing between different economic policies. The parameters of a model generally vary together with changes in economic policy, and from a Keynesian perspective, based simply on the empirical observation of past values of those parameters, there is no way of calculating what values they would assume after a change in economic policy. Such a calculation is believed to be possible only within the perspective of 'classical' theory, where the values of macroeconomic parameters have a theoretical basis in the theory of general economic equilibrium. Only the 'deep' parameters of general economic equilibrium, according to Lucas, are 'structural', i.e. do not vary with the rules of economic policies.

The positive rationale of the 'classical restoration' is that the contradiction between the static general economic equilibrium and the dynamic empirical economic cycle can be overcome by applying the concept of equilibrium, not at the level of actual phenomena, but at a higher level of abstraction of which phenomena are seen as a manifestation. In other words it is assumed that general economic equilibrium refers to the stochastic process of which observed phenomena constitute just one possible realization. The variables appearing in the stochastic process are thus endowed with a complex dynamic behaviour which can 'mimic' phenomenic behaviour without negating the hypothesis that the stochastic process generating those values is one of stationary equilibrium.

This strategy is quite legitimate and typical of scientific progress: the conceptual order (equilibrium, stability) that cannot be found at the level of phenomena is found at a higher level of abstraction (see chapter 4). However, the usefulness of this strategic move is not guaranteed *a priori*; it can be evaluated only by examining the merits of Lucas's scientific contribution.

Lucas's economic vision goes back to the neoclassical picture in its monetarist form.[5] The perfectly competitive market is considered the most

---

[4] Lucas assumes that 'classical' (or pre-Keynesian) macroeconomic theory is correctly defined by the attempt to base the theory of cycles and money on general economic equilibrium. This is philologically questionable, though he is able to cite Hayek: 'The incorporation of cyclical phenomena into the system of economic equilibrium theory, with which they are in apparent contradiction, remains the crucial problem of Trade Cycle Theory' (quoted in Lucas, 1981, p. 215).

[5] We shall see, on the other hand, that the heuristic model differs considerably from the monetarist one (chapter 9).

desirable institutional arrangement for the economic system because of its presumed capacity for very rapid self-regulation and the supposedly related maximization of welfare. Any malfunctions of the market are ascribed to external perturbations arising ultimately from a discretionary and hence erratic Keynesian monetary policy. More generally, they are ascribed to excessive state interventionism in the economy, which is also blamed on the 'scourge of Keynesianism'. Such in essence are the views codified by the Chicago School, particularly by Friedman.

Lucas never pretends to have anything new to say at the level of first principles. He only claims to have pointed out the path whereby Friedman's theses could be given an analytical basis firmly grounded on the principles of general economic equilibrium. Friedman already recognized the need for this in his 'Presidential Address' in 1968, but on that occasion he had to admit that he was unable to work out the necessary analytical steps. Thus Lucas's original contribution is essentially at the methodological and analytical level.

The nucleus of this contribution – generally not shared by the monetarists (see e.g. Laidler 1986) – lies in a systematic application of the so-called 'equilibrium method', which is taken as an extension to macroeconomics of the general-equilibrium approach. It consists in the joint application of two hypotheses: (a) that economic agents act in their own interest; (b) that markets always 'clear', i.e. they are never characterized by excesses of supply or demand. The first postulate is translated in practice into the well known requisite of maximization of utility and profit, which is accepted by the monetarists and by most Keynesians. On the other hand the second one is extremely controversial, contested by the Keynesian economists and by many monetarists. It clearly implies instantaneous adjustment of prices, and this is considered intolerably unrealistic by the critics.

Lucas defends himself by asking to be judged not on the realism of the hypotheses but on the usefulness of his assumptions. He therefore tries to demonstrate that the range of application of the equilibrium method can be extended even to problems which, though crucial for economic policy, have always proved resistant to this type of approach.

In fact Lucas's first contribution to the extension of the equilibrium method deals with the labour market, because 'nowhere is the "apparent contradiction" between "cyclical phenomena" and "economic equilibrium" theory sharper than in labor market behavior' (1981, p. 220). In his famous 1969 article written in collaboration with Rapping, Lucas seeks to demonstrate that the time series of employment can be explained without recourse to any disequilibrium concept such as 'monetary illusion', 'excess labour supply', or especially 'involuntary unemployment' (with the sole possible exception of the 'Great Crisis' of the Thirties). The basic idea can be summed up as follows. Since economic agents possess only limited information, they rationally interpret any variations in the level of prices as expressions, at least in part, of transitory variations in relative prices. Thus, for example, an increase in the level of money wages is to some extent decoded by the workers as a transitory increase in real wages over the level perceived as normal. Hence they decide to work more, expecting to recoup their lost leisure time as soon as their real wages are perceived as being, again for transitory reasons, lower than normal. This, according to Lucas, can explain oscillations in employment and their positive correlation with oscillations in prices and money wages, without casting doubt on any of the 'classical' dogmas: the perfect rationality of the labour market and the capacity for self-regulation of competitive markets, not to mention the neoclassical dichotomy between the real and monetary systems (in particular the null elasticity of the long-term supply curve for labour to variations in money wages).

In this perspective there is no place for involuntary unemployment because the market for labour is always 'cleared' and the workers are always on the labour supply curve: 'Measured unemployment (more exactly, its nonfrictional component) is then viewed as consisting of persons who regard the wage rates at which they could currently be employed as temporarily low and who therefore choose to wait or search for improved conditions rather than to invest in moving or occupational change' (1981, p. 42).

Having thus somehow reconciled the labour market and the equilibrium method, Lucas notes that this type of solution can be generalized to all markets; thus he is led to suggest a way out of the general contradiction between economic cycles and the equilibrium method. According to his hypothesis, economic magnitudes oscillate cyclically because economic agents, finding themselves in a situation of uncertainty, interpret monetary signals rationally as if they were at least in part real signals, thus modifying the dynamics of the quantities which they are able to control. The source of these inevitable misunderstandings, Lucas believes, lies in a monetary policy which is erratic because it suffers from the Keynesian disease of interventionism, which creates unpredictable changes in the behaviour of monetary variables. The above analysis leads to some clear indications for economic policy: 'Insofar as fluctuations are induced by gratuitous monetary instability, serving no social purpose, then increased monetary stability promises to reduce aggregate, real variability and increase welfare' (*ibid.*, p. 234). These arguments are meant to give new support to the adoption of fixed rules of money management, as against discretionary rules. This preference, however, is not based on a presumed ineffectiveness of economic policy – an assumption which is erroneously considered as a corollary of the theoretical theses of new classical economics. It is based, rather, on the awareness of our ignorance:

> Our ability as economists to predict the responses of agents rests, in situations where expectations about the future matter, on our understanding of the stochastic environment agents believe themselves to be operating in. In practice, this limits the class of policies the consequences of which we can hope to assess in advance to policies generated by fixed, well understood, relatively permanent rules (*ibid.*, p. 255).

Moreover, this meets the requirement for a correct relationship between government and citizens, as policy-makers must strive to behave in a credible way.[6]

In the context of this research programme the hypothesis of rational expectations plays an important but not decisive role, as Lucas himself suggests. It is a technical principle of model construction which assures nothing more than consistency between an endogenous mechanism of expectations formation and general economic equilibrium.[7]

8.3   Definition of the business cycle

Lucas, as we have seen, interprets Keynes's macroeconomics as a 'theory of depression', indeed of the 'Great Depression' of the Thirties. In other words he sees it as concerned only with a particular phenomenon, and hence as irremediably dated. In Lucas's own conception, however, macroeconomics is identified with the general theory of economic fluctuations. The business cycle is seen as an inherently systemic phenomenon as it is characterized by the combined oscillations of the principal economic time series.

Lucas's proposed definition is accurate and apparently innocuous, but on closer examination it proves to be misleading. The object is circumscribed in such a way as to make the application of the 'equilibrium method' plausible. However, this definition is rather peculiar (not to say *ad hoc*), and in any case quite restrictive compared to the meaning current in common language and even among economists. Lucas is aware of this, as can be seen

---

[6] Lucas maintains that 'policy makers, if they wish to forecast the response of citizens, must take the latter into their confidence. This conclusion, if ill-suited to current econometric practice, seems to accord well with a preference for democratic decision making' (*ibid.*, p. 126).

[7] Lucas (*ibid.*, pp. 1–2) maintains that

> John Muth's hypothesis of rational expectations is a technical model-building principle, not a distinct, comprehensive macroeconomic theory. Recent research utilizing this principle has reinforced many of the policy recommendations of Milton Friedman and other postwar monetarists but has contributed few, if any, original policy proposals. My own research has been concerned almost exclusively with the attempt to discover a useful theoretical explanation of business cycles.

between the lines on careful perusal of his articles. But he often yields to the temptation to let the reader believe that his proposed theoretical definition applies to the whole complex of phenomena which normally comprise what is called the business cycle, rather than to a very restricted subset of those phenomena.

According to Lucas the main qualitative features of the economic time series which we call 'the business cycle' are movements about trends which 'do not exhibit uniformity of either period or amplitude, which is to say, they do not resemble the deterministic wave motions which sometimes arise in the natural sciences' (1981, p. 217). This is all right as far as it goes. However, the object is restricted to the only invariable regularities that can be found in the available data, i.e. a few 'co-movements' that can be discerned among the aggregate time series:

The principal among these are the following. (i) Output movements across broadly defined sectors move together . . . (ii) Production of producer and consumer durables exhibits much greater amplitude than does the production of nondurables. (iii) Production and prices of agricultural goods and natural resources have lower than average conformity. (iv) Business profits show high conformity and much greater amplitude than other series. (v) Prices generally are procyclical. (vi) Short-term interest rates are procyclical; long-term rates slightly so. (vii) Monetary aggregates and velocity measures are procyclical. (*ibid.*, p. 217)

In other words Lucas chooses to limit the object of the business cycle theory to those regularities which are 'common to all decentralized market economies', so that by definition 'with respect to the qualitative behaviour of co-movements among series, business cycles are all alike'. The ground is thus neatly prepared for the application of the equilibrium method which requires the stationarity of the relevant stochastic processes.[8]

To make sense of his theory, in other words, Lucas has to restrict the definition of the cycle solely to those connotations relating to invariable regularities. He himself recognizes this, but only within an argument which is in danger of being misleading. He declares first of all that he is seeking an equilibrium explanation of the phenomena previously listed.[9] This proves possible only if uncertainty is introduced. The rational economic agent must work out a contingent plan specifying how he will react to unforesee-

---

[8] Lucas observes that 'to theoretically inclined economists, this conclusion should be attractive and challenging, for it suggests the possibility of a unified explanation of business cycles, grounded in the general laws governing market economies, rather than in political or institutional characteristics specific to particular countries or periods' (*ibid.*, p. 218).

[9] Lucas maintains that 'one would like a theory which accounts for the observed movements in quantities (employment, consumption, investment) as an optimizing response to observed movements in prices' (*ibid.*, p. 222).

able events, which implies the formulation of the joint probability distribution for all the stochastic variables which influence his present and future market opportunities. Unfortunately, 'without some way of inferring what an agent's subjective view of the future is, this hypothesis is of no help in understanding his behavior' (*ibid.*, p. 223). At this point the hypothesis of rational expectations enters the picture: 'John Muth . . . proposed to resolve this problem by identifying agents' subjective probabilities with observed frequencies of the events to be forecast, or with "true" probabilities, calling the assumed coincidence of subjective and "true" probabilities rational expectations.' This solution to the dilemma works, however, only in situations where 'the probabilities of interest concern a fairly well defined recurrent event, situations of "risk" in Knight's terminology'. On the other hand the hypothesis of rational expectations, and more generally the equilibrium method, proves inapplicable 'in situations in which one cannot guess which, if any, observable frequencies are relevant' (*ibid.*, p. 223).

Thus Lucas gives the impression of adapting the object to the chosen method, rather than the reverse. In this way he ends up excluding those aspects which, while important, cannot be defined as invariable regularities: international aspects because they depend on the degree of openness of the economy, real wages because they do not show consistent cyclical behaviour, etc. Other aspects are not even mentioned, probably because they are considered too irregular: for example data on productivity and income distribution.

8.4   A single (monetary) shock: a double *non sequitur*

As we have seen, Lucas explains the economic cycle essentially on the basis of impulses seen as exogenous shocks. Precisely because the object of the theory of economic cycles is defined in an extremely restrictive way, we should expect that many factors which might influence the economic cycle will turn out to be exogenous. Surprisingly, however, Lucas imputes the economic cycle to just one type of shock, the monetary shock. The reasoning behind this crucial passage in his argument is very vague, as if it ought to be obvious to everyone: 'It is the similarity from cycle to cycle of comovements among series, as documented by Mitchell, that leads one to a single-shock view of business cycles. *Given* this, Friedman and Schwartz have no alternative but to identify this single shock with monetary instability. What are the other candidates?' (1981, p. 16).

The first part of the argument is far from cogent: its fundamental premise is assumed by definition, and hence its consequence, if true, is true only by definition – that is to say, according to Lucas's peculiar definition of the economic cycle. Even so, the consequence does not necessarily follow from the premise: the regularity of cyclic phenomena depends not so much on the type of exogenous shock as on the internal characteristics of the system (in particular the mechanisms of propagation); this has been well known at least since Wicksell's time.[10] But let us assume for the sake of argument that only one type of shock influences the economic cycle: why should that shock be of a monetary nature? Lucas argues that in a competitive economy quantity choices are determined by agents' reactions to prices, and the latter depend on the quantity of money:

For explaining secular movements in prices generally, secular movements in the quantity of money do extremely well. This fact is as well established as any we know in aggregative economics, and is not sensitive to how one measures either prices or the quantity of money. There is no serious doubt as to the direction of effect in this relationship; no one argues that the anticipation of sixteenth-century inflation sent Columbus to the New World to locate gold to finance it. This evidence has no direct connection to business cycles, since it refers to averages over much longer periods, but the indirect connections are too strong to be ignored . . . All these arguments point to a monetary shock as the force triggering the real business cycle. (*ibid.*, p. 233)

This argument is far from convincing. It is true that over a very long period of time, such as a century, there are solid empirical grounds for the correlation between price movements and the quantity of money; but that has very little to do with the business cycle. With regard to the short-term correlation the link is extremely vague and problematic. This is openly recognized even by Friedman, who speaks of 'long and variable lags'. Lucas himself has to recognize that 'the direct evidence on short-term correlations between money, output, and prices is much more difficult to read', and only 'certain extreme episodes appear to indicate that depressions and recoveries are money-induced' (*ibid.*, p. 233). What is worse, the direction of the causal link between money and prices can by no means be taken for granted. The empirical 'proofs' advanced by the monetarists, based on the erroneous principle of *post hoc ergo propter hoc*, have been effectively confuted by Tobin (1970). In the seventies new 'empirical proofs' based on causality in Granger's sense have been suggested, but their persuasive force is weak (as we saw in chapter 7). Finally, already in the seventies the new classical economists, though they used these questionable tests to support monetarist theses, were forced to recognize that in certain cases the causal link is

---

[10] Wicksell's famous rocking-horse always oscillates in the same way, whether it is hit by a stick, a kick or an earthquake.

reversed. Sargent, for example, reached this conclusion with regard to certain episodes of hyperinflation.[11]

Thus Lucas's argument is marred by a double *non sequitur*. It does not follow from his own definition of a business cycle that the cause of a business cycle is one single type of shock; and in any case, even accepting that conclusion, it does not follow that this shock must be of a monetary nature. One is left with the impression that on this occasion the force of the Chicago tradition is more persuasive than the force of rigorous scientific arguments. It is interesting to observe that many scholars who accept Lucas's equilibrium method have reached radically different conclusions as to the nature of the relevant shocks. According to the adherents of the 'real-equilibrium business cycle' the causes of the cycle are real and have to do with the characteristics of the investment process (such as 'time to build'; see e.g. Long and Plosser, 1983).[12] In the eighties this position became dominant among new classical economists (see chapter 10).

We may legitimately conclude, then, that Lucas's view of the nature of the economic cycle is in no way implied by his methodology of 'equilibrium'.[13]

8.5 The instability of the parameter structure and economic policy

Having analysed what I consider to be the weakest part of Lucas's contribution, I now intend to deal with the part I think is of greatest interest and most lasting value: his criticism of those large-scale econometric models, rightly or wrongly called Keynesian, which are used to predict the behaviour of industrialized economies. Unfortunately his constructive

---

[11] Curiously enough this was recognized by Lucas himself (together with Sargent) in the introduction to their well known book on rational expectations (Lucas and Sargent, eds., 1981, p. xxiv):

> In Chapter 22, Sargent and Wallace reexamine some of the hyper-inflations studied by Cagan (1956) to determine the directions of Granger causality between inflation and money creation. They find stronger evidence of Granger causality extending from inflation to money creation than in the reverse direction, a finding that at first glance would surprise someone committed to a monetary explanation of the hyperinflations.

[12] Some exponents of the equilibrium business cycle have clearly stated that variations in the quantity of money have no significant influence on the economic cycle (see e.g. F. Black, 1982).

[13] Recently Lucas, while reaffirming the basic validity of his own monetary theory of the economic cycle (1987, pp. 4 and 32–3), has recognized that an 'ideal' model of the business cycle should 'hybridize' the monetary point of view of his 1975 model with the 'real' model *à la* Kydland and Prescott, 1982 (*ibid.*, p. 85). Lucas also suggests the lines along which one should proceed in order to obtain this result, which, however, 'is, at present, slightly beyond the frontier of what is technically possible' (*ibid.*). This topic will be discussed in chapter 10.

proposal does not prove equally convincing: the new 'classical' equilibrium models, which are supposed to replace the 'Keynesian' ones, do not seem able to escape that criticism.

Let us begin with the *pars destruens*. As the structure of an econometric model consists of rules for optimal decisions on the part of economic agents, and since these rules vary systematically along with the structures of the main series which characterize the 'environment', it follows that any change in the rules adopted by economic policy, which in fact is interpreted as one of the main series mentioned above, will systematically alter the nature of the econometric models. For the purpose of short-term prediction, according to Lucas, in many cases this problem may prove to be of small importance, since significant changes in the structure of the series analysed, including those directly controlled by economic policy, are not seen as very frequent events. On the other hand these considerations are held to be fundamental for problems involving evaluations of economic policy. In fact in this case comparisons between the effects of alternative economic policy rules based on existing econometric models cannot be considered reliable, whatever validity may be shown by these models in the period for which they were worked out, or in short-term predictions (Lucas, 1981, p. 126).

Hence if we wish to use an econometric model to evaluate the relative validity of alternative economic policies, we need a model capable of elaborating *conditional* predictions. That is to say, it must be able to answer questions like: how would behaviour change if certain economic policies were altered in specific ways? This is possible only if the structure of the model remains *invariant* when the economic policy rules change (*ibid.*, p. 220). This is the crucial point where the new classical economists' equilibrium method intervenes in an essential way. According to Lucas, only an equilibrium model in the sense first defined can show this type of invariance in the structure of the coefficients. By contrast, any disequilibrium model involving elements such as excess demand, involuntary unemployment, etc. – like the Keynesian models – is said to be inherently incapable of passing this type of test.

This argument must be examined very closely because it underlies the presumed superiority of the 'classical' models over the Keynesian ones. Despite the importance of the matter at stake, Lucas's argument is surprisingly weak. He states the problem correctly, recognizing that the invariability of parameters in an economic model cannot be guaranteed *a priori*. Yet he considers it 'reasonable to hope that neither tastes nor technology vary systematically with variations in countercyclical policies' (*ibid.*, p. 220). Economic reality, it would seem, can be divided into two levels: that of phenomena, characterized by erratic movements (disequilibria, in this peculiar sense) and by structural instability of parameters; and a deeper and more basic level – one is tempted to say an 'essential' level – characterized by the parameters of general economic equilibrium, which are considered structurally stable.

So the equilibrium method is meant to bring macroeconomic phenomena, with all their apparent disequilibria – erratic movements and episodes of instability – within the scope of the essential level. By contrast the Keynesian models, from this point of view, stop at the level of phenomena and so fail to transcend the 'appearances' of things. While Lucas does not use such philosophical language, I think the above description may rightly reflect the kernel of his argument.

The rules governing the decisions of economic agents, which characterize economic behaviour at the level of phenomena, generally change when the environment changes. Therefore 'any disequilibrium model, constructed by simply codifying the decision rules which agents have found it useful to use over some previous sample period, without explaining *why* these rules are used' – i.e. because it is condemned to stop at the level of phenomena – 'will be of no use in predicting the consequences of nontrivial policy changes' (*ibid.*, p. 221). On the other hand 'an equilibrium model is, by definition, constructed so as to predict how agents with stable tastes and technology will *choose* to respond to a new situation' (*ibid.*, pp. 220–1), and thus makes the necessary connection showing how the behaviour of phenomena is rooted in the essential level, characterized by equilibrium and stability (both dynamic and structural).

Despite the undoubted fascination of this approach, it must be recognized that the *pars construens* of this research programme is still no more than a conjecture. Are tastes and technology really invariant with respect to changes in the rules of economic policy? Lucas hopes they are, but admits that he does not know for certain.[14]

---

[14] He throws cold water on the excessive enthusiasm of other, less rigorous exponents of new classical economics in passages like this (*ibid.*, pp. 11–12):

> I view 'Econometric Policy Evaluation' [Lucas, 1976] as a contribution to this important question of the relation of theory to econometric work, but sometimes it is read as though it resolved the issue much more decisively than can ever be the case. The paper stressed the importance of identifying structural parameters that are invariant under the kinds of policy changes one is interested in evaluating; and in all of the paper's examples, only the parameters describing 'tastes' and 'technology' were treated as having this property. The presumption seems a sound one to me, but it must be defended on empirical, not logical grounds, and the nature of such a defense presumably would vary with the particular application one has in mind. That is, utility theory does not tell us that utility functions are invariant under changes in the behavior of prices; its application assumes this. The stability of, say, empirical Engel curves over so wide a range of circumstances reflects well on Engel's judgment and is an amazing piece of good luck for us, as empirical scientists, but there is no way that Engel could have assured himself logically that this would be the case.

Still, Lucas feels that there is a 'reasonable hope' that the classical structural parameters are stable. What are we to think of this conjecture? I shall briefly discuss it only in relation to the stability of technology, in order to show that it cannot be taken for granted. There is a respected and consolidated tradition that systematically connects the economic cycle with discontinuous variations in the technological structure. Among the writers who could be cited in this connection are Spiethoff, Schumpeter and Keynes, and also more orthodox scholars such as Robertson, not to mention the recent supporters of the real-equilibrium business cycle. The structural instability of technological parameters does not necessarily imply that they change in response to variations in the rules of economic policy. But I think is is hard to deny that different economic policy rules can significantly influence investment activity in both its quantitative and qualitative aspects, and that this cannot but affect technological progress. It seems to me legitimate, therefore, to conclude that the technological structure cannot be considered invariant with respect to different alternative rules of economic policy (see section 9.4.4).

With regard to those models which incorporate elements of disequilibrium, criticism has concentrated on the most commonly used large-scale econometric models, since they do not satisfactorily explain why certain rules of decision are adopted by economic agents, and hence they cannot explain or predict structural transformations of the economic system. This is not a new argument; it has been used many times in criticizing prevailing econometric practice. We find it clearly sketched out in the last works of Keynes himself, in particular in his critical review of Tinbergen (1939).

Lucas undoubtedly deserves credit for having managed to reformulate this criticism in a much more precise and rigorous version. But there is still no convincing argument to show why such a defect must necessarily characterize *any* disequilibrium model. At the theoretical level there is no reason why one should not postulate a disequilibrium path as an optimal trajectory for reaching certain results, which would permit the solution of the model to be recalculated after a change in the environment. The conclusions that can be drawn from the so-called 'Lucas critique' are for the moment purely negative with regard to both disequilibrium and equilibrium models. In the future, however, there is no reason to assume *a priori* that disequilibrium models may not have an equal chance of circumventing this obstacle.

8.6   The empirical plausibility of Lucas's hypotheses

A detailed examination of the empirical scope of Lucas's scientific paradigm is beyond the limits of the present study. At this stage, however, it may be useful to mention briefly some difficulties which arise in the attempt to apply his theory of the economic cycle to empirical data. To overcome these difficulties, in fact, it is inevitably necessary to reintroduce free parameters, for the total elimination of which Lucas's theory was constructed.

First of all, it should be noted that Lucas manages to provide a basis for the Phillips curve by replacing the free parameter linking variations in prices and money wages to 'excess demand' with a combination of parameters, among which the elasticity of labour supply in relation to real wages plays a crucial role. However, fluctuations in aggregate employment prove systematically too wide, in relation to the fluctuations of inflation, to be interpreted as oscillations along a stable labour supply curve, as Lucas suggests (see Laidler, 1986).

In Lucas's paradigm quantities vary in response to price changes. This seems to imply, *prima facie*, that production and employment should vary with the level of prices, either simultaneously or after a short delay. Data, however, suggest that in many cases quantity variations actually precede variations in price levels.

Moreover, the variations in economic policy rules which occurred in many countries during the early eighties produced different economic effects from those that might have been expected on the basis of Lucas's paradigm. Sudden but well publicized monetary contractions almost immediately generated considerable real effects (reduction of production and employment), whereas only afterwards, gradually, did they produce the desired deflationary effects on prices and money wages.

By means of an opportune series of auxiliary *ad hoc* assumptions, Lucas's paradigm can be rescued from these and other incongruities between theoretical assertions and empirical observations. For example, one can maintain that new economic policies have produced real effects before monetary ones because they did not prove to be credible enough. However, if the credibility argument is introduced into a model of the Lucas type in order to obtain falsifiable predictions, it seems unavoidable – given the present state of theoretical knowledge – to bring in free parameters. In more general terms, that is, Lucas's paradigm manages to avoid using free parameters only as long as it avoids a serious comparison with empirical data. Indeed, as we have seen, Lucas cannot do without free parameters in his theoretical model of the cycle. The 'Lucas principle', therefore, does not offer a criterion for choice between the Lucasian and Keynesian models.

8.7   Lucas's conception of economic science

The fundamental aspects of Lucas's scientific paradigm rest on an extremely reductive conception of science. Macroeconomics itself is looked upon as a strictly demonstrative discipline. Thus only those arguments which lead unequivocally to particular results are accepted as authentically scientific. This implicit postulate in Lucas's scientific paradigm plays a decisive role. Given the available tools, Lucas narrows the object of the analysis enough to render demonstrative arguments applicable.

So we can understand why Lucas declares, whenever he states his most important theoretical or methodological theses, that he feels there are no alternative theoretical options to those explored in his works.[15] If we *a priori* reject non-demonstrative arguments as non-scientific, the range of acceptable theoretical options is enormously reduced. First of all, from the formal point of view, one can accept only analytical models: 'progress in economic thinking means getting better and better abstract, analogue economic models, not better verbal observations about the world' (Lucas, 1981, p. 276). It is recognized that any model which is well enough articulated to provide clear answers to the questions we ask of it will necessarily be 'artificial, abstract, patently "unreal"' (*ibid.*, p. 271). In other words, a model is looked upon as a 'caricature' of reality, which proves the more useful the more effectively it manages to imitate, to 'mimic', the way the relevant economic system reacts to a certain combination of shocks.

The mimic capacities of analytic equilibrium models are clearly limited, however, to a certain type of phenomena: recurrent ones that present a high degree of regularity (see above, chapter 5). This type of analogic mechanism has a limited capacity for adaptation, and will produce erroneous imitations in the case of structural 'surprises'. That is why the object of analysis is limited solely to stationary stochastic processes. This limitation is all the more stringent inasmuch as these models incorporate the hypothesis of rational expectations, whose economic interpretation implies that 'agents have operated for some time in a situation like the current one and have therefore built up experience about the probability distributions which affect them. For this to have meaning, these distributions must remain stable through time. Mathematically, this means that we will be concerned only with *stationary distributions*' (*ibid.*, p. 158).

Lucas's conception of science considerably narrows the range of hypotheses open to scientific treatment. This is due not only to the nature of the object, but also to the level of development of modelling techniques.[16] Here I shall mention only one particularly significant example. Lucas recognizes that it might be useful to work out an equilibrium model assuming that markets are not perfectly competitive. But this proves impossible, at least at

[15] At this point it is worth pondering the words of Popper quoted in the epigraph to chapter 14.
[16] 'Developments in a particular substantive field, such as the study of business cycles, will be influenced strongly by technical developments in our ability to construct explicit model economies' (*ibid.*, p. 281).

the present stage of development of modelling techniques. Only 'the hypothesis of competitive equilibrium . . . permits group behavior to be predicted from knowledge of individual preferences and technology without the addition of any free parameters' (*ibid.*, p. 290).

If one looks at the nature of economic theory from this point of view, 'a "theory" is not a collection of assertions about the behavior of the actual economy but rather an explicit set of instructions for building a parallel or analogue system' (*ibid.*, p. 272). Thus the heart of the theory, even according to Lucas, is what I have called a heuristic model (see chapter 1). It is no accident that Lucas, together with Sargent, has worked out a notably precise and articulated version of the heuristic model inspiring their theoretical contributions. A further investigation of Lucas's scientific paradigm must necessarily deal with this basic contribution.

8.8   Conclusions

The research programme worked out by Lucas in the seventies has profoundly influenced macroeconomics. Although many of the basic conjectures have not stood the test of time and have been weakened or abandoned by Lucas and most new classical economists, the kernel of this research programme, which I call the Lucas's heuristic model, is still inspiring the research carried on by new classical economists.

The criticisms developed in this chapter regarding Lucas's paradigm of the seventies do not necessarily apply to the subsequent research of Lucas and the other new classical economists. Most contributions have abandoned the extreme monetarism of the seventies as well as the idea that a competitive equilibrium is always an optimum or that economic policy is necessarily ineffective. A few contributions try to analyse the non-neutral effects of money (see e.g. Lucas 1986) or the convergence to rational-expectations equilibria (see e.g. Lucas, 1986 and Marcet and Sargent, 1988). There are also contributions which try to abandon the assumption of a representative agent (see e.g. Lucas 1986 and Diaz-Giménez and Prescott 1989).

However, a few basic ideas have survived and still inspire the research in progress of Lucas and the other new classical economists. Most of them are summarized in what I call Lucas's heuristic model, which I will analyse in some detail in the next chapter.

9

Lucas's heuristic model

> While in the physical sciences the investigator will be able to measure, on the basis of a *prima facie* theory, what he thinks important, in the social sciences what is treated as important is often that which happens to be accessible to measurable magnitudes. It can hardly be denied that such a demand quite arbitrarily limits the facts that are to be admitted as possible causes of the events in the real world. (Hayek, 1974)

9.1   Introduction

In this chapter I intend to discuss the heuristic model of Lucas (for the definition of 'heuristic model' here adopted see section 1.4 above). The task is made easier by the fact that Lucas, together with Sargent, has given us a thorough version of it (Lucas and Sargent, eds., 1981).

For convenient comparison I will give an algebraic representation of the model, using the symbols adopted by Lucas and Sargent, in section 9.2. I shall also provide a representation of the model in the language of block diagrams, to aid an intuitive perception of its meaning, and to facilitate comparison with Keynes's heuristic model, which I shall reformulate in the same language in chapter 11.

In section 9.3 I will consider a few criticisms raised against Lucas's heuristic model (in particular by Keynesian economists and followers of Sims's VAR econometrics). I shall reject these criticisms insofar as they are based on alleged logical weaknesses, but I will show in section 9.4 that the applicability scope of Lucas's methodology is very restricted. Conclusions will follow in section 9.5. In appendix 9A I will briefly set out and discuss Sims's heuristic model which has been recently counterposed to that of Lucas and Sargent.

9.2   Description of the model

A heuristic model is meant to provide solutions to a problem. The problem considered by Lucas is defined with extreme clarity: 'We observe an agent, or collection of agents, behaving through time; we wish to use these observations to infer how this behavior would have differed had the agent's environment been altered in some specified way' (Lucas and Sargent, eds., 1981, pp. xi–xii).

Lucas's heuristic model describes the cognitive-decisional process through which the 'representative'[1] economic agent adapts to the environment.

The representative agent is characterized by a state variable whose value at time $t+1$, $x_{t+1} \in S_2$, depends on the state at the preceding time x_t, on the state of the environment at time t, $z_t \in S_1$, as well as on the action chosen at time t, $u_t \in U$:

$$x_{x+1} = g(z_t, x_t, u_t) \tag{9.1}$$

The function g: $S_1 \times S_2 \times U \to S_2$ expresses the 'technology' of the system. The state of the environment evolves through time according to the following relation:

$$z_{t+1} = f(z_t, \epsilon_t) \tag{9.2}$$

where the 'innovations' $\epsilon \epsilon \epsilon$ are independent extractions of a given stationary probability distribution Φ which expresses the degree of environmental uncertainty affecting the economic system. The function f: $S_1 \times \epsilon \to S_1$ describes the 'law of evolution' of the environment which, like Robinson Crusoe on his island, the economic agent must take into account but can in no way modify or influence. It is further assumed that the economic agent intentionally chooses an action u_t on the basis of his situation:

$$u_t = h(z_t, x_t) \tag{9.3}$$

where h expresses the decisional rule of the economic agent.

If we wish to study the economic agent's reactions to changes in the environment, we must first of all define more precisely what is meant by the latter. By changes in the environment we mean a variation of its 'law of evolution' f. Lucas and Sargent consider only one particular case: a systematic change in the way the variables of economic policy react to the evolution of the situation. We expect that the economic agent, faced with a change of this kind, will modify his decisional rule in the following way:

$$h_t = T(f_t) \tag{9.4}$$

As we see, in order to evaluate the consequences of changes in the policy rules one must know the function T. This is very difficult, because often our observations refer exclusively, or prevalently, to a given environment. To

---

[1] Lucas's representative agent is an ideal decisional unit that 'represents' the typical, or 'average', features of the economic agents acting in a given economy.

be able to estimate a function T one would have to vary f and see how h varies. This poses no problems in experimental disciplines like ethology or psychology, where the environment can be easily modified in a controlled way. In economics that is not possible. International comparisons may suggest some information about reactions to different environments (see e.g. Lucas, 1973), but such information is hardly reliable, not only because the data are difficult to compare but also because the economic system itself varies from one country to another.

A non-experimental solution to the dilemma must therefore depend on a theoretical analysis of the criteria which determine the economic agent's choice of decision rule h. Here enters the criterion of rationality, which is the key to this approach. It is assumed that the economic agent selects that decisional rule h which allows him to maximize an objective function V: $S_1 \times S_2 \times U \to R$, given f and g. If this maximization problem is soluble, the knowledge of the objective function V makes it possible to calculate the function h that would be chosen in any assumed environment, or:

$$h_t = T(f_t, \Phi, g_t, V) \tag{9.5}$$

The interrelationships described up to this point represent Lucas's heuristic model in its most general form. Figure 6 gives a block-diagram representation of Lucas and Sargent's general heuristic model, in order to provide a synoptic intuitive view of it. As can be seen, the interweaving between the internal structure of the system and the structure of the environment is extremely complex, and implies a degree of structural instability which is difficult to handle with analytic methods. Since Lucas has no intention of renouncing such methods, which he considers an indispensable guarantee of scientific rigour, he is forced to simplify the problem drastically so as to make it soluble by exact quantitative methods.

Lucas's preferred strategy is to assume that h and g are linear and V is quadratic. These assumptions allow him to exploit the properties discovered by Simon (1956) ('certainty equivalence').

Under these assumptions the problem of optimization can be broken down into two simpler parts: the choice of an optimal rule h_2 for prediction of the future evolution of the environment which depends only on the latter through f and Φ, and – given this prediction – the choice of an optimal decisional rule h_1 which depends only on the internal structure of the system, that is on V and g. In other words, h can be written as a compound function:

$$h(z_t, x_t) = h_1[h_2(z_t), x_t] \tag{9.6}$$

where $h_2(z_t) = z_t$ denotes the optimal prediction of the evolution of the environment which can be expressed as a function $h_2: S_1 \to S_1$, of the current state z_t. Although this function is in general non-linear, in practice it is

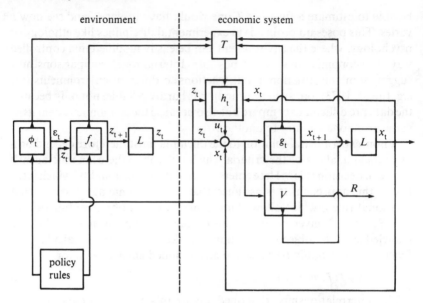

Figure 6 General heuristic model of Lucas and Sargent

assumed that h_2 is a linear predictor which minimizes the square of the residuals. The second advantage of the criterion of certainty equivalence is that it permits a theoretical derivation of the decisional rule h_1 from preferences V and technology g_t 'as if' the economic agent knew the future evolution of the environment with certainty, despite the fact that in reality the environment is stochastic (thanks to the properties of 'certainty equivalence').

Lucas's heuristic model is therefore reformulated as in figure 7. The cognitive process is separated from the decisional one, which allows one to circumscribe the problem of structural instability solely to the formation of expectations. The internal functional structure of the system becomes completely independent of the environment and of the uncertainty which characterizes it. The problem remains difficult but, limited in this way, it may be solved through the hypothesis of rational expectations. According to Lucas, in fact, assuming that the subjective distribution of z equals the objective distribution, on the basis of purely theoretical considerations one can find out the function T_t and hence the way in which the optimal predictive rule will vary in response to a systematic change in the environment.

Thus the initial problem is solved. Lucas's 'operative' heuristic model permits the evaluation of the effects of different rules of economic policy

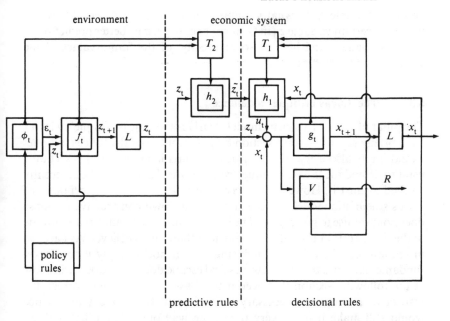

Figure 7   Operational heuristic model of Lucas and Sargent

(induced variations of f and/or Φ) on the structure of the system, while still assuming that economic agents operate in a stochastic environment.

In any application of Lucas's heuristic model, expressed in equations (9.1)–(9.6), z_t and S_1 must be concretely specified. It is thus necessary to give a list z_{1t} of exogenous variables which enter directly as arguments of function g_t (which describes the technology) and V (which describes the preferences). An awkward problem arises as soon as one tries to specify function f, which describes the evolution of the environment. In fact all the additional exogenous variables z_{2t}, which interact with z_{1t}, must enter as arguments of this function – even if they do not have a significant direct influence on the function of technology and preferences. Economic agents should not ignore these additional variables, for if they do they risk obtaining a lower value of the objective function.

According to Lucas, *economic* reasoning is in general useful only for working out *a priori* the variables of vector z_{1t}, but not for working out those of vector z_{2t} because function f_t is exogenous and does not depend on economic factors. The way out is found in an application of Granger causality, which, as we know (see above, chapter 7), is considered by Lucas and the other new classical economists as 'non-conditional' upon *a priori* theoretical assumptions. In this view, it is possible to discover, simply by applying suitable tests, what variables belong to z_{2t}. Any variable which 'causes' a certain variable z_{1t} in Granger's sense permits better prediction of its future values, and hence also, indirectly, of the future values of the system's state variables.

9.3   The 'Lucas critique': a defence

The pillar of Lucas's heuristic model clearly is the 'Lucas critique' (which I have briefly summarized in section 8.5). A rebuttal of the 'Lucas critique' would imply also a rejection of Lucas's heuristic model. In this section I want to defend the 'Lucas critique' from the attacks that have been recently levelled against it. However, its acceptance does not imply acceptance of Lucas's heuristic model. On the contrary, his own constructive response does not promise to go very far. The first reason is to be found in the latitude of the 'Lucas critique' itself, which is wider than Lucas believes. As I argued in section 8.5, there is no convincing reason not to apply it to market fundamentals, and thus the new classical escape does not work. I will show in the following section that even if this basic intuition were correct, the restrictive assumptions necessary to implement this strategy in practice would still make it not a very promising way out. We are left with an important but generic prescription: whenever we are interested in policy evaluation exercises we should look for parameters with the highest possible degree of invariance to environmental changes. This is sound methodological advice but by itself it does not help us to choose *a priori* between different families of models: the relative stability of parameters is an empirical issue which may vary in different geographical areas and historical times. Thus it cannot support a preference in principle for new classical models over Keynesian models. In addition, we should recognize that there is an alternative research programme which appears able to cope with the same problems. It consists in collecting information and giving it serious theoretical thought in order to understand how economic agents react to structural change (see above, chapter 5).

The 'Lucas critique' had a great impact on macroeconomics. It is very difficult to find another single paper as influential as this one in the last twenty years. The research activity directed to building, revising and applying large multi-equation econometric models, which was a flourishing business before the publication of this paper, declined abruptly. Many macroeconomists all over the world were convinced by Lucas's argument to abandon the Keynesian camp for the new classical one. It was also accepted, at least in its destructive part, not only by the new classical economists but also by many Keynesians (a good example is Tobin, 1980 a and b). However, in the eighties the 'Lucas critique' began to be increasingly questioned, criticized and even rejected.

We may identify two families of criticisms. According to the first one, the 'Lucas critique' is logically sound but not very stringent in practice. The 'Lucas critique' applies whenever there is a change in policy rules, but it is contended that genuine policy changes in this strong sense are very rare. This objection is raised in similar ways by two opposite camps: by Keynesian macroeconomists willing to defend the basic tenets of the 'neoclassical synthesis' (Blinder, 1986), and by 'atheoretical' macroeconometrists refusing any commitment to 'incredible *a priori* restrictions' (Sims, 1982).

This empiricist argument should be rejected: firstly because we should not confuse the logical level with the empirical level; secondly because even if we were able to prove that genuine changes in policy rules were rare in the past, we don't know if this will or will not be true in the future. We could get out of indeterminacy only if we could rely on a theory of perceived structural change. But neither Lucas nor these critics are willing to follow a research programme of this kind.

The second family of criticisms is more interesting because it challenges the 'Lucas critique' on its own logical ground. What is denied is nothing less than the logical possibility of a genuine policy change, whenever the agents are fully rational in their decisions and expectations. A policy change is modelled by Lucas as an exogenous change in deterministic parameters that define a certain policy, which is implemented once and for all with no one – apart from the economic adviser and the policy authorities – 'knowing beforehand that the change may occur and no one doubting afterward that the change is permanent' (Sims, 1987, pp. 306–7). But, so the criticism goes, the agents must recognize, if their expectations are consistently rational, that the parameters of the policy 'rule' are liable to change. So we must assume that the agents consider the parameters which define the policy rule as stochastic variables over which they formulate a probability distribution. We thus have a meta-policy rule (a second-order policy rule, we might say) which is assumed to be time-invariant in policy-evaluation exercises. This would again raise Lucas's criticism, or we would have an infinite regress. What Lucas calls a change in policy rule is thus nothing but a realization of the second-order policy vector (the elements of which are parameters of the first-order policy vector).

In other words, according to this criticism, a consistent application of the rational-expectations hypothesis able to avoid an infinite regress implies that there is only one possible stationary stochastic process, the one we happen to live in. Therefore we cannot compare different stochastic processes characterized by different policy rules, but only different realizations of the same stochastic process.

I consider this criticism invalid both in its destructive and in its constructive part. What it really shows is just one of the possible paradoxes raised by the rational-expectations hypothesis. According to the strong substantive interpretation (see above, section 6.3), a rational equilibrium must be *permanent*, so that by definition there cannot be any genuine structural change: any apparent change must be consistent with the time-invariant probability distributions which characterize the 'equilibrium' stationary stochastic process.[2] In this case there cannot be any room for economic policy, since 'an analysis that maintains the assumption of a fixed probabilistic structure permits no policy advice to be given or choice to be delineated. Vector autoregressions become tools for passive, intervention-free forecasting of various types' (Sargent, 1984, p. 413). The economic adviser may still study the effects of different realizations of policy variables (of the first or superior order). So there is still some room for forecasting, although its role is restricted to making explicit what was already implicit in the rational agent's knowledge. But by definition there is no way of choosing a certain realization of the stochastic process, otherwise there would be a systematic force not captured by the stochastic process and again we would contravene the rational-expectations hypothesis in its strong substantive interpretation.

To this criticism I would object that the logical structure of the Lucas critique is sound, provided that we abandon the strong version of the substantive interpretation of the rational-expectations hypothesis. This interpretation excludes the possibility of systematic mistakes not only *ex ante* but also *ex post*: here lies the real root of the paradox. If instead we accept the weak version which excludes systematic mistakes *ex ante* but not *ex post*, the problem raised by Sims vanishes.

Having ascertained that the problems raised by Lucas are to be taken very seriously, we should inquire whether the way out suggested by Lucas in his heuristic model is acceptable or not. I have argued in section 8.5 that this way out does not look very promising because it is still subject to the 'Lucas critique' though for reasons different from those underlined by Sims. In any case, as I will show in the next section, there are methodological objections which severely limit its range of application.

9.4   Limits of Lucas's heuristic model

9.4.1   The concept of equilibrium

Lucas's heuristic model is constructed in such a way as to provide correct foundations for macroeconomic models built, according to its instructions, on what he considers to be the solid ground of general economic equili-

---

[2] This is one of the paradoxes which spring from an extreme rationalist point of view. See above, sections 2.7 and 6.2.

brium. It is no accident that the economic system is essentially characterized by tastes and technology, as in every model of general economic equilibrium.

Despite the fundamental role played by the concept of equilibrium in Lucas's research programme, on close examination we find that this concept is never satisfactorily explained.

At some points the concept of equilibrium is used in a syntactic sense[3] and at others in a semantic sense, without the link between the two being clarified. Nor is the link specified between these two meanings and the dynamic one, which as we have seen is prevalent in Keynes and in many scientific contexts. This creates an almost inextricable tangle of misunderstandings, which I shall try to sort out.

From the syntactic point of view, equilibrium is interpreted as the solution of a formal system. As we saw in chapter 2, this is fundamentally incorrect because, in the absence of a properly explained dynamic framework, the concept of solution does not enable one to discriminate between equilibrium and disequilibrium. Nonetheless the 'usual' concept of equilibrium, i.e. the concept typical of a deterministic system (which is attributed to Keynes) is counterposed to the concept of equilibrium typical of a stochastic system. In the first case, according to Lucas, equilibrium exists when 'nothing changes in the system', so there can be no reconciliation between general economic equilibrium and the business cycle. In the second case equilibrium is seen as a stochastic process which proves compatible with the empirical evidence. This permits a reconciliation between general economic equilibrium and the business cycle.

This argument, based on the dynamic implications of different concepts of 'solution', seems to me profoundly erroneous. First of all it is not true that in a deterministic system equilibrium implies that 'nothing changes in the system'. We may in fact have a mobile equilibrium when the system is characterized by purely exogenous dynamic behaviour. Such dynamic behaviour in equilibrium may have any desired degree of complexity, which by definition derives exclusively from the exogenous dynamic impulse and is isomorphic with it. In this sense there is no difference at all between a dynamic concept of equilibrium and a stochastic one. A stochastic equilibrium is compatible with any complex dynamic behaviour because stochastic shocks produce exogenous dynamic impulses which have exactly the same kind of effect on the dynamics of the stochastic system as exogenous factors have in a deterministic system. The question of whether or not cycle theory is compatible with general economic equilibrium thus has nothing to do with what concept of equilibrium is used.

---

[3] See e.g. Lucas, 1981, p. 178.

Lucas also provides a semantic definition of equilibrium based on the two requisites of self-interest and cleared markets (see section 8.2), whose dynamic implications remain obscure. One possible interpretation is to consider the two requisites as the only possible sources of endogenous change which are considered by Keynesian models and which Lucas means to exclude by his definition of equilibrium. Keynes's underemployment equilibria are suboptimal but do not imply an endogenous change in the system. In Keynesian models, on the contrary, there are many other sources of endogenous dynamic behaviour, such as the dynamic multiplier and the accelerator.

There is another possible interpretation. It can be assumed that Lucas's semantic concept, contrary to what usually happens (see above, chapter 2), is not to be interpreted as a specification of the dynamic concept, and thus is not entirely consistent with the latter. The thesis is supported by an analysis of the Lucasian model of the cycle 'in equilibrium'. That model is essentially characterized by one or more mechanisms of endogenous dynamic behaviour which are termed 'propagation mechanisms'. For example, in Lucas's 1975 model (see above, section 8.3) we find the following two mechanisms:

(a)   A mechanism of perceptive delay which prevents immediate awareness of past values of the relevant variables (Lucas, 1981, p. 181). This assumption permits the introduction of a certain degree of self-correction of errors, but cannot explain their cumulative character.

(b)   A mechanism of acceleration, since the adjustment of capital stock to the behaviour of the economy requires time. This assumption, together with the foregoing one, permits an explanation of the cumulative character of errors in the business cycle.

The above-mentioned propagation mechanisms are therefore essential in a model of the cycle 'in equilibrium', in order to explain the self-correlation of residuals in wave form which can be seen in the empirical evidence. Thus we end up with the paradox that Lucas's cycle in equilibrium is necessarily characterized by endogenous dynamic behaviour, i.e. disequilibrium in the 'usual' dynamic sense, which is also the sense found in Keynes. The use of a semantic concept of equilibrium incompatible with the dynamic concept generates serious terminological ambiguities and several methodological inconsistencies.

9.4.2   The concept of disequilibrium

As we have seen, Lucas's concept of equilibrium does not necessarily coincide with the dynamic concept of equilibrium. At this point we may well ask why Lucas gives such weight to the distinction between equilibrium and disequilibrium. His own answer is trenchant but not fully argued. The equilibrium hypothesis is seen as a 'condition of intelligibility' for economic processes.

By non-intelligible Lucas apparently means 'arbitrary' (*ad hoc*).[4] He has in mind the adjustment mechanisms that come into play when there is an excess of supply or demand, or those that characterize the hypothesis of adaptive expectations. In such cases the practice of traditional econometrics is based on the use of 'free parameters', to be determined by purely inductive means. The good econometric 'fit' obtained through this methodology is rightly considered by Lucas to be misleading, since the parameters involved are not determined *a priori* on the basis of theoretical considerations. From this substantially correct observation Lucas derives the principle that such a theoretical foundation can indeed never be possible when the situation under analysis is one of disequilibrium. This principle is clearly untenable. A disequilibrium path may very well be the optimal solution to a problem (see chapter 3). Moreover it is not correct to maintain, as Lucas does, that any affirmation not based on the postulates of classical theory is arbitrary. This argument cannot be used in general against an alternative theory, such as the Keynesian one, which is based on a different set of postulates. The first requisite (self-interest) might have been accepted, with some qualifications, even by Keynes. The second requisite for intelligibility (market clearing) finds no justification whatever. The fact that 'free parameters' are generally used to analyse the dynamic behaviour of a system in disequilibrium does not demonstrate the impossibility of such an analysis, suitably based on parameters' values restricted *a priori* on the basis of rigorous theoretical considerations.

Lastly, the argument regarding arbitrary postulates is not at all conclusive. Any model is characterized by arbitrary hypotheses. This is true even of Lucas's models, as many critics have pointed out. All we can say in general is that *ceteris paribus* it is sound methodological advice to minimize the number of arbitrary hypotheses. Thus if we manage to eliminate one or more arbitrary hypotheses without introducing any new ones, that is certainly a positive step. But the comparison between new classical models and Keynesian ones is much more tricky because some arbitrary hypotheses can be eliminated only by introducing others.[5] The choice, therefore, must be based on criteria of a different nature.

The concept of involuntary unemployment is a particularly important

---

[4] In chapter 2 we considered a possible source of this opinion. If we adopt a 'rationalist' perspective based on a rigorously static substantialist concept of rationality, then disequilibrium appears non-intelligible as it implies a logical contradiction.

[5] See above, section 8.6, on this issue.

case in point. Lucas considers involuntary unemployment to be a non-intelligible concept; he interprets it as a disequilibrium concept which violates the principle of voluntary exchanges in a market economy, and/or the principle of maximization which must characterize the behaviour of rational agents. The concept of involuntary unemployment does not imply that there are economic agents who do not optimize (as is demonstrated in a considerable and increasing number of models),[6] nor does it imply the existence of a disequilibrium (in the dynamic sense). But it certainly does imply the existence of an excess labour supply, and hence the existence of a disequilibrium in Lucas's sense.

In a trivial and misleading sense it is doubtless true that any action on the part of a rational agent can be considered voluntary. Even when the victim of a mugging has to choose between his money and his life, the decision to hand over his money can be seen as voluntary in that he makes the optimal choice between those which are open to him. But when Keynes speaks of involuntary unemployment he means something else. He wants to emphasize that the range of options before the worker is reduced by comparison to a certain standard which is considered normal, or at least possible in the short term (full employment equilibrium). This forces the rational worker to choose an option which is suboptimal compared to the optimal choice in the standard range of options. Unemployment, therefore, is involuntary in the sense that the standard range of options is reduced, regardless of the workers' volition, by a level of effective demand which is insufficient to guarantee full employment. There is nothing unintelligible about the concept of involuntary unemployment seen in this light.

9.4.3 *Dynamic instability and ergodicity: a forgotten requisite*

In the last chapter we saw that the equilibria analysed by Lucas are conceived as stationary stochastic processes. The fact that they are stationary imposes a long series of restrictive hypotheses on the range of applicability of the heuristic model, and these considerably reduce the empirical usefulness of Lucas's equilibrium method (see the definition of the business cycle discussed in section 8.3). This method basically consists of exercises in what might be called 'stochastic' comparative statics, based on comparison of the properties of different stationary stochastic processes.

As this analogy suggests, for such a method to make sense one more condition is required, which Lucas unfortunately overlooks. The stationary 'equilibrium' stochastic process must also be 'dynamically stable', or

---

[6] See e.g. Hahn, 1987.

'ergodic', in the terminology of stochastic processes.[7] An ergodic process is defined precisely as a stochastic process whose limit is independent of the initial values. But within Lucas's heuristic model taken literally there is no way to demonstrate – or even to argue – the ergodicity of the stochastic process, because that would mean considering the system's behaviour in disequilibrium, which is excluded by definition.

When the environment changes, that is to say when – in Lucas's hypothesis – the rules of economic policy change, the transformation cannot be perceived and understood immediately. Hence a learning process begins which does not necessarily converge towards classical equilibrium. What is worse, if one adopts Lucas's method of pure equilibrium implying the non-intelligibility of disequilibrium positions, there is no way to argue about the robustness of the alternative equilibria under consideration. In other words, Lucas's heuristic model, not to mention the analytical models built according to his instructions, prove to be useless for the very purpose for which they were primarily constructed – the evaluation of alternative economic policies. Such use cannot be justified on the basis of considerations lying within Lucas's heuristic model because that would require an examination of the behaviour of the system in disequilibrium, which is non-intelligible within the bounds of Lucas's theoretical and methodological universe.

9.4.4 Structural instability and uncertainty

The point of departure for Lucas's heuristic model is the accusation that Keynesian models do not take account of the structural instability of the economy. As far as Keynes is concerned this accusation is certainly wrong, for Keynes observed on many occasions, in particular in his 1939 review of Tinbergen, that the most important condition for the validity of an econometric model is the homogeneity and uniformity of the environment during the relevant period of time (CW, vol. 14, p. 316).

On the other hand it must be acknowledged that there are serious grounds for this criticism with regard to most econometric models of Keynesian inspiration. The importance of structural instability, however, is limited by Lucas himself in such a way as to make it scarcely relevant. The

---

[7] This requisite has been underlined by Davidson (1982–3). Davidson's argument, though substantially correct, is not completely flawless. He maintains that stationarity is too weak a validity condition, as it is a necessary but not sufficient condition for Lucas's method to be considered consistent. Only the stronger condition of ergodicity would be both necessary and sufficient to this end. However, stationarity and ergodicity in this context should be considered as independent conditions (as is apparently recognized by Davidson himself in a note to his paper), as independent as a condition of stationary equilibrium and a condition of dynamic stability of such equilibrium (see above, chapter 3).

restriction of structural instability solely to the formation of expectations is especially perplexing. There is no reason to believe that the environment has no influence on the tastes and technology which characterize an economic system. As far as tastes are concerned, it is obvious that extra-economic factors of a cultural nature can systematically influence consumers' preferences. As for technology, innovation, which is at least partly exogenous, must certainly be considered as an integral part of the environment which influences the dynamic behaviour of the economic system. One might perhaps object that Lucas is studying only the rules of economic policy. But these too may influence the technology adopted. This is true not only for industrial policy, which aims to directly influence the system's technological structure, but also for macroeconomic policy itself. For example an induced variation in the interest rate can significantly influence investment and hence also embodied technological change. Even if one believes in the existence of a natural interest rate – or in the ineffectiveness of economic policy – it is hard to deny that different economic policy rules can induce different degrees of structural uncertainty. Indeed it is on this basis that Lucas declares his preference for fixed rules which minimize structural uncertainty. It can be demonstrated that variations in the degree of systemic uncertainty induce significant modifications in the technology of the system. For example an economic policy which accentuates the degree of systemic uncertainty encourages the adoption of more flexible technologies (see chapters 5 and 12, as well as Vercelli, 1986 a and b).

Even if one accepts the restriction of structural instability solely to the process of expectation formation, the solution of the problem depends crucially on the assumption of rational expectations, and is subject to all the objections and limits which that hypothesis involves. A particularly delicate dilemma arises with regard to the specific problem which the hypothesis of rational expectations is meant to solve. Rational expectations refer, here as elsewhere in Lucas's interpretation, to an economy which is considered structurally stable. To this end the economic structure has been stabilized by reducing the range of analysable phenomena to a small subset to which the hypothesis applies. This procedure is decisive for the validity of the result: it makes no sense to refer the hypothesis of rational expectations (in the strong 'substantivist' interpretation outlined in chapter 6) to an unstable system. This is recognized even by those who support the hypothesis. The trouble is that a model of rational expectations can be given a determinate solution only by assuming that the equilibrium is a 'saddle point'. As is well known, from the formal point of view a model with these characteristics is structurally unstable.

The contradiction between the structural instability of the model and the structural stability attributed to the reality which the model is meant to represent leads to a difficult problem. A rational-expectations model must be structurally unstable to be soluble, but can be applied only to structurally stable processes (see chapter 6). If we replace the model with a structurally stable one the solution becomes indeterminate, and this is not compatible with the hypothesis of rational expectations in Lucas's substantivist interpretation.

If we accept that the reality described by the model is structurally unstable, then the slightest error in specification, or even in the collection of data, would make the future behaviour of the phenomenon under analysis unpredictable: and this again is incompatible with Lucas's version of the hypothesis of rational expectations. In both cases we encounter the problem of uncertainty, in the strong sense used by Keynes and Knight, which is incompatible both with rational expectations in the substantivist interpretation and with 'certainty equivalence', i.e. with the two crucial hypotheses on which Lucas's operative heuristic model is based.

9.4.5   Rationality and causality

We have already seen that Lucas's concept of rationality, while central to the structure of his arguments, is in fact very limited. (Here I am referring to the rationality which Lucas attributes to economic agents in his macroeconomic models and not to that attributed to policy-makers or model-builders.) Rationality is seen exclusively in its substantive aspects; no attention is given to the procedural aspects (despite a few occasional references to learning processes), or, especially, to the creative aspects. This implies that the 'environment' remains rigidly beyond the reach of any action of control or transformation on the part of economic agents. The environment, in fact, is defined as the whole complex of variables over which economic agents have no control, but which influence their decisions. An exception is made only for the authorities who decide economic policy. These are conceived as *dei ex machina* endowed with the power to modify the rules of economic policy, which as we have seen constitute an essential part of the environment.

On the other hand the Lucasian environment, though conceived in a very limited sense, plays a fundamental role in explaining the dynamics of the economic system. The 'Lucas critique' is nothing but the recognition that the phenomenic structure of the economic system is crucially affected by changes in the environment. Thus we may observe that although Lucas conceives of economic phenomena as stochastic, the situational determinism typical of neoclassical economics is not substantially affected. The environment moulds the parameters that describe the systematic elements of economic processes, as well as those that describe the probabilistic distributions of errors.

A correct description of the environment is therefore crucial for correct prediction of the dynamic behaviour of the economic system. Causality, in Granger's sense, plays a key role in sorting out all the main variables that make up the environment for each particular problem. We shall examine the reasons for this in some detail.

In every concrete application of Lucas's heuristic model it is necessary to specify concretely what variables characterize the environment. Some of these variables are suggested *a priori* by economic reasoning. In general, however, given the residual nature of the concept of the environment, we must expect them to be significantly influenced by another set of variables, which must be taken into consideration if we want to avoid erroneous predictions regarding the future of the environment. According to Lucas these latter variables cannot be detected except through *a priori* theoretical reasoning. He solves the problem by using the empirical causality tests proposed by Granger, Sims and their followers, which as we know (see chapter 7) are considered not to be conditioned by *a priori* theoretical hypotheses. Prediction of the future dynamics of the environment is in fact assisted by any variable which in Granger's sense directly or indirectly causes the 'law of evolution of the environment'.

This procedure works only on the assumption – erroneously made by Granger, Sims and some other supporters of this concept of causality, and also accepted by Lucas, Sargent and the other new classical economists – that the results of the tests are completely independent of *a priori* theoretical hypotheses. As we have seen, this assumption cannot be accepted, and so Lucas's argument collapses. This problem cannot be avoided by replacing Granger's idea of causality with an alternative one, since for the reasons shown in chapter 7 no concept of causality is meaningful without previous specification of its theoretical background.

The way out must therefore be sought in a different specification of the environment. A necessary premise for this, though far from a sufficient one, is to avoid confusing the distinction between system and environment with the distinction between endogenous and exogenous. The environment interacts with the system: if we are to analyse this interaction we must consider it at least partly endogenous to the process under examination. While this is a very difficult task, we cannot manage without studying how the environment interacts with the economic system, introducing the forgotten but crucial perspective of 'creative' (or 'option-making') rationality.

9.5   Concluding observations

Lucas's heuristic model focusses on the link between a changing environment and the economic system. Here, in Lucas's opinion, lies the original sin of Keynesian theory, which cannot be overcome without abandoning the whole Keynesian methodology. But the proposed way out does not solve the problem, for it is open to the same criticisms which Lucas directed at Keynesian models, despite the use of a long chain of simplifications which define away the initial problems.

What is worse, Lucas's heuristic model is not strictly applicable to the fundamental problem for which it was developed, i.e. the evaluation of the effects of alternative economic policies. For such an application, in fact, we must necessarily have recourse to exercises in stochastic 'comparative statics' which make no sense unless we can demonstrate the 'dynamic stability' of the equilibria being compared. The fact that the equilibria are actually stationary stochastic processes alters the terminology (the stochastic process must be ergodic), but it in no way alters the crucial importance of this requirement. Lucas cannot adequately argue the economic significance of the comparisons, because having declared disequilibrium to be non-intelligible he is not in a good position to study the 'dynamic stability' or ergodicity of the compared stationary stochastic processes. One cannot thus seriously appraise alternative policy rules while remaining rigorously within Lucas's heuristic model.

Appendix 9A The heuristic model of Sims

Granger causality has both historically and logically underpinned a recent flourishing research programme aptly dubbed 'atheoretical econometrics'. This research programme basically accepts the principle of strategic interdependence brought forward by the 'rational-expectations revolution', but radically challenges 'rational-expectations econometrics' founded on the heuristic model of Lucas and Sargent. I have briefly summarized and rejected the main criticisms levelled by 'atheoretical econometrics' against rational-expectations econometrics in section 9.3. In this appendix I will rapidly survey and criticize the *pars construens* of this research programme. (This is nothing but an extension to Sims's heuristic model of the criticisms already developed in chapter 7 against the inductivist interpretation of Granger causality.)

In this appendix I will heavily borrow from Cooley and LeRoy (1985). At the same time these authors radically criticize Lucas's and Sims's heuristic models. However, the two critiques are independent: I share the second critique but I reject the first, as I have explained in section 9.3.

The aim of VAR uninterpreted models is to obtain with much less effort the same results that could be obtained through VAR models interpreted according to Lucas's heuristic model. Indeed, superior results are claimed for policy evaluation, since in this case it is not limited to radical changes in regimes which are considered to be very rare. The basic idea is that VAR reduced forms, though uninterpreted, are perfectly adequate to describe, forecast and control economic systems. By contrast, any approach which requires VAR models to be subsumed under some theoretical structure is implicitly seen as useless. The underlying philosophy is openly instrumentalist and resumes Friedman's criticism of structural models as against mere reduced forms. It is ironic that this same extreme instrumentalism led Sims to abandon his monetarism of the seventies (see Sims, 1980 a and b, 1982). Granger causality and VAR macroeconometrics built on it are theoretically agnostic. Sims contends against Lucas and Sargent that existing Keynesian models are not useless for policy evaluation though the theoretical restrictions may appear 'incredible'. In fact, provided that a certain policy instrument is proved exogenous by a Granger or Sims test, the quality of the forecasts does not depend on the structural form but on the reduced form (see Cooley and LeRoy, 1985, p. 289).

A vector autoregression (VAR) is a regression of a vector of variables on its own past values:

$$x_t = \sum_{i=1}^{n} \Pi_i \, x_{t-i} + u_t, \qquad E(u_t u'_t) = \Sigma \tag{9A.1}$$

where x_t is a vector of observable random variables, Π_i is a square matrix of parameters and u_t is a vector of mean-zero, serially uncorrelated unobservable variables. The errors in (9A.1) are not assumed to be contemporaneously uncorrelated. It is customary to premultiply (9A.1) by the unique triangular matrix with units on the main diagonal that diagonalizes the error covariance matrix:

$$T x_t = T \sum_{i=1}^{n} \Pi_i \, x_{t-i} + \eta_t, \qquad E(\eta_t \, \eta'_t) = D \tag{9A.2}$$

where $\eta_t = T u_t$ and $D = T \Sigma T'$ is a diagonal matrix. The η_t are termed the orthogonalized innovations.

The main purposes of Sims's research programme are the following:

(a)   *Description.* Vector autoregressions give a useful compact description of a few features of stochastic processes. In particular they 'provide a convenient way of summarizing the second moments of time-series data' (Sargent, 1984, p. 408). Under weak restrictions on the coefficient matrices, the VAR model (9A.2) can be inverted and written in moving average form:

$$x_t = \sum_{i=0}^{\infty} \Gamma_i \eta_{t-i} \tag{9A.3}$$

where the η_t are contemporaneously and serially uncorrelated.

(b)   *Forecasting.* 'Since VAR models allow complete flexibility and generality (except for the linearity assumption) in specifying the correlations between future, present and past realizations of the system variables, they have a natural application to forecasting' (Cooley and LeRoy, 1985, p. 286).

(c)   *Causality tests.* These have been discussed above in chapter 7.

(d)   *Tests of theories.* Many theories in macroeconomics have the implication that one variable of the system does not Granger-cause another. Thus it is possible to test whether a certain theory is consistent with empirical evidence. For example in the seventies Sims found that income does not Granger-cause money, and this was then taken to support monetarism against Keynesism (Sims, 1972, and 1977).

(e)   *Heuristic search.* VAR models describe stylized facts about causal orderings of macroeconomic variables which may suggest new explanatory hypotheses.

(f)   *Impulse response analysis.* In a moving-average representation (9A.3) of a VAR model, each variable can be written as a function of the orthogonalized innovations, so that the response of the ith element of x_{t+k} to the innovation in the jth variable at date t is just the i,j element of the matrix Γ. A tabulation of these responses for $k = 0, 1, \ldots$ is called an impulse response function.

(g)   *Variance decomposition* (or innovation accounting). Variance decomposition aims to indicate what proportion of each variable's forecast error depends on each of the orthogonalized innovations in the VAR model. Since the covariances among the innovations are zero by definition, the variance of each variable is represented as a weighted sum of the variances of each variable, with weights corresponding to the elements of the matrix Γ_k.

(h)   *Policy evaluation.* Sims has recently contended (1980a, 1982, 1986) that, whenever a stochastic variable is exogenous in his sense, VAR model forecasts conditional on different hypothetical realizations of the policy variable may offer a criterion for evaluating the effects of different policies. This methodology would be applicable not only to 'permanent' policy changes but any kind of policy interventions.

VAR models are certainly useful for descriptive purposes. They are also useful for forecasting, provided that the stochastic process will not be affected by structural changes (as is implicitly assumed by Sims: see section 9.3). They may also have a heuristic value like any method suggesting empirical generalizations. However, they cannot by themselves suggest actual explanatory hypotheses because for that the empirical generalization must be embedded in the framework of a fully fledged theory. (Although there are different conceptions of explanations, this requirement is agreed upon by most epistemologists; see the survey by Suppe, ed., 1977.) For the same reason, we cannot rely on such tests of theories.

We have already commented on the validity scope of causality tests in chapter 7. Again they may be useful for descriptive, forecasting and heuristic purposes but not for a satisfactory causal analysis.

The success of impulse response analysis and innovation accounting depends on the identification of conditional correlation with causal orderings (see the examples brought forward by Cooley and LeRoy, 1985, p. 301). Since this identification is unacceptable for reasons we have already examined in section 7.5, we are left with a sophisticated disaggregated analysis of correlations which may be useful for description and forecasting but not for explanatory purposes.

Finally, the validity of policy analysis through VAR models is strongly questioned by the 'Lucas critique', whose validity I have defended in section 9.3 against the attacks of Sims. VAR parameters are 'shallow' parameters and we cannot rely on their invariance following a certain policy intervention. This problem is overcome by Sims only by assuming that the existing stochastic process is in fact permanent and its structure cannot be changed. However, in this case there is no room for genuine policy advice and VAR econometrics can be used only as a forecasting tool.

We may thus conclude that VAR econometrics represents an interesting research programme for descriptive, forecasting and heuristic purposes but we should recognize that it has a very limited use for theory testing, explanation and policy evaluation.

10

The real equilibrium business cycle and Lucas's attempt at a synthesis

We will not postulate the existence of states of equilibrium where none exists, but only where the system is actually moving toward one. When, for instance, existing states are in the act of being disturbed, say by a war financed by government fiat, or by a 'mania' of railroad building, there is very little sense in speaking of an ideal equilibrium coexisting with all that disequilibrium. It seems much more natural to say that while such a factor acts there is no equilibrium at all. When it has ceased to act, and when we observe that readjustment sets in which we interpret as a movement toward equilibrium, then and only then the ideal equilibrium becomes the goal of an economic process, the nature of which can be elucidated by reference to it. Then and only then the ideal equilibrium becomes what we have called it before, the 'theoretical norm' of the economic variables. (Schumpeter, 1939, p. 70)

10.1   Introduction

In the eighties new classical economists split on many fundamental issues. Branching is typical of any evolutionary process in nature as well as in the history of science. The same thing has happened to the Keynesian school, and indeed to most successful schools in the history of economic thought. The identification of the different branches is becoming increasingly difficult, and is very sensitive to different definitional criteria. Even the boundaries of the school are not easy to locate.[1] Among the main points of disagreement within the school, the following are particularly important:[2]

> the nature of the equilibrium business cycle,
> the scope and the implications of Lucas's critique,
> the role, if any, of policy-advising,
> the correct econometric methodology.

[1] It has been discussed, for example, whether or not an author such as Sims should be included in the school (see Hoover, 1988, p. 273).
[2] For a general overview on these topics see Hoover, 1988.

As a case study I will consider just the first point. The equilibrium approach to the business cycle (the so-called 'equilibrium business cycle', hereafter EBC) has been the central focus of the school, at least up to now.[3] In this field there has been a major switch from the monetary approach (monetary business cycle: MBC), initiated by Lucas's seminal model of 1975, to a real approach (real business cycle: RBC) initiated by Kydland and Prescott (1982) and Long and Plosser (1983). Although the causal hypotheses and the policy conclusions have radically changed, there is a profound methodological kinship between the two streams which I will discuss in section 10.2. This confirms that new classical economists may be identified as a school mainly because they adhere to a common methodology rather than to common substantive points[4] (this is less true for the Keynesian and monetarist schools). In section 10.3 I will provide a brief account of Kydland and Prescott's model, which most authors (including Lucas) have taken as the paradigmatic example of the RBC. In section 10.4 I will summarize the main criticisms raised by Lucas and other authors against the existing versions of RBC models. In section 10.5 I will consider Lucas's attempt at a synthesis of MBC and RBC equilibrium models. In section 10.6 I will summarize my own point of view, introducing a few further criticisms of the whole EBC research programme. Conclusions follow in section 10.7.

10.2   The real business cycle and Lucas's heuristic model

The RBC research programme should be interpreted as a rigorous application of Lucas's operational heuristic model. Lucas's first monetary model (1975) and Kydland and Prescott's real model (1982) are nothing but different realizations of the same methodological perspective: the perspective of the 'equilibrium business cycle' which underlies Lucas's heuristic model. Cyclical fluctuations are seen as equilibrium movements in the sense that throughout the cycle agents optimize and markets clear. While in the monetary version the business cycle is seen as the optimal adaptation of a representative agent to unpredictable fluctuations in the general price level induced by erratic monetary policies, in the real version the business cycle is seen as the optimal response of a representative agent to unpredictable fluctuations in technology. The problem is always to reconcile empirical

---

[3] Even this might change in the future. Lucas maintains in his latest book (1987) that business cycles might after all not be very important in terms of foregone wealth. The main emphasis of the research of new classical economists might thus shift towards growth theory. A possible sign of this shift is Lucas's Marshall Lecture (1988).

[4] The main substantive point which is common to new classical economists is just a strong belief in the self-adjusting properties of a competitive market.

evidence on economic fluctuations with general equilibrium. The reconciliation is reached only under the same restrictive assumptions as those of Lucas's heuristic model: certainty equivalence and rational expectations.

RBC theorists accept Lucas's distinction (borrowed by Frisch) between impulse and propagation. However, they deny that the impulse which generates the business cycle is a monetary one. Historically the first stimulus to this switch came from the literature on Granger-causality. While in the seventies the tests of Granger-causality (from now on G-causality) had apparently confirmed that the causal nexus runs from money to income (Sims, 1972, 1977), in the early eighties new, more sophisticated tests of G-causality pointed out that money loses its incremental predictive power over output as soon as interest rates are taken into account. Similar results are obtained through VAR methods (Sims, 1980b).

RBC models assume that fluctuations are mainly stimulated by shocks impinging on the real economy. The model suggested in 1982 by Kydland and Prescott, which rapidly became the paradigm for almost all new classical RBC models, identified the real shocks with perturbations affecting the technology of the system. This assumption has become standard in subsequent literature, although nothing prevents the exploration of the effects of different real shocks in the context of the RBC theory.

Like Lucas's model, RBC models are essentially a variation on the single-sector neoclassical growth model. Real impulses are conceived as random variations in technology. Information about these shocks is assumed to be incomplete. As in Lucas's model there is a problem of signal extraction from background noise, and this crucially affects the cyclical fluctuations. To the extent that workers think the shocks are transitory, the real wage seems high relative to future real wages. Workers then supply more labour in the current period in order to enjoy more leisure tomorrow when they expect real wages to be lower. At the same time the producers, to the extent that they believe the shock to be persistent, decide to add to the stock of capital. Since new capital takes time to be produced ('time to build'), output will increase for some time after the shock disappears. Producers will then try to reduce the excess capital and slow down investment until capital depreciation brings the economy back onto the steady-state path.

10.3   The basic real business-cycle model

To discuss some details of a paradigmatic RBC model I will follow Lucas's expository strategy, beginning with a 'basic' version of the seminal model put forward by Kydland and Prescott (hereafter KP). This basic model expresses the kernel of KP's contribution and may thus be considered as the prototype of existing RBC models.

The study of this very simple basic model (much simpler than the one in the published version and other versions in the subsequent literature) should give an intuitive grasp of the essentials of the subject. It will also facilitate the discussion of Lucas's point of view on RBC models, and thus also of his most recent, slightly modified views on the business cycle.

KP's RBC model is a very good illustration of Lucas's heuristic model which we analysed in the preceding chapter. For this reason it is chosen by Lucas as the 'most useful' prototype of RBC models: 'it is the only model I know that is theoretically coherent . . . while yet having been developed to the point where its implications can be compared to observed time series in a quantitatively serious way' (Lucas, 1987, p. 33).

KP's model is a highly simplified competitive system, in which a single good is produced by labour and capital with constant-returns technology. All consumers are assumed to be identical and to live forever. The *only* shocks to the system are exogenous, stochastic fluctuations in labour productivity, interpreted as stochastic shifts in the production technology.

Let the typical household be endowed with n^o units of time for each period, and let its current period utility depend on goods consumed c_t and leisure $n^o - n_t$, where n_t is labour sold to firms. Preferences are assumed to be

$$E\left\{ \sum_{t=0}^{\infty} \beta^t U(c_t, n^o - n_t) \right\}$$

The technology is expressed by

$$\sigma_t = F(k_t, n_t, x_t)$$

where σ_t expresses the units of output that can be produced with k_t units of capital and n_t man-hours of labour while the technology shock is x_t. Let us assume that the shocks x_t follow a Markov process with transition probabilities

$$G(x',x) = Pr\{x_{t+1} \leqslant x' | x_t = x\}$$

The technology F is homogeneous of degree one in (k_t, n_t), so we can interpret all variables in per-household terms. Output σ_t is divided into consumption c_t and gross investment i_t and capital evolves according to

$$k_{t+1} = i_t + (1-\delta)k_t$$

Households own all the factors of production and rent them to profit-maximizing firms in each period at wages and capital rentals w_t and u_t (with the price of current output normalized at unity). Households' expectations about future factor prices are rational.

As in Lucas's heuristic model we have a representative agent defined by a well specified technology F, tastes U and the 'law of evolution of the environment' G. The state of each household represented is described by three variables: its own holdings of capital y_t, the capital stock in the economy as a whole k_t, and the current technology shock x_t. At each date, the action a chosen by the typical household is the vector (c, n, y') describing its consumption, labour supply, and capital holdings at the end of the period. The immediate return from any such action is just $R(a) = U(c, n^o - n)$. Owing to the assumption of perfect competition, the opportunity set Ω from which the action is selected is determined by the current factor prices $w(k, x)$, $u(k, x)$ which depend on the economy's state (k, x) but not on the individual's holdings. Thus:

$$\Omega(y,k,x) = \{(c,n,y'):c + y' \leqslant w(k,x)n + u(k,x)y + (1-\delta)y, c \geqslant 0, 0 \leqslant n \leqslant n^o, y' \geqslant (1-\delta)y\}$$

In an equilibrium, the next period capital stock for the economy as a whole, k', will be some function $h(k, x)$ of today's state. The rational-expectations hypothesis implies that this function is known by agents, along with the functions G, w and u. Then the household value function $v(s)$ must satisfy:

$$v(s) = \max_{(c,n,y')\in\Omega} \{U(c, n^o - n) + \beta \int v(y', h(k, x), x')dG(x', x)\}$$

This equation describes the decision problem faced by a household with regard to its consumption, labour supply and savings, given current factor prices $w(s)$ and $u(s)$ and given expectations about the way prices will behave in the future. These expectations, in turn, can be calculated from knowledge about the current state of the system (k, x), the way the distribution G of future exogenous shocks depends on this state, and the way the capital stock of the economy evolves, h. In other words, the system has been isolated from the environment according to the instructions of Lucas's heuristic model. Thus the representative household's decisions (c, n, y') will be a given function of the state (y, k, x) that sets the terms of this maximum problem.

The system is in a rational-expectations equilibrium when the savings behaviour each household believes others will follow coincides with the savings behaviour each household finds it optimal to follow, given its expectations about others. The equilibrium behaviour of the capital stock can be simulated by drawing shocks $\{x_t\}$ from the assumed distribution G and running the difference equation $k_{t+1} = h(k_t, x_t)$. Since the values of consumption, employment and factor prices are all functions of (k_t, x_t), the model generates time series for these variables as well. The stochastic difference equation obtained can generate behaviour that closely resembles an economic time series: the variables show erratic, serially correlated fluctuations around their mean values. In addition, in this case, the function $h(.)$ has a clear economic interpretation in terms of preferences and technology: 'a favourable technology shock shifts out current production possibilities; this induces high capital accumulation which spreads this benefit forward into future periods' (Lucas, 1987, p. 40).

Lucas observes that the basic model is only a point of departure for a satisfactory analysis of empirical evidence: 'the employment movements predicted by the model have lower amplitude (relative to output movements) than do actual employment variations. Consumption is more volatile and investment much less so in the model as compared to actual data' (*ibid.*).

In order to reduce these discrepancies between theory and facts RBC theorists have introduced a few modifications of the original basic model. In their published model KP modified both preferences and technology. The current value of 'leisure' $n^o - n_t$ was replaced by a distributed lag of its current and past values as an argument of the current utility function. This has the effect of increasing the intertemporal substitutability of leisure without altering the assumed intertemporal substitutability of consumption. On the technology side, the assumption that investment at date t augments the stock of production capital at date $t + 1$ was replaced with a gestation lag scheme. Finally it is assumed that technology shocks consist of 'permanent' and transient components, in a mix that cannot be observed by agents.

The effect of these modifications is to increase the dimensions of the state space, thus improving the model's ability to fit actual evidence. However, this ability would be trivial if KP were unable to justify the value assigned to free parameters. This is why they try to estimate as many parameters as possible from a wide variety of out-of-sample evidence. For example, the fact that people work about one-third of the time pins down one preference parameter; the observation that investment projects take something like a year to complete is used to fix a technological parameter, etc. The number of free parameters – including the critical parameters which define the technology shocks that drive the system – is reduced to about six. KP then choose values for the remaining parameters such that certain low-order moments (variances, covariances, autovariances) predicted by the model will match the corresponding moments from the collection of time series in the sample they used.

The logic behind the model is very close to that of Lucas's MBC when real shocks are substituted for monetary shocks. A favourable technology shock that increases the current productivity of both labour and capital is the analogue of Lucas's expansionary shock in monetary demand. Both kinds of shock make it attractive to work and produce in the current period rather than under the conditions expected to prevail in the future: thus in both cases employment and output rise in the current period. In both cases

168

the shock may be temporary or permanent. Insofar as the demand shock is purely monetary it is seen as transient; insofar as the supply shock is due to technical progress it is seen as 'permanent'. Therefore a monetary shock is the analogue of a transitory technology shock. Insofar as the shock is perceived as permanent and signals higher productivity for future periods, new investment projects are initiated to exploit this favourable contingency. The projects so initiated will increase output and employment until they are completed, spreading the effects of this shock – even if it should turn out after the fact to be transient – forward into future periods. They also carry within them the seeds of a future downturn, both because they increase the capital stock – possibly inappropriately – and because workers will be less willing to supply labour in future periods.

10.4   Criticisms

RBC models have been criticized by many authors. In my opinion, the following criticisms are particularly embarrassing for the supporters of this type of model.[5]

(1)   A crucial magnitude of the model is the average time necessary 'to build' new capital goods. In their simulations KP choose the average construction time reported in empirical studies. However, it is difficult to accept the idea that this magnitude is a constant, as one would expect the 'time to build' to vary with economic conditions. The speed of construction is a function of costs which producers are prepared to bear, and this depends on expected profits.

(2)   A second crucial assumption is intertemporal substitutability of leisure, which is supposed to explain strong responses in labour supply as a response to weak price signals. Recent empirical research by Ashenfelter (1984) and Mankiw, Rotemberg and Summers (1985) casts serious doubts on the possibility that intertemporal substitutability of leisure is high enough to account for actual cyclical fluctuations in labour supply and output.

(3)   In order to test the empirical validity of the model, KP have to give well defined values to the parameters. They claim to have parameterized the model on the basis of well established microeconomic and long-run information. This has been questioned by many authors. In particular, for example, let us consider a parameter that KP consider very important in determining the properties of

[5] For a longer list see Summers, 1986 and Hoover, 1988, pp. 49–52.

the model: the share of household time devoted to market activities. KP claim that it is one-third, while according to serious recent research (Eichenbaum and Singleton, 1986) its average value over the past thirty years is of about one-sixth.

A second example is the average real interest rate. KP give the value of 4 percent, but over the thirty-year period studied its actual value averaged only about 1 percent (Hoover, 1988).

(4)   What are called 'technology shocks' are in fact 'productivity shocks'. Moreover they arise mainly from labour hoarding (see Fay and Medoff, 1985, p. 653) which is a consequence rather than a cause of the business cycle.

A few other criticisms will be mentioned in the next two sections. New classical economists are working hard on new RBC models able to overcome the criticisms. I will here consider only the recent attempt by Lucas to hybridize the RBC model with his MBC model.

10.5   Lucas's attempt at a synthesis between MBC and RBC

In the preceding section I left aside a further criticism often levelled against the RBC. This class of model – at least in the prevailing version inspired by KP – completely ignores any role in the EBC for monetary variables. This is clearly recognized by Lucas: 'Nominal variables – the quantity of money, the general price level, and nominal rates of interest – play no role in the Kydland-Prescott model . . . One consequence of this omission is that these theories cannot shed light on the problem of inflation or on the observed associations between movements in money and prices and real activity' (1987, p. 70).

Lucas sees this as a serious problem, though it would be possible to graft onto the model a monetary sector with passively responding money, so as to accommodate the empirical evidence (exhibited, for example, by Friedman and Schwartz, 1963). In this case money would not play any active causal role, contrary to what Lucas argued in the 1970s (see section 8.4). But more recently Lucas has not insisted on his previous argument on causality. The crucial problem with the RBC is seen in the difficulty of explaining large empirical fluctuations in the absence of 'shocks' having the right order of magnitude. RBC models cannot be reconciled with empirical evidence 'not because the evidence documents an independent "causal" role for money, but because these real movements appear too large to be induced by a combination of purely real shocks and the kind of "propagation mechanism" Kydland-Prescott constructed' (1987, p. 71). This problem is not apparent in KP's model because they do not collect independent empirical evidence on the size of the so-called 'technology shocks', but choose a value *ad hoc* for the variance of the technology shock so as to be consistent with observed GNP variability.

According to Lucas this problem can be solved only by integrating a neoclassical cash-in-advance theory of money[6] with a KP-type RBC. This is judged by Lucas as 'slightly beyond the frontier of what is technically possible'. The trouble is that a model of this kind cannot be solved through a system-wide maximum problem as Kydland and Prescott did with their model. In Lucas's opinion money introduces a 'wedge of inefficiency' that makes it impossible to use this method of solution. Thus what Lucas tries to do with his 'integrated model' (which could be called the 'monetary–real business cycle': hereafter MRBC) is just to conjecture a few dynamic properties in qualitative terms. He assumes the same specification of preferences and technology as in KP's model. Trading follows the alternating pattern used by Lucas in his cash-in-advance model in order to motivate the use of money: agents trade in securities at the beginning of a period and then use cash so acquired to buy some of their consumption goods later on in the period. Work and investment goods are 'credit goods' in the sense that they are paid for at the end of the period. Money supply is erratic and modelled as a stochastic process, whose parameters remain fixed over time and known to agents. Lucas wants to examine under what conditions we should expect non-neutralities relevant to an equilibrium business cycle. In this context a real 'response' may occur only when a change in money conveys information about the way money or other variables will change in the future. Under these assumptions only anticipated changes in money are allowed to matter. In particular: 'for a monetary contraction to induce a real contraction, then, it would have to set up anticipations of a subsequent expansion, inducing agents to cut back on cash-using activities like working and spending' (Lucas, 1987, p. 88).

Lucas believes that inflation-tax effects of this type are unlikely to contribute very much to the explanation of major depressions or even relatively minor post-war recessions since 'the predicted interest rate movements are in the wrong direction, and . . . effects of this type [cannot] stimulate the kind of investment response that plays such an important role in the propagation mechanism of Kydland and Prescott's model and in many earlier models' (*ibid.*).

Surprisingly enough Lucas believes that the way out can be found by introducing some sort of nominal price rigidity. This sounds like the

---

[6] I do not need to be specific here on Lucas's theory of money as expressed in Lucas, 1984 and Lucas and Stokey, 1987. This theory is clearly summarized by Lucas himself in chapter 6 of his recent book on the business cycle (1987). On this subject see also Hoover, 1988, pp. 127–34.

traditional solution of Keynesian macroeconomics, but Lucas takes pains to specify nominal price rigidity in such a way as to make it consistent with his heuristic model. After a concise survey of the main existing alternatives, Lucas argues that the only acceptable way of modelling price rigidity is to link it with limited information in a manner similar to that which he had already examined in his MBC models. This is because, in his opinion, the central issue for a theory of nominal price rigidity lies not in the nature of the game agents are assumed to be playing, but rather in the information they are assumed to have about the state of the system at each date.[7] In a framework of full information unanticipated changes in money are neutral; they can produce non-neutral effects upon the business cycle only in systems with private information. In that case, according to Lucas, it may well be in the private interest of individual agents to specialize their individual information systems to adapt for unit changes of a purely monetary origin. As a result, agents react to monetary shocks as though they were real shocks.

In particular, it does not seem implausible to Lucas that in a model such as KP's, adapted so as to admit limited information on the part of agents, shocks of monetary origin would be 'misread' by agents as signalling changes in technology or preferences, and hence would trigger the same kind of dynamic response that technology shocks do in the model they reported (Lucas, 1987, p. 100).

The 'hybrid' MRBC model requires a disaggregated version of KP's model. We need a plurality of agents and goods in order to justify the presence of money and private information. One advantage of the hybrid model is that it might be used to show how much of the empirical business cycle depends on real shocks and how much on monetary shocks. This is important not only for descriptive purposes but also for the sake of economic policy. According to Lucas, insofar as the business cycle is induced by real shocks, the KP model implies that economic fluctuations are the best response to shocks originating in 'nature'. A policy designed to stabilize economic behaviour would thus be undesirable as it would induce inefficiencies that would more than offset the benefits from reduced risk. On the contrary, insofar as the business cycle is induced by monetary shocks, efficiency gains are possible through policies that stabilize the supply of money. This conjecture by Lucas is questionable because even the MBC

---

[7] The following passage is particularly clear:

> In so far as the monetary information necessary to permit agents to correct for what are, or ought to be, unit changes is public ... then one would expect this information to be used, independent of the form of interaction among agents. If, on the other hand, this information is *not* public, this simple 'correction' will not be possible and other possibilities present themselves. I think the construction of a satisfactory theory of a money-induced business cycle must involve exploiting these possibilities as well. (Lucas, 1987, p. 95)

describes the optimal adaptation of the economic system to environmental changes. Moreover one can think of changes in the real part of the environment which could improve the performance of the economy even in the RBC.[8] This set of questions cannot be answered unless we study the irreversible effects of short-run fluctuations, and it is doubtful whether this is possible in an EBC framework. However, it seems reasonable to assume that the ability to partition existing fluctuations into those due to real shocks and those induced by monetary shocks would improve not only our knowledge of empirical business cycles but also our ability to evaluate and select the available economic policies.

Lucas, then, may be justified in believing that his choice to focus on the MBC was taken 'with good judgement'. I agree with him that his hybrid disaggregated model would be superior to other existing EBC models because of its wider and more persuasive coverage of possible causes of the business cycle. Unfortunately this model – as Lucas himself stresses – is at the moment not yet operational and thus does not pass the tests of scientific acceptability set by Lucas's heuristic model (see above, section 8.7).

From my point of view the non-operational character of Lucas's model is not a sufficient reason to ignore it. But even a fully operational version of this model would still be subject to the criticisms raised against Lucas's heuristic model. The only real step forward would be in the suggested innovation which is particularly difficult to make operational in an EBC context: the abandonment of the hypothesis of the representative agent. In any case there are further problems which are common to all varieties of EBC models; these I want to raise in the next section.

10.6   The prospects of equilibrium business cycle theory

I am now in a position to express a few thoughts on the prospects of the EBC research programme.

First of all, it is perplexing that the exact nature of the so-called 'technology shocks' has so far not been sufficiently clarified, despite the crucial role of 'prime mover' of business cycles which is attributed to them by RBC theorists. What are called 'technology shocks' are in fact simply productivity shocks. The definition given to them is thus misleading because it involves an implicit explanation of productivity shocks which is not justified either theoretically or empirically. What is worse, as we have already noticed, existing evidence suggests that fluctuations in labour productivity arise mainly from labour hoarding. To the extent that this is so, the so-called technological shocks should be interpreted as an effect

---

[8] Moreover Lucas does not offer any reason why the hypothetical inefficiencies introduced by a stabilization policy in the RBC should 'more than offset' the reduction of risk.

rather than as the cause of the business cycle. The actual cause of the business cycle thus remains unexplained by RBC models.

This is not to deny that technological shocks might actually exist and could play a part in the explanation of empirical business cycles; but they should be specified in a different, more accurate and more structured way. Personally I feel quite sceptical about the possibility of including the cyclical effects of temporary technological shocks within the framework of an aggregate model. I share Schumpeter's view that the essence of technological change can be captured only by shifting our attention towards disaggregated models. Lucas's disaggregated MRBC model should thus be more promising in this sense. However, even this model has so far proved unable to take in the specific aspects of technical change. That is why Lucas can lump together technical change and changes in the structure of demand:

In such a many-good elaboration of the model, shifts in the composition of product demand would be modeled in a way very similar to the way Kydland and Prescott model technology shifts . . . From the point of view of producers, a new-found ability to make widgets with given inputs comes to very much the same thing as the ability to produce widgets that people like better than the old ones. (Lucas, 1987, pp. 96–7)

In addition, I believe that the effects of technical change on economic behaviour (including business cycles) are a consequence of 'permanent' shocks rather than temporary ones. This point of view prevails in a recent series of RBC models (see King *et al.*, 1987 and King, Plosser and Rebelo, 1988 a and b). However, even this new research programme is unable to overcome a crucial problem common to all EBC models, both monetary and real.

A common feature of the whole of this research programme is the idea that business cycles are set in motion by shocks which are perceived as offering new favourable opportunities. Such a favourable surprise was to be fairly strong if it were to match actual fluctuations. It is very doubtful that this requirement is consistent with the basic tenet of the EBC, i.e. that the economy is in equilibrium throughout the cycle. As we know from chapter 3, the stability of the general equilibrium is jeopardized by shocks of such a nature. Convergence towards equilibrium cannot be expected unless favourable surprises are negligible (see Fisher, 1983). Thus Schumpeter's basic intuition that a sizeable technological shock triggers a disequilibrium process of structural adjustment seems to be vindicated.

10.7 Conclusions

In this chapter I have briefly surveyed a few aspects of what Lucas believes to be 'the current frontier of business cycle theory', i.e. Kydland and

Prescott's variety of RBC models. These models apply the methodology of Lucas's heuristic model and are thus open to the same criticisms as those we have already discussed in chapter 9. In addition this class of models raises a set of specific problems which are so far unsolved. Even Lucas's attempt at a synthesis between KP's RBC model and his own MBC model, though stimulating, has so far been unsuccessful as it has not yet reached the degree of operationality required by his own scientific paradigm. In particular, in addition to the long list of criticisms existing in the literature, I have argued that technological shocks are often to be identified with sizeable favourable surprises due to unpredictable technological progress. This undermines the dynamic stability of general equilibrium which is necessary for applying the equilibrium method typical of the EBC theory.

Keynes's heuristic model: general observations

A theory cannot claim to be a *general* theory, unless it is applicable to the case where (or the range within which) money-wages are fixed, just as much as to any other case. (Keynes, GT, p. 276)

11.1 Introduction

It is not my intention to propose yet another interpretation of Keynes's *General Theory*. I shall concentrate exclusively on one very limited aspect of his mature work: the logical scheme of the arguments developed in the *General Theory*, which may be called his 'heuristic model'. This scheme, expressed in 'semi-formalized' language, consists of a causal 'plot' and a set of 'instructions for use' which remain partly implicit.

It will be useful to begin with a reconstruction of the causal links that make up the basic structure of the heuristic model and of the whole *General Theory*. In chapter 12 I shall deal more specifically with the 'instructions for use' and the underlying 'conception of economic science'.

Keynes sees macroeconomics as a discipline based on probabilistic arguments which aim to persuade a rational audience. These arguments are ordered sets of propositions, whose structure is dictated by links of epistemic probabilistic causality (see chapter 7).

At first sight the causal structure of the heuristic model, in the version here proposed, will look very much like that of the analytic models used in textbooks to illustrate Keynes's theory. Thus my exposition might at first seem pointless, but it aims to emphasize certain peculiarities of Keynes's contribution which, despite their considerable importance, are tradition-ally neglected. In addition the following exposition will help to bring out what in my view is the meaning, as well as the theoretical and empirical value, of the Keynesian method.

11.2 The causal outline of the heuristic model

Keynes sets out the causal structure of the heuristic model in two successive stages. In the first stage, developed in the first eighteen chapters of the

General Theory, he constructs a 'particular' model which is based on the provisional assumption that money wages are constant. In the second stage he deals with the case of flexible wages (chapters 19–21). The model is thus complicated and extended into a (relatively) 'general' version, including further relationships of interdependence.

In both stages the method of exposition may be defined as 'constructivist'. Keynes begins with the basic problem under analysis (diagnosis and therapy of involuntary unemployment), first studying the direct causal determinants, then the first-order indirect determinants (i.e. direct causes of the direct causes), and so on until he comes to exogenous determinants which are controllable through economic policy.[1] Hence the order of exposition of the causal links is the reverse of the causal order itself.

11.2.1 The particular heuristic model (fixprice)

Keynes divided the economic structure into four markets: the labour market, the goods market, the capital market and the money market. The markets are examined in this sequence, which is the opposite of the causal order that connects them in the analysis. The causal analysis of the particular heuristic model is thus divided into four successive phases which correspond to the analysis of the four markets.

The labour market (chapter 2 of GT)

Keynes sets out to demonstrate that the traditional analysis of the labour market becomes indeterminate when its postulates are adjusted to fit reality. According to the 'classics' both the employed labour in a certain economy (N) and the real wage rate at which it is employed ($v = w/p$) are simultaneously determined on the labour market by the intersection of the labour demand curve (N^D) and the labour supply curve (N^S). (See table 3 for a list of the principal symbols used in this chapter.) The demand curve is given by the points at which the marginal productivity of labour equals the real wage. The supply curve is given by the points at which the marginal disutility of labour equals the real wage. The labour demand curve is negatively sloped because the marginal productivity of labour is assumed to decrease with respect to employment. The supply curve is positively sloped since the disutility of labour is assumed to increase when the amount of labour supplied on the market increases. The assumption that the solution must lie on the labour demand curve is what Keynes calls the 'first classical postulate', whereas the assumption that it must lie on the supply curve is

---

[1] In the preparatory studies for the *General Theory* Keynes makes it clear that the final objective of the causal analysis is 'to select those variables which can be deliberately controlled or managed by central authority in the kind of system in which we actually live' (CW, vol. 13, p. 483).

Table 3. *Principal symbols used in this chapter*

A	autonomous expenditure
c	marginal propensity to consume
c_0	exogenous consumption
C	aggregate consumption
d'	marginal labour disutility
D	aggregate demand
e	marginal efficiency of capital
E	aggregate expenditure
G	public expenditure
i	rate of interest
I	investment
$1/k$	velocity of money
L_1	transactional demand for money
L_2	speculative demand for money
M	money supply
M_2	residual money supply
N	employment
N^D	demand for labour
N^S	labour supply
p	cost of living
s	marginal propensity to save
S	savings
U	unemployment
$\hat{U}$	involuntary unemployment
$v = w/p$	real wages
w	money wages
w_0	'historical' level of money wages
Y	aggregate income
Y^*	effective demand
Z	aggregate supply
λ	average labour productivity
λ'	marginal labour productivity
θ	exogenous determinants of money wages

(All monetary variables are measured in wage units; equilibrium values are starred.)

called the 'second classical postulate'. The two postulates hold simultaneously only at the point where the two curves meet. This is the labour market equilibrium according to the traditional analysis (see figure 8(a)). The empirical validity of the two postulates depends respectively on the behaviour of entrepreneurs aiming to maximize profit and on the behaviour of workers aiming to maximize utility. A corollary of this analysis, therefore, is that the market equilibrium, given the technical and psychological conditioning factors, reflects both the wishes of the entrepreneurs and those of the workers. In particular this is true of the level of unemployment: from the 'classical' point of view there can be no unemployment which is not voluntary.

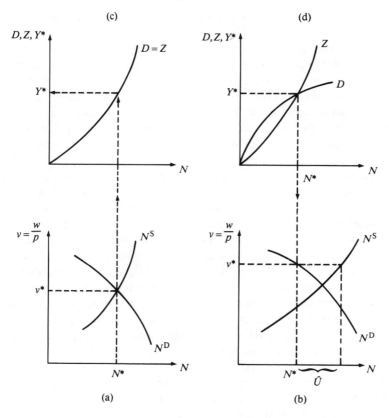

Figure 8   Labour market and effective demand

The weak point of the above analysis lies, according to Keynes, in the assumption that the second classical postulate is necessarily always satisfied. The fact is that while entrepreneurs are able to control both real wages and employment to conform to the first postulate, the workers are not able to guarantee that the second postulate will also be generally satisfied. Indeed both the value of the real wage and that of employment are largely outside the workers' control. Employment is determined by entrepreneurs on the basis of predictions regarding levels of effective demand, and is thus substantially exogenous to the labour market. Wage bargaining between entrepreneurs and workers concerns money wages more than real wages, and wage differentials rather than average wage levels. To determine real wages, once money wages are determined on the labour market, one must know the level of the cost of living. The latter depends on a whole series of factors independent of the labour market, such as harvests, the dynamics of import prices, the degree of plant utilization, etc. Keynes therefore rejects the second classical postulate, while accepting the validity of the first. This implies that the solution of the model becomes indeterminate *per se* unless employment is fixed exogenously by effective demand (see figure 8(b)). Here the full-employment equilibrium is only one extreme case among the possible equilibrium states. All the other possible values represent situations of 'under-employment equilibrium'. These situations also describe equilibrium states, because the market adjustment mechanism alone proves unable to restore full employment. Such circumstances result in an 'excess supply' of labour (involuntary unemployment); but, contrary to the view of the 'classical' theory of competitive markets, in general such an excess cannot significantly influence the market price (the real wage), which lies outside the full control of the workers. So the 'classical' equilibrating mechanism can function only as a consequence of the behaviour of the entrepreneurs. In a situation of excess labour supply, in fact, entrepreneurs would be prepared to employ more workers at a lower real wage, if at the same time there were an unsatisfied effective demand for goods on the commodity market. But as soon as effective demand was fully satisfied the adjustment mechanism would no longer work even for the entrepreneurs. The trouble is that this limit is generally reached before the level of full employment. Why? That is the main question which Keynes aims to answer in the following stages of the argument.

This problem does not exist in the 'classical theory' because it accepts Say's Law, which maintains that at every level of production supply creates its own demand. On this assumption there can be no limit to the increase in employment until full employment is reached. Adherence to Say's Law makes it impossible for classical theory to deal with the characteristics of a developed capitalist economy.

The market for goods: effective demand (chapter 3 of GT)

It follows from the analysis of the labour market that in order to determine employment the level of effective demand must be known. This level is represented by the point where the aggregate demand curve meets the aggregate supply curve. In the 'neoclassical theory' the effective demand proves indeterminate, since according to Say's Law the curve of aggregate demand and the curve of aggregate supply coincide (see figure 8(c)). If supply creates its own demand, and forces exist which push output to its maximum possible level, then demand will always be equal to the output produced under full employment. In this theoretical context the problem of effective demand does not exist. It arises only as a corollary of the rejection of Say's Law, to explain the divergence between maximum virtual production and actual production. Thus it becomes possible to understand the so-called 'paradox of poverty in the midst of abundance'. An insufficient effective demand is bound to stop the increase in employment short of the full employment level. Unfortunately 'the richer the community, the wider will tend to be the gap between its actual and its potential production' (GT, p. 31).

Keynes's theory, developed in chapter 3 of the *General Theory* to explain effective demand, has been the object of endless controversy. Without going into these in detail, I shall merely summarize the interpretation which I consider most convincing.[2] Effective demand is given by the point where the aggregate demand curve and the aggregate supply curve cross. The aggregate demand curve expresses the yield expected from the sale of the product at a given level of employment, while the supply curve expresses the minimum yield corresponding to any employment level that can justify the corresponding level of output. On the assumption of decreasing returns the two curves may be supposed to behave as in figure 8(d).

As long as aggregate demand is greater than aggregate supply, the total return can be increased by raising output (and employment); however, if aggregate demand is less than aggregate supply a reduction in the level of output is called for. The crossing-point is therefore a very short-term ('daily') equilibrium, as at each instant it satisfies all the dynamic tendencies implicit in the entrepreneurs' expectations. Short-period equilibrium presupposes also that the entrepreneurs' short-term expectations are correct. This happens at the point where the aggregate supply curve and the aggregate expenditure curve cross. In the contrary case a process of revision of expectations would begin, causing a rapid convergence of the daily equilibrium to the short-term equilibrium. Since in the short term we can assume that the supply curve is invariant, employment is crucially determined in that case by the aggregate expenditure function.

The market for goods: aggregate expenditure and the propensity to consume (chapters 8 and 9 of GT)

To determine the aggregate expenditure its two components, consumption and investment, have to be determined separately. This distinction is necessary because the behaviour of each of them has different causes and different consequences. Keynes begins with consumption. He surveys the main determinants of expenditure: both objective (variations in wages, discount rates, etc.), and subjective (enjoyment, improvidence, generosity, etc.). He concludes that in the short term consumption is mainly determined by income. This conclusion departs radically from the views of the 'classical theory', whose proponents believe that consumption is deter-

---

[2] For an accurate exposition of this interpretation see Casarosa, 1981.

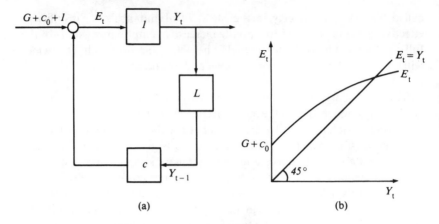

Keynes after Lucas

(a)

(b)

Figure 9 Income–expenditure feedback

mined by the maximization of the consumers' utility functions under budget constraints. Thus it is a function of the system of prices (including wages and interest rates), while income levels appear not as an independent variable but only as a 'constraint' which does not modify the function itself. Keynes, by contrast, expresses consumption as a fraction of income which tends to decrease as income rises (see figure 9(b)). In fact, in his opinion people tend to increase their consumption when their income increases, but not to the same degree. This arises both from the viscosity of spending habits during cyclic fluctuations, and from the reduced pressure of primary needs. The gap resulting from this divergence, according to Keynes, becomes more and more difficult to fill by means of adequate investments. Hence attention must be shifted first to the role of investment in determining effective demand, and then to the factors that influence investment itself.

The multiplier (chapter 10 of GT)
Analysis of the consumption function reveals that if the supply curve is constant, effective demand depends on the interaction between income and expenditure. In fact consumption depends on income, but together with investment it determines expenditure which in turn is translated into income, and so on. The interaction between income and expenditure which underlies the multiplier can be interpreted as a feedback mechanism (see figure 9(a)). The system is stable because, as Keynes himself showed clearly, the marginal propensity to consume has a value between zero and one. The equilibrium value of this process of interaction would still be indeterminate (three equations for four variables) if it could not be assumed that investment is mainly exogenous. Keynes considers this assumption reason-

182

able (as he will explain when analysing the capital market); thus one can work out the equilibrium value of income and aggregate expenditure as a function of investment.[3] In particular, it proves possible to determine the increase in income generated by a given increase in investment. This is done by calculating the product of the latter and a coefficient, called 'multiplier', that generates an increase in income equal to a multiple of the increase in investment. Keynes uses this multiplier to determine effective demand, on the restrictive hypotheses assumed after the third chapter. However, if there is reason to believe that short-term expectations are wrong or the supply curve changes significantly during the period under consideration, then the multiplier no longer suffices to determine effective demand and we must revert to the analysis sketched in chapter 3 of GT, conducted in terms of aggregate supply and demand.

The capital market (chapters 11, 13 and 14 of GT)

Here too the analysis begins with a critique of the 'classical' theory, according to which investment is determined in the 'capital market' by the normal market mechanism. Investment, savings and interest rates are determined simultaneously by the point of intersection of the capital demand curve (investment) and the capital supply curve (savings), while the interest rate acts as the price equilibrating supply and demand (see figure 10(a)). Here again Keynes shows that the 'classical' theory becomes indeterminate as soon as it is amended to take account of actual reality. Since savings depend crucially on income, as is already implicit in the consumption function, there will be as many capital supply curves, and hence as many solutions, as there are possible values of income.

The theory must therefore be reformulated appropriately. First of all it must be understood that savings have no causal influence on the determination of investment:

Saving, in fact, is a mere residual. The decisions to consume and the decisions to invest between them determine incomes. Assuming that the decisions to invest become effective, they must in doing so either curtail consumption or expand income. Thus the act of investment in itself cannot help causing the residual or margin, which we call saving, to increase by a corresponding amount. (GT, p. 64)

If savings are determined by investment in this way, the possible equilibrium points coincide with the investment curve. This leaves one function

---

[3] The multiplier of the *General Theory*, unlike that found in Kahn (1931) and in 'The means to prosperity' (1933a), is largely conceived as static. Victoria Chick (1983) has collected and classified the passages in the *General Theory* where the multiplier is conceived as static and those in which an alternative conception, closer to the dynamic one, seems to emerge. In the first group of passages Keynes slips into a syntactic conception of equilibrium which is not only unjustified in itself (see chapter 2 of the present study) but conflicts with the dynamic conception which prevails in the *General Theory*.

Keynes after Lucas

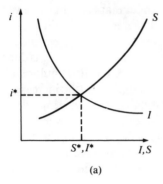
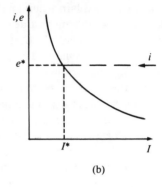

(a)   (b)

Figure 10   Capital market

for two unknowns: investment proves irremediably indeterminate in the capital market unless the interest rate is assumed to be exogenous (see figure 10(b)). This is just the path Keynes chose to take, demonstrating in the next stage of the argument that the interest rate is determined in the money market.

In Keynes's argument the reversal of the causal order between savings and investment is essential from the semantic point of view.[4] If one accepted the 'classical' theory's causal order, the only effect of the increasing gap between full-employment income and consumption, which so worries Keynes, would be to accelerate capital accumulation and increase the future welfare of consumers. In fact the 'classical' economists consider saving as an autonomous decision involving the substitution of future consumption for present consumption. This makes it possible to free productive resources (capital and labour) from the production of consumer goods, in order to use them for production of investment goods. That is why savings are seen as the highest economic virtue. For Keynes, on the other hand, the decision to save is purely residual and is not automatically translated into a decision to invest. In fact the act of saving implies a desire for wealth as such, or rather for a capacity to consume unspecified goods at unspecified dates. Saving slows up commodity circulation, since exchange value ceases to be a means of acquiring use values and becomes an end in itself. A potential demand for use values is 'frozen' by savings, but this demand does not specify which goods will be actually in demand and when.

---

[4] The question of whether these observations on the order of causation are compatible with the assumption that savings and investment are necessarily equal is one I shall not discuss here. I will merely observe that this assumption on Keynes's part is certainly unsatisfactory as regards both the question itself and the supporting arguments. Here too Keynes slips into a purely syntactic (or logical) conception of equilibrium.

184

The capital demand curve is also redefined conceptually, and rechristened the 'curve of the marginal efficiency of capital'. It retains a certain formal analogy with the classical curve, but its derivation and its significance are profoundly different. Keynes does not reason in terms of marginal productivity of capital, but in terms of a hierarchy of investment plans according to their expected profitability. The plans which are carried out will be those whose expected profitability is not less than the market interest rate. The other plans are discarded, since the funds necessary to finance them can be more profitably employed if lent at the market interest rate. The lower the market interest rate, therefore, the greater the investment – as in the 'classical' capital demand curve.

But the curve of marginal efficiency of capital is distinguished from the 'classical' curve in the following ways:

(a)   The yield of capital does not depend on its productivity, but only on its scarcity. Hence Keynes considers it as a kind of nonproductive rent, which in principle could be eliminated.

(b)   No particular link is implied between interest rate and capital intensity (Pasinetti, 1974), which avoids the logical difficulties that characterize the classical theory of capital.

(c)   'The schedule of the marginal efficiency of capital is of fundamental importance because it is mainly through this factor . . . that the expectation of the future influences the present' (GT, p. 145). The fluctuations of the marginal efficiency of capital caused by the state of expectations, according to Keynes, constitute the principal cause of the economic cycle (see chapter 23 of the *General Theory*).

*The money market and the determination of the interest rate
(chapters 15, 16, 17 of GT)*

At the end of the long analysis outlined above, Keynes reached the conclusion that one must first determine the interest rate in order to determine investment, and hence indirectly, income and employment. The interest rate does not depend on the capital market (as the 'classical' economists maintained), but on the interaction between the supply of money and the demand for money. Thus money plays a fundamental role in the Keynesian theory of employment: the rigid 'classical' dichotomy between monetary and real variables no longer exists (see chapter 12).

In most of the *General Theory* Keynes assumes that money supply (measured in wage units) is essentially exogenous, as it is controlled by the monetary authorities. With regard to the demand for money, the basic reason why money may be preferred to other capital goods, which offer a positive interest rate, is that it is 'liquid', i.e. it can be immediately exchanged at practically no cost for any other commodity: 'its utility is

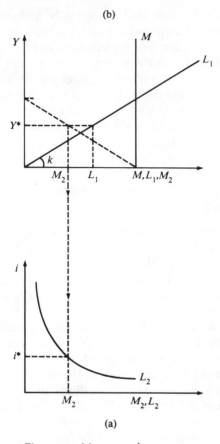

Figure 11   Money market

solely derived from its exchange-value' (GT, p. 231). For this reason Keynes calls the money demand curve the 'liquidity preference curve'.

The significance of interest is related to the concept of liquidity. In fact Keynes, unlike the classical economists, understood interest as 'a measure of the unwillingness of those who possess money to part with their liquid control over it' (GT, p. 167).

The demand for money must be ascribed to three different motives: (a) the *transactional* motive, to permit the normal transactions involved in the functioning of an economy; (b) the *precautionary* motive, to hold a reserve for dealing with unforeseen and unavoidable expenses; and (c) the *speculative* motive, to realize a profit through a more accurate assessment of the future than that prevailing on the market.

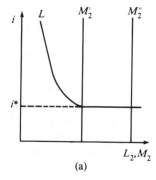
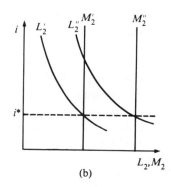

Figure 12   Liquidity trap

The demand for money arising from the first two motives (L_1) depends basically on the level of economic activity as measured by the level of the national income Y (see figure 11(b)). The demand for money arising from the speculative motive (L_2) depends instead on the interest rate (see figure 11(a)). This is the channel through which the quantity of money (M) influences the real economic system. The role of money depends on the uncertainty of the forecasts made by economic agents. Otherwise it would always be more advantageous to hold interest-bearing securities. If this is true, an increase in 'superfluous' money M_2 (i.e. money not absorbed for transactional and precautionary purposes) can be absorbed by the public only if the incentive to hold wealth in non-liquid form decreases, which means only if the interest rate falls. The market mechanism assures that an increase in money supply will reduce the interest rate and hence increase investment: 'If, however, we are tempted to assert that money is the drink which stimulates the system to activity, we must remind ourselves that there may be several slips between the cup and the lip' (GT, p. 173).

To the 'slips' previously examined (the possibility of perverse shifts in the propensity to consume and the marginal efficiency of capital) is added another which operates on the money market: 'whilst an increase in the quantity of money may be expected, *ceteris paribus*, to reduce the rate of interest, this will not happen if the liquidity preferences of the public are increasing more than the quantity of money' (*ibid.*). This difficulty is usually called the 'liquidity trap'. It can be formalized (as in figure 12(a)) by tracing a liquidity preference curve whose elasticity with respect to interest becomes infinite at a certain level of interest rate (i^*). At that level the public's desire to hold wealth in liquid form becomes unlimited, since the interest rate no longer sufficiently compensates for the sacrifice and the risk of holding wealth in non-liquid form. Any further increase in money supply would no longer affect the interest rate. The same effect could arise from a perverse shift in the liquidity preference function such as to compensate for the positive influence of an increased money supply (see figure 12(b)).

In any case the liquidity trap, which Keynes actually mentions briefly only a very few times in the *General Theory*, does not necessarily prevent an expansionary monetary policy from effectively stimulating economic activity, as a few critics have erroneously maintained. Keynes is convinced that in certain circumstances monetary policy may even have a substantial influence on the real behaviour of the economy. In this respect he again opposes the views of the 'classical' economists, who hold that monetary variables can have a durable influence only on other monetary variables, not on real magnitudes such as income (measured in wage units) and employment.

Here again Keynes maintains that the 'classical' theory is true only on the assumption of full employment. In the latter case, in fact, the increase in effective demand caused by the increase in the money stock cannot be translated into a corresponding increase in the aggregate supply of commodities. The excess demand results only in price rises. Still, in a situation characterized by the under-employment of productive factors, the increase of the money stock can mobilize unused resources, with real consequences which are not purely transitory.

The logical structure of the fixprice heuristic model (chapter 18 of GT)

As we have seen, Keynes disaggregates the economy into four markets (labour, commodities, capital, money). He analyses these in sequential order, and to each he first applies the partial equilibrium method typical of the traditional Cambridge school (Marshall and Pigou) to show the inadequacy of that approach. In fact, the characteristic magnitudes of each of these markets remain indeterminate unless one takes account of the exogenous causal impulse deriving from the market that follows it in the series. A chain of variables emerges, in which the order of exposition is opposite to the order of causation. In the order of exposition the two extremes are the real wage and employment on the one hand, and the money supply on the other.

In chapter 18, before going on to the second stage of the argument and studying the effect of variations in money wages, Keynes summarizes the heuristic model with exogenous wages elaborated in the first seventeen chapters. We in turn should now briefly go over the causal sequence of the first stage to see how the different pieces of the heuristic model are combined into an overall view of the short-term functioning of the capitalist economic structure (see figure 13).

Keynes shows first that the traditional analysis of labour market equilibrium remains in itself indeterminate because the 'second classical postulate' is invalid. There remains only one relation (the labour demand curve) with which to determine two variables: real wages and employment. Any point on the labour demand curve, in the sector where demand is less than supply of labour, may be a point of equilibrium. To determine which of these possible solutions actually characterizes the real equilibrium, we must know an exogenous variable: effective demand. But from the 'classical' viewpoint this too turns out to be indeterminate in the market for goods, since according to Say's Law the aggregate demand curve and the aggregate supply curve coincide. So we must take another backward step, recognizing that the aggregate demand for commodities derives from the sum of expenditure on consumer and investment goods. Keynes then goes on to consider, in order, the determinants of consumption and investment. According to the 'classical' economists consumption is determined by the maximization of the utility functions under budget constraints. In Keynes's view this procedure leaves aggregate consumption indeterminate, since it would depend partly, and especially, on aggregate income. By establishing a privileged link between consumption and income Keynes brings out an important corollary of his rejection of Say's Law: the existence of a complex interaction between income and expenditure. This interaction is expressed by an interdependent model with three equations and four unknowns.

The market for goods also remains indeterminate. Investment is then considered exogenous, as it is determined not in the commodity market but in the capital market, by factors independent of the interaction between income and expenditure. But here too, as in the labour market, the 'classical' theory fails to stand up because the capital supply curve proves indeterminate with respect to the interest rate (since it depends partly on income), and in any case has no determining causal influence. Only one relation (the capital demand curve) remains for two unknowns (investment and the interest rate). A further backward step must therefore be made, taking the value of the interest rate as determined in the money market. Here too the money demand curve plays the determining causal role once account is taken of the money supply, which is exogenous.

Thus we reach the end of the causal line. At this point one cannot refer to a further 'market'. The analysis remains indeterminate. To close the model we must take a leap from political economy to economic policy (see figure 13).

11.2.2 The general heuristic model (flexprice)

In the first eighteen chapters of the *General Theory* Keynes sets up a heuristic apparatus which enables him to carry out conceptual experiments, simulating the effects of alternative economic policies. This makes it

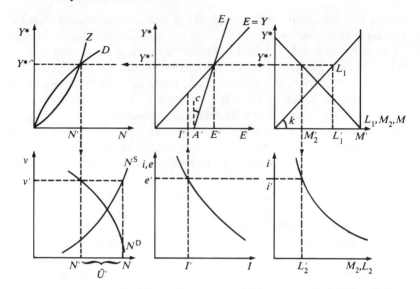

Figure 13   The fixprice heuristic model of Keynes: a Cartesian-diagram representation

possible to follow the way an impulse deriving from a particular economic policy rule is transmitted into the economy. Thus we can work out which rule is preferable, and eventually see how the whole mechanism should be modified.

To carry out this plan, Keynes is forced to consider money wages as flexible, and to take account of the probable repercussions of alternative economic policy rules on the structure of the parameters. Hence in Book V of the *General Theory* (chapters 19–21) he proceeds to complicate the heuristic model to produce a version which may be considered (relatively) general.

Structural instability of parameters and alternative economic policies

The first conceptual experiment concerns the economic policy of *laissez faire* following the traditional prescriptions of the classical free-trade theory. The results are negative for the case of fixed wages, because the 'particular' heuristic model shows that the economic system is unable to regulate itself – i.e. to eliminate involuntary unemployment by moving back to an equilibrium position of full employment. We must now see if these conclusions hold also for the real world, characterized by flexible wages.

The 'classical' economists of the thirties blamed the persistence of unemployment on the presence of trade unions which, by exploiting their 'monopoly' position in the sale of labour services, managed to keep wage levels too high to make full employment possible. The remedy proposed by these economists was to reduce money wages, using external pressure to induce what a perfectly competitive market would have done by itself. The second and decisive conceptual experiment, then, was to analyse the consequences of this type of economic policy in the model.

Keynes excludes the effectiveness of such a policy within the labour market because the reduction in money wages would probably be accompanied by an identical reduction in prices, so deflation would have no direct effect on real wages and unemployment. This does not deny the possibility of an indirect effect through effective demand via monetary channels. In fact the heuristic model (if one momentarily ignores the structural instability of its parameters), makes it possible to claim that if there is unemployment it is because the quantity of money measured in wage units is not sufficient to mobilize all the available resources. A reduction in money wages would have the effect of increasing that quantity, and hence of reducing unemployment, insofar as the transmission mechanism is unimpeded by its numerous 'slips' (perverse shifts in the liquidity preference function, the marginal efficiency of capital and the propensity to consume). Even so, exactly the same results can be obtained without reducing money wages, by increasing the nominal quantity of money. Hence there is no *prima facie* reason to prefer the 'classical' prescriptions to an expansionary monetary policy.

On the other hand there would be a number of reasons not to prefer the first type of economic policy, which Keynes examines in chapter 19 of the *General Theory*. Note in particular the following:

(a)   a wage cut might set off a deflationary spiral which would lower the curve of marginal efficiency of capital;

(b)   the schedule of liquidity preference might shift upwards if the wage deflation shook the confidence of economic agents;

(c)   cuts in money wages might lead to a redistribution of income from workers to entrepreneurs and from these via price deflation to *rentiers* – in other words in favour of classes with a lower propensity to consume. This would further reduce the effective demand, creating more unemployment.

Thus in Keynes's opinion the trade unions, in resisting indiscriminate cuts in money wages, prove to be better economists than the academics. However, though an expansionary monetary policy is preferable to a policy of wage cuts, it is not sufficient. It must be supplemented by external interventions made necessary by the failures of the transmission mechanism (see above, section 11.2.1). The basic problem is rooted in the probabilistic nature of the causal transmission. A long chain of probable causes is very unreliable. The way out is found by Keynes in interventions in the market of goods in order to sustain effective demand directly. This can be done supporting consumption and investment through an opportune budget policy. Progressive income taxation would generate a redistribution of wealth in favour of the classes that have a greater propensity to consume. Public works financed with public loans ('deficit spending') would generate income without destroying any. These and other analogous tools of economic policy, which Keynes analyses in some detail in the *General Theory*, may permit public regulation of investments ('socialization of investments'), and thus make possible the full utilization of available resources.

Variations in money wages and effective demand
According to Keynes money wages vary partly because of exogenous factors (social and institutional factors that affect the results of wage bargaining), and partly because of endogenous factors. Suppose we begin the analysis with a situation characterized by very high levels of unemployment, and then progressively increase effective demand. Money wages would at first remain approximately constant, at a level depending partly on extra-economic factors. However, as soon as employment reached levels approaching full employment, money wages would begin to increase, accelerating more and more until, with full employment, any further increase in effective demand would be wholly translated into increases in money wages. In other words, an expansionary policy has purely real effects at very high levels of unemployment and purely monetary effects under full employment; at intermediate levels there are both real and monetary effects. Keynes characterizes the latter as positions of 'semi-inflation', reserving the term (absolute) inflation for the full-employment situation. In Keynes's view the semi-inflation positions have 'a good deal of historical importance. But they do not really lend themselves to theoretical generalisations' (GT, p. 302). Hence we must observe a series of precautions in attempting to give them a graphic representation. The function shown in figure 14 is meant to aid an intuitive perception of the link which Keynes established between the money wage level and employment. However, a few fundamental qualifications must be kept well in mind:

(a)   For the sake of simplicity the function is drawn as a continuous curve, but it should actually be understood as discontinuous: 'In actual experience the wage-unit does not change continuously in terms of money in response to every small change in effective demand; but discontinuously – these points of discontinuity are

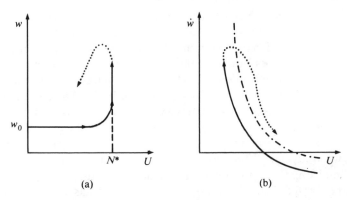

Figure 14   Money wages and unemployment

determined by the psychology of the workers and by the policies of employers and trade unions' (GT, p. 301).

(b)   The function is not reversible, since in fact money wages are less flexible downwards than upwards (for this reason I have drawn arrows on the curve).

(c)   This function clearly implies the existence of a Phillips curve. The explanation suggested by Keynes (GT, p. 253) particularly emphasizes the link between workers' bargaining power and the rate of unemployment:

> Although the struggle for money-wages is, as we have pointed out above, essentially a struggle to maintain a high relative wage, this struggle is likely, as employment increases, to be intensified in each individual case, both because the bargaining position of the worker is improved and because the diminished marginal utility of his wage and his improved financial margin make him readier to run risks.

However, it is clear from the preceding observations that in Keynes's version the 'Phillips curve' is in no way conceived as stable and thus as usable by economic policy. This example gives a significant indication of how the 'Keynesians' of the seventies (especially the proponents of the so-called 'neoclassical synthesis') have misunderstood Keynes's method.

11.3   Conclusions

In my concluding observations it is useful to summarize and further develop the analysis of the role of money wages in the *General Theory*.

From the very first pages of the *General Theory* Keynes admits that money wages may be influenced by the level and the variations of employment, but he strongly denies that variations thus induced in money wages can directly produce a feedback effect within the labour market. Any such effect will be directly determined by effective demand. In principle, however, Keynes does not deny the possibility of an indirect influence exerted through effective demand. He thus recognizes the existence of a 'wage feedback',[5] which has been disregarded by both followers and critics although it plays a decisive role in Keynes's contribution. Before facing the problem, however, Keynes is forced to expound the theory of effective demand by assuming *pro tempore* that money wages are exogenously given. That is why the *General Theory* can examine this subject only in chapter 19, after completing the exposition of the particular heuristic model. This has caused no small difficulty[6] for most of the critics;[7] it has led them, among other things, to underestimate the importance which Keynes attributes to wage feedback.

In the first eighteen chapters he already takes account, though only implicitly, of the influence exerted by possible variations in money wages on the variables determining effective demand (money, investment and consumption), which are measured in money units. Here it is assumed that the monetary effect is proportional to the cause, so that there is no alteration in the above magnitudes measured in wage units (apart from any exogenous

---

[5] See Appendix 11A. It may be useful to eliminate one possible source of misunderstanding straightaway. Recognizing the existence of a wage feedback and its importance does not essentially contradict the widespread idea that the labour market occupies a passive and residual position in Keynes's theory. This assertion is certainly true for the first eighteen chapters of the *General Theory* and is rightly indicated as a decisive difference from 'classical theory'. Book V, however, introduces qualifications which from this point of view are only secondary, because: (a) variations in money wages depend only partly on labour market conditions; and (b) variations in money wages have an ambiguous influence on effective demand, and in any case this influence is mediated by economic policy. Hence, while labour market conditions depend univocally on the effective demand, the symmetric causal influence is of uncertain sign.

[6] Keynes shows that he is perfectly aware of the misunderstandings that may arise from this problem. On many occasions he apologizes for the delayed introduction of flexible wages. Here is an example: 'It would have been an advantage if the effects of a change in money-wages could have been discussed in an earlier chapter . . . It was not possible, however, to discuss this matter fully until our own theory had been developed' (GT, p. 257).

[7] Particularly significant, in this connection, is Hicks's authoritative testimony (1974, pp. 59–60):

> One of the things in the *General Theory* which caused most trouble to its first readers (I speak from experience) was the habit of working in what were called 'wage units' . . . All expositors of Keynes (including myself) have found this procedure a difficulty. The wage-theorem could not be understood until one had grasped the rest of the theory; yet the rest of the theory (when expounded in the way Keynes expounded it) could not be understood without the wage-theorem. We had to find some way of breaking the circle. The obvious way of doing so was to begin by setting out the rest (multiplier, liquidity preference and so on) on the assumption of *fixed* money wages. Then, with that behind one, it was fairly easy to go on to the wage-theorem. That is what we did – I still think it was what we had to do – but the consequences of doing it were serious.

influences which alter the proportions). So money wages serve as an effective standard for the monetary magnitudes whose variations have no importance for the real configuration of the economy. Hence the choice of the 'wage unit' as a unit of measure. This has led many critics to maintain that the specificity of Keynes's argument depends on the rigidity of money wages, or at least on the postulate of their total irrelevance for the real configuration of the economy.[8] But Keynes does not limit himself to analysing the effects just described. As we have seen, after chapter 18 he analyses the non-neutral effects which are added to the former ones, enriching and qualifying the argument previously developed. One cannot disregard this part of Keynes's contribution, as is usually done,[9] without profoundly altering its meaning.

Appendix 11A The fixprice and flexprice heuristic models of the *General Theory*

Here I shall give a synoptic representation of the heuristic model with fixed wages described by Keynes in the first eighteen chapters of the *General Theory*, as well as of the model with flexible wages presented in Book V.

In figure 13 (see above) I have 'assembled' the Cartesian diagrams, representing the single markets, into one comprehensive scheme. In figure 15 the same general scheme is represented in the language of block diagrams. Finally, figure 16 shows a block diagram of the heuristic model with flexible wages. A comparison between figures 15 and 16 will bring out the basic differences between these two models.

Appendix 11B The labour market in Keynes

The interpretation I have suggested for Keynes's labour market theory, as given in Volume II of the *General Theory*, is far from uncontroversial.[10] The traditional

---

[8] The clearest version of the postulate is Hicks's so-called 'wage-theorem': 'When there is a general (proportional) rise in money wages, says the theorem, the normal effect is that all prices rise in the same proportion – provided that the money supply is increased in the same proportion (whence the rate of interest will be unchanged)' (1974, pp. 59–60).

[9] In other words, any interpretation based on the fixprice heuristic model, disregarding the qualifications introduced in the flexprice heuristic model, in the end proves profoundly misleading. A particularly significant case is that of the IS-LM model (see appendix 11C).

[10] This interpretation is not new as it has been maintained by a few authors in recent years. One of the first versions of this type of interpretation is sketched in Clower, 1960.

Keynes after Lucas

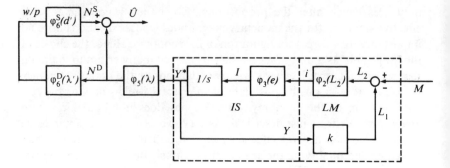

Figure 15 The fixprice heuristic model of Keynes: a block-diagram representation

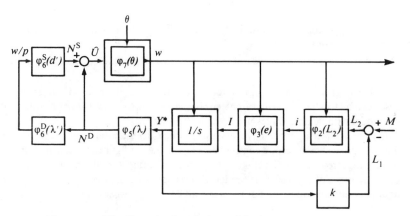

Figure 16 The flexprice heuristic model of Keynes

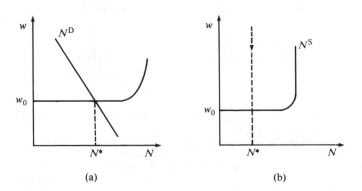

(a)   (b)

Figure 17 Labour market and money wages

196

interpretation, whose most influential early version is that of Modigliani (1944), is based on supply and demand curves expressed in terms of money wages (assuming given prices); it derives results of a Keynesian type from particular assumptions about the form of the supply curve.

The latter, as expressed graphically in figure 17, 'is assumed to be perfectly elastic at the historically ruling wage rate, say w_0 ... But as soon as all those who wanted to be employed at the ruling real wage rate w_0/p have found employment, wages become flexible upward' (Modigliani, 1944, p. 47).

Given the labour supply, the equilibrium point of the labour market is determined in one of two alternative ways: either one accepts the hypothesis that employment is determined exogenously by effective demand, which permits the equilibrium money wage to be calculated immediately, or one draws a labour demand curve with a negative slope, which together with the supply curve simultaneously determines money wages and employment (see figures 17(a) and (b)).

This category of interpretations meets a few embarrassing difficulties:

(a)   The labour supply curve, expressed in terms of real wages (second classical postulate), is criticized by Keynes as a causal determinant of real wages and employment, but he does not see it as being devoid of any theoretical function. It still serves to define the labour supply at a certain real wage, and it constitutes the maximum limit of employment. On the other hand there is no reason to think that a segment of it must be inelastic to variations in real wages, as would be implied by the preceding assumptions (remember that prices are taken as given).

(b)   In the interpretation under discussion an increase in effective demand would raise real wages together with employment (above the critical threshold of semi-inflation), whereas there is no doubt whatever that in the *General Theory* it is assumed that real wages decrease with an increase in employment.[11]

(c)   The labour supply curve, by definition, expresses the decisions that would be voluntarily made by workers in the absence of external constraints (i.e. different from those of the labour market). Any equilibrium point lying on the labour supply curve is thus incompatible with the existence of involuntary unemployment.[12]

(d)   The labour demand curve is unequivocally expressed by Keynes in terms

[11] For example see the following passage: 'with a given organisation, equipment and technique, real wages and the volume of output (and hence of employment) are uniquely correlated, so that, in general, an increase in employment can only occur to the accompaniment of a decline in the rate of real wages' (GT, p. 17). Modigliani, on the other hand, maintains that 'the supply of labor will not increase unless the money wage rate rises relative to the price level' (Modigliani, 1944, p. 47). In the latter case an increase in employment occurs, *ceteris paribus*, along the labour supply curve, and hence with increasing real wages.

[12] 'The equality of the real wage to the marginal disutility of employment presupposed by the second postulate, realistically interpreted, corresponds to the absence of "involuntary" unemployment' (GT, p. 14).

of real wages (according to the first classical postulate, which is explicitly accepted in the *General Theory*). It is extremely hard to 'translate' his analysis in terms of money wages: first of all because whatever slope one gives to the demand curve (assuming given prices), one assumes that variations in money wages are unaccompanied by analogous price variations (this is ruled out repeatedly by Keynes, who at most is prepared to admit a brief delay in the adaptation of money wages to price variations). Moreover, drawing the curve with a negative slope (as is usually done) would make both real and money wages decrease together with the increase in employment if the equilibrium shifted along the demand curve. Keynes, on the contrary, insists that money wages and real wages move in opposite directions.[13] (On the other hand, drawing the demand curve with a positive slope would only aggravate the problem: there would still be a positive correlation between money and real wages, and in addition real wages would rise with the increase in employment.)

(e)   Finally, the version where employment is endogenously determined is in clear contrast with the often repeated Keynesian thesis that employment is determined by effective demand.

The above reasons seem to me sufficient to justify a preference for the interpretation suggested in the present work.

Appendix 11C **Keynes's heuristic model and IS-LM**

The IS-LM model, proposed by Hicks in 1937, has long been presented in textbooks as a substantially faithful representation of Keynes's *General Theory*.[14]

Recently an increasing number of economists have taken the view that the IS-LM model fails adequately to represent many important aspects of Keynes's thought. Not long ago Hicks himself admitted and clarified a few questionable features of his model (1974, 1980–1).

An analysis of the relation between Keynes's heuristic model and the IS-LM model may be useful for a better understanding of some aspects of these recent controversies, and may further clarify certain peculiarities of Keynes's heuristic model.

The fixprice heuristic model describes an interaction among four variables: money, interest, investment and income (see figure 18). The interdependence among these four variables is conceived in causal and hence asymmetric terms.[15] To pass

---

[13] 'In the short period, falling money-wages and rising real wages are each, for independent reasons, likely to accompany decreasing employment' (GT, p. 10).

[14] This opinion has never been shared by the Keynesian authors who have been more critical of neoclassical positions (for example J. Robinson, Garegnani, Pasinetti).

[15] There can be no legitimate doubt that Keynes was fully aware of the importance of so-called 'monetary feedback'. Keynes's causal successivism does not exclude the existence of important interdependences (see e.g. Vercelli, 1979).

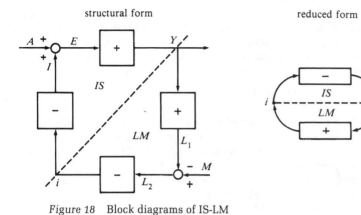

Figure 18   Block diagrams of IS-LM

from Keynes's particular heuristic model to the IS-LM model it is necessary to conflate the relations existing between these four variables into a pair of relations between two of the variables. Hicks chooses interest rate and income, but that is not the only possible choice.[16] The pair of relations thus obtained may be represented on a two-dimensional Cartesian plane.

At this point we can bring out the most important differences between the particular heuristic model (fixprice) and the IS-LM model. Some of these differences show the convenient features of the IS-LM model:

(1)   The IS-LM model simplifies the heuristic model, which Keynes expressed in semi-formal language. This makes it possible to formulate Keynes's model in rigorously analytic terms.

(2)   It becomes possible to assess the final effects of the 'monetary feedback' between income and the demand for money. Keynes clearly has serious problems with his purely qualitative sequential method when it comes to evaluating the final effect of the interaction between the real market and the money market. It cannot be denied that the reformulation of the fixprice heuristic model in analytical terms, insofar as it may be considered legitimate, offers a solution to this problem.

(3)   The simplifications of the *particular* heuristic model prove on the whole to be acceptable if it is assumed that the long-term expectations are stable. On that assumption the labour market, which does not appear at all in the IS-LM model, plays only a passive and residual role and can easily be supplemented with a further diagram representing a causally sequential subsystem.

The above considerations help to explain the great success of the IS-LM model. Keynes's approval of Hicks is also comprehensible. However, the matter does not

---

[16] Hicks has recently (1974) maintained that it would be better to choose investment and income as poles of the dichotomy.

end here. Keynes's *general* theory is the one represented by the *flexprice* heuristic model. The IS-LM model, as a simplified representation of Keynes's *fixprice* heuristic model, takes no account whatever of the further fundamental complications and qualifications introduced by Keynes in Book V of the *General Theory*. Among others I would point out the following basic differences:

(a)   The IS-LM model assumes fixed prices as well as constant money wages. Thus the underlying theory is compatible with the 'classical' theory in both its theoretical results and in relation to economic policy.

(b)   The sequential scheme of causality that characterizes Keynes's heuristic model is made completely implicit by the IS-LM model. So it is no longer possible to analyse the processes whereby an impulse is transmitted, and hence to assess its structural repercussions. This is particularly serious in view of the probabilistic character of the Keynesian causal links. The conditional probability of an endogenous causal event in consequence of an exogenous event depends crucially on the conditional probability of the intermediate events. The transmission mechanism thus has important consequences for the final result.

(c)   The IS-LM model completely ignores the structural instability of the economic system. Hence it is not suitable for evaluating the effects of alternative economic policies. It is true that structural instability could be represented in a way by discontinuous shifts of the two curves following economic policy interventions. But having lost sight of the structure of sequential causality which underlies Keynes's flexprice heuristic model, it is impossible to evaluate the effects of the actions and structural feedbacks set off by variations in economic policy rules. In any case the plausibility and the basic determinants of structural instability would remain irremediably without foundation, because uncertainty is completely ignored by the model.

To sum up, the IS-LM model offers a profoundly distorted representation of Keynes's *general* theory, because its genesis and its use are not controlled within his heuristic model. It is however a fairly faithful analytic representation of some aspects of the *fixprice* heuristic model (although here too the criticisms under (b) and (c) above apply to some extent). As with any such analytical model, to use it correctly one must never lose sight of the more general conceptual picture.

The above critical observations do not imply that the IS-LM model should be discarded. In view of the advantages listed previously, it may well be useful for teaching or as a preliminary step in analysis. But one should always be aware of its considerable distance, not only from reality, but also from Keynes's general heuristic model itself. The basic qualifications involved in that model remain to be considered at a later stage.

Money and production in Schumpeter and Keynes: two dichotomies

The use of money is enough in itself to make a free market system potentially unstable . . . the higher the degree of development, or sophistication, that it exhibits the greater does the danger of instability become. (Hicks, 1982, p. 9)

12.1   Introduction

There is one crucial aspect of Keynes's heuristic model which has so far remained implicit. One major objective of the *General Theory* is to resolve the classical dichotomy between money and production by showing that 'money enters into the economic scheme in an essential and peculiar manner' (GT, p. xxii). As early as 1932 Keynes made it clear that what was really needed in economics was a 'monetary theory of production'.[1] The ultimate reason for systemic market failures in a developed capitalist economy is seen precisely in the influence of money on production. According to Keynes orthodox economists are unable to explain market failures and persistent unemployment because they do not have a method capable of coping with the monetary aspects of modern economies. They have always maintained that production is not affected by money[2] in an essential way, at least in the long period. Money is considered simply as a technical device for facilitating real exchanges. Production is believed to be merely 'veiled' or, at best, 'lubricated' by money.

In order to clarify Keynes's position on this issue I think it is illuminating

---

[1]   In the autumn of 1932 Keynes changed the title of his course of lectures from 'The Pure Theory of Money' (their title since the autumn of 1929) to 'The Monetary Theory of Production'. The essay with the same title, drafted in 1933, shows a clear progress in this direction.

[2]   We will assign to the word 'money', throughout this chapter, the broad meaning of the financial relations of a certain economy, considered not only in their quantitative aspects but also in their qualitative aspects. Quantity and quality of credit relations are thus included in the definition.

to compare and contrast it with the position of Schumpeter, another distinguished critic of this aspect of orthodox economics. Both Schumpeter and Keynes reacted against the received view, claiming that money does affect production in an essential way. At first sight their approaches to the problem appear completely foreign to each other. (Schumpeter's harsh criticisms of the *General Theory* are too well known to be recalled here.)[3] However, a deeper analysis shows that notwithstanding the profound differences between the two approaches, there are also a few illuminating similarities. All in all they may be seen as basically complementary, and should be integrated in a creative way to build up the foundations of a satisfactory theory of the impact of money on production.

In this chapter I shall examine the issue from a particular and limited point of view. Each of the two authors based his attack against monetary orthodoxy on a fundamental dichotomy. In Schumpeter's case the opposition was between 'circular flow' and 'development', whereas Keynes focussed on the opposition between 'cooperative economy' and 'entrepreneur economy'. In both cases the first term is meant to define the empirical scope of the received view. The validity of 'monetary orthodoxy' is not altogether denied, but it is restricted to the concept of 'circular flow' or 'cooperative economy'. To deal with the second term, however, both Schumpeter and Keynes feel the need to suggest radical theoretical innovations. One might say that both the *Theory of Economic Development* (Schumpeter, 1911) and the *General Theory* were written for just that purpose. Here, however, we are not going to compare the results of these formidable innovative analyses; we shall consider only a few aspects of the two basic dichotomies.

In section 12.2 I will briefly set out the Schumpeterian dichotomy, while in section 12.3 I will summarize the main features of the Keynesian one. The two dichotomies are then compared and appraised in section 12.4. After the conclusions (section 12.5), I will try in appendix 12A to clarify the foundations of the perspective on money emerging from this chapter.

12.2 Schumpeter: circular flow versus development

Schumpeter's view of the impact of money on production cannot be understood without reference to the crucial dichotomy between circular

---

[3] See e.g. Schumpeter, 1936, 1952, 1954. I shall briefly discuss some of these criticisms in section 12.5. However, in his posthumous article on Mitchell (1952) Schumpeter seems to praise Keynes as the leading contemporary representative of the view, shared by himself, according to which 'the capitalist economy is a profit economy in which economic activity depends upon the factors which affect present or prospective pecuniary profits' (1952, p. 253).

flow (or 'static state') and development. As is well known, circular flow encompasses all the cases in which adaptive forces prevail in the economy so that the Walrasian equilibrium method may be satisfactorily applied. According to Schumpeter this is apparently the general case in a capitalist system. There is just one exception, which however is so crucial as to require a profound modification of the analysis.

The exception is the process of technological change which is considered the 'prime mover' of capitalist development (Schumpeter, 1939, p. 106). In fact, the 'disturbances of equilibrium arising from innovations cannot be currently and smoothly absorbed' (*ibid.*, p. 101). This is why the equilibrium method cannot be applied to the study of the process of development: 'evolution is a disturbance of existing structures and more like a series of explosions than a gentle, though incessant transformation' (*ibid.*, p. 102). The distinction between circular flow and development is fundamental for our purposes, because money really affects production only in the process of development. As a matter of fact, 'money has, in the circular flow, no other role than that of facilitating the circulation of commodities' (Schumpeter, 1911, p. 53). In contrast, in the process of development, money and credit 'perform an essential function'. The main reason is the following: credit creation makes possible a rapid redistribution of resources in favour of innovators, 'enabling the entrepreneur to withdraw the producers' goods which he needs from their previous employments, by exercising a demand for them, and thereby to force the economic system into new channels' (*ibid.*, p. 106).

A thorough understanding of the Schumpeterian view of the impact of money on production thus requires a deeper analysis of the dichotomy between circular flow and development.

Development may be defined as a succession of discontinuous structural changes in the channels of the circular flow due to endogenous mutations of internal factors.[4] Each qualification in the definition is necessary for the equilibrium approach to be seriously jeopardized. In the absence of even

---

[4] The following passage contains one of the clearest definitions of the Schumpeterian concept of 'development':

> By development . . . we shall understand only such changes in economic life as are not forced upon it from without but arise by its own initiative, from within. Should it turn out that there are no such changes arising in the economic sphere itself, and that the phenomenon that we call economic development is in practice simply founded upon the fact that the data change and that the economy continuously adapts itself to them, then we should say that there is no economic development. By this we should mean that economic development is not a phenomenon to be explained economically, but that the economy, in itself without development, is dragged along by the changes in the surrounding world, that the causes and hence the explanation of the development must be sought outside the group of facts which are described by economic theory. (Schumpeter, 1911, p. 63)

only one of them, we fall back into the set of phenomena ruled by the adaptive forces of the circular flow and analysable through the 'static' method of general equilibrium. Of course this would also imply the irrelevance of money and credit. Therefore we have to clarify the above definition of development and make it as precise as possible.

First of all we must clarify exactly what Schumpeter means by 'change in the channels of the circular flows'. The 'channels of trade' may be visualized as the flows of a block diagram which represents the economic system.[5] This analytically precise picture of the circular flow is inspired by a hydraulic analogy similar to the one Schumpeter uses in his analysis of circular flow. The change in the channels of trade can thus be understood as a change in the structure of the flows (the connective matrix, i.e. the network of oriented connections between the variables of the system) and/ or as a change in content of one or more blocks.[6] This implies a change in the equilibrium values of the system.[7] However, not every change in the equilibrium induced by a change in the functional structure implies 'development' in the Schumpeterian sense. This change must be triggered by internal factors, i.e. the parameters of a Walrasian general equilibrium: tastes, technology and production factors.[8] Schumpeter believes that change in tastes and in quantity, quality and distribution of productive factors is continuous and may be absorbed by adaptive forces. In contrast, technological change is considered discontinuous,[9] and this makes it the crucial feature of development.

Technological innovation is understood by Schumpeter as a spontaneous and internal disturbance which produces a 'creative' (i.e. 'non-

[5] See appendix 2A.
[6] If attention is restricted to the linear case (as is usual with block diagrams), a change in the channels of trade may be defined as a change in the functional structure of the system. (For the concept of 'functional structure' and related concepts, see appendix 4A.)
[7] Schumpeter is perfectly aware of this as he writes that development is a 'spontaneous and discontinuous change in the channels of the flow, disturbance of equilibrium, which forever alters and displaces the equilibrium state previously existing' (1911, p. 64).
[8] See for example the following passage (Schumpeter, 1939, p. 73):
> Factors of change internal to the economic system are changes in tastes, changes in quantity (or quality) of factors of production, changes in methods of supplying commodities. One of the services that our equilibrium system renders consists precisely in assuring us that this classification of internal factors is logically exhaustive, for everything else in the system is deducible from tastes, quantity and distribution of productive resources, and productive functions.

It is interesting to observe on this point the analogy with Lucas's point of view (see chapter 8). From a Schumpeterian point of view Lucas's theory would be considered as fairly adequate for circular flow, but unable to cope with development.
[9] Technological change is conceived as a discontinuous change in the system that so 'displaces its equilibrium point that the new one cannot be reached from the old one by infinitesimal steps. Add successively as many mail coaches as you please, you will never get a railway thereby' (1939, p. 164, n.1).

adaptive') response which will 'discontinuously and forever' displace the equilibrium configuration. In other words development, unlike circular flow, requires that both the disturbance and the reaction of the system be 'internal'. This implies that the structural change that characterizes development cannot be fully exogenous.

The concept of development is thus accurately delimited by Schumpeter. Its meaning does not coincide with the common-sense one, since its scope is much more restricted. By contrast, the complementary term – circular flow (or 'static state') – has a much wider range of applicability than the words suggest. Circular flow encompasses not only the stationary state but also steady growth,[10] since in steady growth structural change is absent and the dynamic behaviour of the system is continuous and exogenous. But even unsteady growth does not necessarily imply development in Schumpeter's sense, unless structural change is endogenous and discontinuous.[11]

According to Schumpeter, money affects production only in the context of the development process, and only in the restricted sense of 'credit creation' for financing innovations. In circular flow, not only the role of money but also 'the role of credit would be a technical and subordinate one in the sense that everything fundamental about the economic process could be explained in terms of goods' (Schumpeter, 1928, p. 381). In that case production could and would be financed substantially by current gross revenue, and only small discrepancies would need to be ironed out. By contrast, development would be inconceivable without credit creation: 'as innovation, being discontinuous and involving considerable change and being, in competitive capitalism, typically embodied in new firms, requires large expenditure previous to the emergence of any revenue, credit becomes an essential element of the process' (*ibid.*, p. 380).

Summing up, it could be said that according to Schumpeter Walrasian equilibrium economics works perfectly well whenever the dynamic behaviour of the economic system can be considered to be controlled by a stable

[10] This is stressed by Schumpeter himself (1939, pp. 371–2):

> We can also allow, without leaving the precincts of statics, change variations, provided reaction to them is merely adaptive, in the sense of an adaptation capable of being brought about by infinitesimal steps. And we can, finally, deal with the phenomenon of mere growth of population or capital and, consequent thereupon, of the National Dividend. For these changes occur continuously, and adaptation to them is essentially continuous. They may condition discontinuous changes; but they do not, directly and by their mere presence, bring them about. What they do bring about automatically are only variations at the margins . . . From this it follows that mere growth is not in itself a source of instability of either the System or the Order of Capitalism.

[11] A case in point would be Pasinetti's model of unsteady growth (1981) in which structural change is considered as continuous and exogenous.

equilibrium.[12] This is generally true, in Schumpeter's opinion, because the economic system has been found to be stable, and its stability to be amenable to rational proof, under static conditions (1928, p. 364). And even under non-static conditions 'there is rather more stability than we should expect' (*ibid.*, p. 372). As a matter of fact Schumpeter, for the sake of 'localizing' the causes of instability which cannot be disregarded, takes some pains to prove that economic life is dominated by a stable equilibrium even when 'conditions are not entirely constant'. (This is the case with exogenous and/or external dynamic impulses as well as with growth of population, capital and 'National Dividend'.)

At the end of this analysis Schumpeter concludes that there is only one fundamental cause of instability inherent in the capitalist system: the process of innovation (*ibid.*, p. 385). It is this process which 'by its mere working and from within . . . destroys any equilibrium that may have established itself or been in the process of being established' (*ibid.*, p. 383). The instability induced by technical change is not just the ordinary kind of dynamic instability, because the pre-existing equilibrium is not only destabilized but altogether destroyed. The economic system is thus characterized by structural instability[13] in the sense that a disturbance (innovation), which at first might appear relatively small, is enough to produce a discontinuous structural change.

Structural instability is induced by the process of credit creation, which gives the system a certain degree of technological flexibility – i.e. that particular kind of structural instability which allows a rapid pace of technical change. This effect of credit on production is *physiological*, in the sense that it ensures the survival and evolution of the capitalistic economic system. Schumpeter recognized that the structural instability implied by sophisticated financial relations may also create 'possibilities', although not more than possibilities, of recurrent catastrophes and crises (*ibid.*, p. 384); but he never considered them serious enough to deserve a detailed treatment in the theoretical part of his works. These pathological effects, by contrast, lie at the centre of the contributions of Keynes.

12.3 Keynes: cooperative economy versus entrepreneur economy

Keynes founded his criticism of monetary orthodoxy on a dichotomy which is analogous, though not identical, with that of Schumpeter. In the preparatory drafts of the *General Theory* he expressed this dichotomy as an

---

[12] Schumpeter believes that a dynamically unstable equilibrium is useless for economic analysis (see e.g. the epigraph to chapter 10).

[13] On the distinction between structural and dynamic instability see above, chapters 3 and 4.

opposition between a cooperative economy (or real-wage economy)[14] and an entrepreneur economy (or money-wage economy). He then changed the terminology, but not the underlying theoretical foundation, in the published text of the *General Theory* where he preferred to speak of an opposition between a barter economy and a monetary economy. In this chapter, I will adopt the first terminology, because the second might be misleading. As a matter of fact this opposition has nothing to do with the mere presence or absence of money. As Keynes himself stressed in the preparatory drafts of the *General Theory*, a 'barter' economy 'does not exclude the use of money for purpose of transitory convenience' (CW, vol. 29, p. 67); therefore it is 'better to call it a *real-wage economy*, or a *cooperative economy* as distinct from an *entrepreneur economy*' (*ibid.*). A barter economy may well be characterized by monetary exchanges, but, as in the case of the Schumpeterian circular flow, it is not affected by money[15] in its fundamental behavioural rules.

A cooperative economy is defined as an economy in which the productive and distributive decisions are taken jointly by all the producers in such a way as to maximize production and consumption for the community as a whole (see Keynes, CW, vol. 29, pp. 66 and 77).

An entrepreneur economy is defined as an economy in which the fundamental productive and distributive decisions are taken by the entrepreneurs in order to maximize their own profits: 'an entrepreneur is interested not in the amount of product, but in the amount of money which will fall to his share. He will increase his output if by so doing he expects to increase his money profit, even though this profit represents a smaller quantity of product than before' (CW, vol. 29, p. 82). This implies that in an entrepreneur economy Say's Law does not necessarily hold, since the level of effective demand which maximizes the profits of entrepreneurs may be insufficient to mobilize all the existing productive resources. Therefore in an entrepreneur economy effective demand is crucial and unemployment may

---

[14] In his contribution to the *Festschrift* for Professor Spiethoff (1933) Keynes calls a cooperative economy by the different name of 'real exchange economy' (see Keynes, CW, vol. 12, p. 408).

[15] We should remember here the special meaning which Keynes attached to the word 'money':

> Money is *par excellence* the means of remuneration in an entrepreneur economy which lends itself to fluctuations in effective demand. But if employers were to remunerate their workers in terms of plots of land or obsolete postage stamps, the same difficulties could arise. Perhaps anything in terms of which the factors of production contract to be remunerated, which is not and cannot be a part of current output and is capable of being used otherwise than to purchase current output, is, in a sense, money. If so, but not otherwise, the use of money is a necessary condition for fluctuations in effective demand. (Keynes, CW, vol. 29, p. 86).

The same concepts are developed in chapter 17 of the *General Theory*.

be chronic. That is why, in Keynes's opinion, the theory of 'classical' economists, which is based on Say's Law, works perfectly well for a cooperative economy but fails in an entrepreneur economy. (Analogously, according to Schumpeter, equilibrium theory is appropriate for circular flow but not for the development process.)

In both kinds of economies there may be money, but only in an entrepreneur economy does it affect production in an essential way. In a cooperative economy, money only plays the role of an exchange device. This does not interfere with the dominance of adaptive forces which can assure the maintenance of a full-employment equilibrium. In an entrepreneur economy, there can be many virtual equilibria, which are, all but one, characterized by different degrees of involuntary unemployment. Each of these equilibria may be considered as dynamically stable, at least reasonably so, but there may arise sudden, discontinuous jumps from one equilibrium configuration to another, due to changes in the conventional expectations of entrepreneurs and/or *rentiers*. In other words, in a k-uncertain milieu (see section 4.2 above) such as that produced by sophisticated financial relations, we have a multiplicity of equilibria which are dynamically stable but structurally unstable. A small disturbance may be enough to provoke a big jump from one equilibrium to another with qualitatively different characteristics. The structural instability analysed by Keynes is 'pathological' in that it weakens and distorts the adaptive forces of the economic system. Since it depends on developed financial relations it may thus be called, more specifically, *financial fragility*.[16]

At this stage of the analysis we should add that the Keynesian dichotomy is slightly complicated by the addition of a third paradigm which he calls a 'neutral economy'. A neutral economy is an entrepreneur economy made to behave in the same manner as a cooperative economy.[17] In other words, in a neutral economy the second classical postulate and Say's Law are satisfied exactly as in a cooperative economy. In this case classical economics applies without problems of any kind. According to Keynes classical theory, as exemplified in the tradition from Ricardo to Marshall and Pigou, has always assumed 'that the conditions for a Neutral Economy

---

[16] This terminology was introduced by Minsky, 1975 and 1982. The somewhat different definition here adopted has been introduced in Vercelli, 1984a; for more details see appendix 12A.

[17] Keynes believes that this is, at least in principle, possible through opportune interventions of economic policy. The main purpose of the *General Theory* can be seen precisely as an attempt to give a foundation to this sort of policy. In the passages of the preparatory drafts where the distinction is introduced, particular emphasis is put on income policy conceived as 'a mechanism of some kind to ensure that the exchange value of the money incomes of the factors is always equal in the aggregate to the proportion of current output which would have been the factor's share in a cooperative economy' (Keynes, CW, vol. 29, p. 78).

are substantially fulfilled in general' (*ibid.*, p. 79). Keynes believes, by contrast, that

the conditions for a Neutral Economy are not satisfied in practice; with the result that there is a difference of the most fundamental importance between a cooperative economy and the type of entrepreneur economy in which we actually live. For in an entrepreneur economy, as we shall see, the volume of employment, the marginal disutility of which is equal to the utility of its marginal product, may be 'unprofitable' in terms of money. (*ibid.*, p. 79)

The dichotomy between a cooperative economy and an entrepreneur economy, together with the accessory concept of neutral economy, plays a crucial role in the mature thought of Keynes: it clarifies his reasons for opposition to classical theory and thus lays the foundations for his trailblazing contributions.

12.4   A comparison between the two dichotomies

To begin with we may observe a couple of interesting analogies between the two dichotomies put forward by Schumpeter and Keynes.

In both cases the first, 'classical' term (circular flow and cooperative economy) is characterized by a prevalence of the adaptive forces controlled by a (possibly shifting) stable equilibrium. Money does not essentially affect production because it does not affect the equilibrium but only the adjustment path.

The second term refers to the innovative part of Schumpeter's and Keynes's contributions, and these are as different as the theories themselves. However, there is a formal analogy between Schumpeterian technological flexibility and Keynesian financial fragility. In both cases sophisticated financial relations induce a disposition to discontinuous and irreversible structural change triggered by 'internal' disturbances. This property may be interpreted as a case of structural instability (see chapter 4 above).

Of course these analogies should not obscure the profound differences between the two dichotomies and the two underlying theoretical points of view. According to Schumpeter the aggregative character and the short-period perspective of the *General Theory* prevent a thorough understanding of the crucial features of capitalist development[18] related to discontinuous

---

[18] According to Schumpeter, Keynes is led by the short-period assumptions to 'abstract from the essence of the capitalistic process' (Schumpeter, 1954, p. 1447). Analogously, the aggregative approach 'keeps analysis on the surface of things and prevents it from penetrating into the industrial processes below, which are what really matters. It invites a mechanistic and formalistic treatment of a few isolated contour lines and attributes to aggregates a life of their own and a causal significance that they do not possess' (Schumpeter, 1939, p. 44).

structural changes in technology. More specifically, the short-term assumption rules out any serious analysis of technological change, while aggregation obscures any change in the structure of production and masks the redistributive role of credit creation in favour of innovators.

These criticisms hit the mark, but they do not rule out the possibility of integrating the two approaches in a broader common framework. Indeed such an attempt at synthesis is urgently needed if we want to overcome the limitations of both theories. Keynes himself appears to be aware of the severe limitations in the scope of his own analysis implied by the aggregative and short-term assumptions. He always stressed the role of money in redistributing wealth among different social classes and different productive sectors. This is altogether clear in the early works up to the *Treatise*,[19] and in the *General Theory*, despite its prevailing aggregative character, he does not appear to have changed his mind: the redistributive and allocative effects of monetary changes are recalled in many crucial passages of the analysis.[20]

Similarly, notwithstanding his witticism 'in the long run we are all dead', Keynes did not completely overlook the importance of long-period phenomena, particularly capital accumulation. In the *Treatise* he explicitly approved the Schumpeterian vision of accumulation and of technical change.[21] And after all, even in the *General Theory*, at the centre of the analysis we find the process of investment whose changes necessarily affect both the quantitative and qualitative aspects of accumulation and development.

To sum up, the short-period and the aggregative assumptions aim to simplify the essential features of the Keynesian message. The best way to make sense of these simplifying assumptions is the following: if we can find an essential role for money under strict conditions, *a fortiori* we will be in a good position to find an even broader and deeper role for money if these conditions are relaxed. Keynes basically succeeded in this task, discovering two fundamental consequences of money in an entrepreneur economy, which had been previously neglected or played down (even by authors such as Schumpeter):

[19] The following statement is particularly relevant: 'The fact that monetary changes do not affect all prices in the same way, to the same degree, or at the same time, is what makes them significant. It is the divergence between the movements of different price-levels which are at once the test and the measure of the social disturbances which are occurring' (Keynes, 1930, p. 94).
[20] Suffice it to recall here that the portfolio approach to the role of money in the accumulation process worked out in chapter 17 of the *General Theory* is intrinsically disaggregated.
[21] 'In the case of Fixed Capital . . . Professor Schumpeter's explanation of the major movements may be unreservedly accepted' (Keynes, 1930, pp. 95–6).

(a)   the 'adaptive forces' of the economy do not assure convergence towards the 'optimal' full-employment equilibrium, but only, generally speaking, towards an unemployment equilibrium;

(b)   the uncertainty induced by sophisticated financial relations is not only an effect of the 'fits and starts' of development, but a real determinant factor in economic behaviour.

Neither Schumpeter himself nor the orthodox economists saw the decisive importance of these two crucial characteristics of a monetary economy. It is their influence that bars a satisfactory application of 'classical' or equilibrium economics even in the short run and from an aggregate point of view. In this case adaptive forces may be at work but only in a pathological way (assuring convergence towards an equilibrium which in general is characterized by unemployment). Moreover, the high degree of uncertainty implies a considerable degree of financial fragility. Schumpeter, by contrast, assumes full employment of productive factors, at least in his pure theory of development. He believes that high unemployment is either exogenous or induced by the process of development itself, in which case it is only a temporary phenomenon.[22] Likewise, a significant degree of uncertainty is seen as an effect of the primary wave of cyclical development, although it may strongly influence the secondary wave,[23] so that in the pure theory of the primary wave perfect foresight is assumed.[24]

To summarize the principal results of the comparison, it should be emphasized that Schumpeter was able to point to one very strong case ('development') in which adaptive forces do not rule in the economic process, while maintaining that in all other cases adaptive forces do rule and money is not important. Keynes was able to show that in an entrepreneur economy adaptive forces may not predominate even in the short run and

[22] 'Great unemployment is only the consequence of non-economic events, as for example the World War, or precisely of the development which we are investigating. In neither of the two cases can its existence play a fundamental role in the explanation' (Schumpeter, 1911, p. 67).

[23] 'The cyclical clusters of errors, excesses of optimism and pessimism and the like are, as we have seen, not necessarily inherent in the primary process (which process would produce ups and downs and, be it particularly remembered, also losses without errors) although they can be adequately motivated by it . . . part of the phenomena of the secondary wave consists, in fact, of nothing else' (Schumpeter, 1939, p. 146).

[24]   Anxious as we are just now to work out only the pure logic of our subject, and to avoid anything of a consequential or incidental character, however important it may be in practice, we will even retain, for the moment, the heroic assumption that not only the full increase in the new product, which will be brought about by more and more firms taking up production, and the incident fall in its price have been perfectly correctly foreseen by the first in the field, but also that those who came later also foresaw correctly what possibilities were left to them. (Schumpeter, 1939, p. 135)

disregarding technological change, if we relax the assumptions of full employment and perfect foresight. In both cases the basic reason is found in the existence of sophisticated financial relations.

12.5 Conclusions

Keynes and Schumpeter analysed the impact of money on production through two fundamental dichotomies which are at the same time institutional and methodological: the dichotomy between circular flow and development and that between the cooperative economy and the entrepreneur economy. A cursory examination of the differences and analogies between the two dichotomies suggests that the two approaches are complementary in their essential meaning, though not in language and in detail. In both cases the basic role of money is seen as that of giving the economic system a certain degree of structural instability which facilitates discontinuous structural changes. Those examined by Schumpeter are mainly physiological in the sense that they make possible the survival and development of the capitalist system; those examined by Keynes are mainly pathological in the sense that they obstruct the performance of an individualistic economic order.

Still we can detect a common logical and historical root. The first effect of the introduction of money in the exchange process is to separate purchase and sale, temporally and spatially. This implies a certain degree of structural flexibility which overcomes the strict limitations imposed first by the double coincidence of wants, and then by limited markets and rigid configurations of relative prices, distributive shares and productive coefficients (see appendix 12A).

These considerations may offer an interpretative key for understanding the development of financial relations from commodity money to sophisticated credit instruments. We could advance the hypothesis that financial innovations have been introduced whenever the need to increase the structural flexibility of the economic system has been felt.[25] Unfortunately, the development of financial relations seems to have progressively increased not only physiological instability but also pathological instability, giving rise to financial fragility, inflation, unemployment and crises.

Neither Keynes nor Schumpeter gave full weight to this basic ambiguity

[25] This idea is adumbrated by Schumpeter: 'nothing, therefore, is so likely to give a wrong impression of the operation of credit as taking a mechanistic and static view of it and neglecting the fact that our process, by virtue of its own working, widens the limits which, *ex visu* of a given point of time, seem to be rigid fetters' (Schumpeter, 1939, p. 122).

of financial relations and their development. Schumpeter focussed his attention on the fundamental physiological aspects of structural instability (technological flexibility), while Keynes focussed his attention mainly on a few basic pathological aspects (financial fragility). By merging the two points of view we could work out a more balanced and articulated view of the role of money in production.

A promising line of research would be a suitable application of the method of 'shifting equilibrium' (adumbrated in the *General Theory*)[26] to long-run evolutionary problems. Each stage of the sequence should be interpreted as a long-period equilibrium, not in the temporal sense but in the logical sense of taking full account in the model of the effects of investment on the quantity and quality of the capital stock. This would permit a proper analysis to be made of structural change in technology and/ or in other features of the economy. In the context of this sequential method, however, long-period equilibria should be considered as transitory states.[27] As we know, Keynes did not have much to say about technical progress and long-run structural change, but his theory may be extended in this respect without necessarily conflicting with his heuristic model, once it is freed from the strait-jacket of the short period.[28] The main task, phrased in Keynes's own terms, would thus be to develop a theory aiming to explain the evolution of the aggregate supply curve as a consequence of the introduction and diffusion of technical progress, and of other changes in the parameters describing the economic structure (e.g. tastes) and the environment (not only policy rules but also institutional structure and the ecological milieu).

---

[26] Keynes distinguishes there between the theory of stationary equilibrium and the theory of shifting equilibrium 'meaning by the latter the theory of a system in which changing views about the future are capable of influencing the present situation' (GT, p. 293). The first point of view is that typical of classical economics, as we know from Lucas (see above, chapters 8 and 9). Keynes makes a further distinction within this category between an economy which is unchanging (stationary state), and one subject to change, but where all things are foreseen from the beginning (as in steady-state-growth theory) – or, it should be added, today, where expectations are 'rational'. For the method of shifting equilibrium in Keynes see also Kregel, 1976.

[27] This point of view is thus quite different from that of Kalecki and a few Keynesian writers who suggested that the long period should be considered as nothing but a sequence of short periods. It is however very close to the spirit, if not to the letter, of Keynes's heuristic model in which, as we have seen, equilibria are never considered as permanent or natural positions.

[28] The attempt by a few authors to extend Keynes's theory to the long period, by using a growth theory of Keynesian inspiration, can only be considered as a very preliminary step towards a satisfactory long-period theory, owing to the implicit assumption of structural invariance.

Appendix 12A **Money and structural flexibility**

This appendix aims to clarify the foundations of the propositions put forward in this chapter. The concept of structural flexibility introduced in appendix 5A is summarized and to some extent developed as a fundamental property of money.

As has been shown in chapter 5, structural flexibility may be seen as a particular aspect of structural instability (introduced and discussed in chapter 4 in its most abstract and general sense). Intuitively a system can be defined as 'structurally unstable' whenever its structure is liable to change in qualitative terms as a consequence of a change in the environment. This definition is also suitable, at an abstract level, for the concept of structural flexibility.

Here, in order to avoid confusion, we shall use the term 'structural flexibility' whenever structural instability is considered as a physiological property of the system, and 'structural rigidity' whenever structural stability is considered as a pathological property of the system. By contrast, where structural instability is considered as a pathological property the term 'structural fragility' will be employed, and whenever (structural) stability is considered as a physiological property the term (structural) 'solidity' will be used.

This terminological convention, synoptically set out in table 4, is quite close to current practice. For example, in the financial field, structural instability is seen as a pathological property and is called (financial) *fragility*, while structural stability is seen as a physiological property and thus is called (financial) *solidity*. In the productive and technological field, on the other hand, structural instability in the sense of 'propensity to structural change' is seen as a physiological property whenever it allows a prompt adaptation to unexpected circumstances and a smooth introduction of technical change. A high degree of 'propensity to structural change' may thus be called productive or technological *flexibility*, while a low degree of this property would be called productive or technological *rigidity*.

The distinction between physiological and pathological aspects implies an evaluation by a subject. Hence a correct use of the concepts classified in table 4 requires a specification of the subject making the evaluation and of its objective function. We should be aware that different subjects may give different evaluations. For example, what is seen as an increase in labour flexibility by the employer may be perceived as an increase in job rigidity by the employee. The same factors which extend the set of options for the employer may reduce the set of options for the employee. This is important for understanding many conflictual economic processes in industrial societies, and also for analysing the tricky nexus between the micro and macro dimensions of these concepts.

Variations in the micro dimensions of structural flexibility (or fragility) have ambiguous repercussions on the macro magnitudes. This is not only because of the usual problems of aggregation or the impossibility of providing a cardinal measure of these dimensions. There is an even more basic and difficult problem: a variation in

214

Table 4. *Varieties of structural stability and instability*

	Structural instability	Structural stability
Physiological	flexibility	solidity
Pathological	fragility	rigidity

the degree of structural flexibility (fragility) of an agent may have sizeable repercussions on the degree of structural flexibility of other agents.

In certain circumstances there is a sort of redistribution of a given set of options among different subjects. A case in point might be labour flexibility, where the basic issue is whether a few basic options regarding the use of the labour force should remain in the option sets of labour or should be transferred into those of employers. In this case we may speak of zero-sum flexibility by analogy with the well known terminology of game theory, although in this case it might be impossible to calculate a 'sum'. Likewise we may speak of positive-sum and negative-sum structural flexibility (fragility) when the overall effect on the macro set of options is positive or negative. For example, in principle an increase in financial fragility of a unit increases the overall macro financial fragility because of spill-over effects on other units. Thus we can say that financial fragility is a case of positive-sum structural fragility. An increase in liquidity of households induced by a shift from bonds and stocks towards money deposits could reduce the liquidity of firms, and thus it could also reduce the overall liquidity of the economy. In this case we cannot rule out the possibility of a negative-sum exchange flexibility (liquidity).

A further difficulty arises from the likely chance that trade-offs may occur among different varieties of structural flexibility (or fragility). A case in point is a trade-off between an increase in intertemporal exchange flexibility (liquidity) which discourages productive investment, and technological flexibility which is enhanced by productive investment.

An important unifying explanation of the origin and evolution of money seems to be related to the ubiquitous need to overcome different sorts of structural rigidities. At the same time, unfortunately, this process has also increased the structural fragility of the system. This should not come as a surprise in the light of the foregoing analysis. The progressive development of financial relations has progressively developed the degree of structural instability of the economic system in both its physiological and its pathological aspects. The problem of money management has always been that of filtering out the physiological aspects from the pathological aspects.

The first instance to be considered is the role of money in enhancing the exchange flexibility of a community (initially with respect to other communities and then also inside the community itself). Money of course makes it possible to overcome the rigidity of the 'double coincidence of wants', thereby extending the set of exchange opportunities. When monetary economies become sophisticated enough to offer a wide variety of substitutes for money, though with different degrees of exchange flexibility, this property may be called liquidity.

A second crucial role that money has played since the very beginning of its history is that of overcoming the rigidity of a given distribution of income and wealth. Kings, emperors and, more recently, governments have exploited seigniorage rights in order to attract resources from citizens through inflation. The quantity of money is still a very important factor in regulating the functional and personal distribution of income and wealth. Money inflation is seen as a possible 'solution' to distributional conflicts (although sometimes it also causes them). In this sense money inflation has been defined as a social 'mollifier' (Bronfenbrenner and Holzman, 1963) – an expression which vividly describes its role as an instrument of structural flexibility. We may call this sort of flexibility 'distributional flexibility' induced by unexpected changes in the quantity of money.

Unexpected inflation changes not only the relative prices of productive factors but also the relative prices of goods. In this case money makes it possible to overcome the rigidities of a given allocation of resources. These rigidities may depend on downward stickiness of prices or on inertial behaviour. In these circumstances unexpected changes in the quantity of money may help to readjust the structure of relative prices and thus the allocation of resources. We may call this property 'allocative flexibility'.

A particularly important aspect of allocative flexibility refers to the reallocation of resources through credit in favour of innovating entrepreneurs. This property of money, which may be called 'technological flexibility', has been particularly stressed by Schumpeter (for a more detailed analysis of this point see Vercelli, 1988). Through innovation, technological flexibility extends the set of economically viable technologies (though the repertoire of actually viable technologies may even shrink as many existing technologies become obsolete with the introduction of new ones).

This list of aspects of structural flexibilities influenced by financial relations is not an exhaustive one but it should be enough to support the claim that a major role of money is to enhance the structural flexibility of the economy. The entire evolution of money, credit and financial relations may be seen as a progressive injection of structural flexibility into the economic system. Even the worn-out traditional image of money as oil facilitating a smooth functioning of the economic mechanism may be seen in the same light.

The trouble is that this progressive increase in the physiological aspects of structural instability also adds to the danger of an increase in its possible pathological consequences, i.e. (financial) fragility. This is only a virtual increase in financial fragility, which may be 'repressed' through suitable money and credit management so as to filter out the physiological aspects from the pathological aspects.

Keynes always stressed the crucial nexus between money and structural flexibility. In the works which preceded the *General Theory* he stressed in particular the role of money in enhancing the distributional and allocative flexibilities of the economy. In the *General Theory* he concentrates his attention on liquidity, interpreted as intertemporal exchange flexibility.

The trade-off between money-induced structural flexibility and financial fragility always occupied a central place in his reflections. In the *General Theory* this is interpreted as a perverse interaction between intertemporal liquidity preference and structural instability induced by a sudden change in long-run expectations. Both are seen as a consequence of economic behaviour under k-uncertainty. Liquidity gives agents time to learn, and learning in these conditions may imply sudden switches in conventionally based long-term expectations.

Keynes believes that the market by itself is unable to 'filter out' the physiological consequences of sophisticated financial relations from the pathological consequences. This is the main reason why he maintains that the state must intervene to sustain productive investment jeopardized by an excessive liquidity preference of agents stabilizing their long-run expectations.

The evolution of financial relations increases the structural flexibility of the market, but it also increases the weight of speculative expectations (regarding the 'psychology of the market') compared to entrepreneurial expectations (regarding 'the prospective yield of assets over their whole life'): 'as the organisation of the investment market improves, the risk of the predominance of speculation does . . . increase' (GT, p. 158). Hence the progressive increase in exchange flexibility is, according to Keynes, the origin of the expectational fragility of a mature 'money economy'. There is a temptation therefore, to reduce the exchange flexibility introduced by money which is at the root of the problems: 'the introduction of a substantial government transfer tax on all transactions might prove the most serviceable reform available, with a view to mitigating the predominance of speculation over enterprise in the United States' (GT, p. 160). The only radical way to avoid structural instability in a money economy would be to deprive decision-makers of the intertemporal flexibility (liquidity) acquired through hoarding money: 'the only radical cure for the crises of confidence which afflict the economic life of the modern world would be to allow the individual no choice between consuming his income and ordering the production of the specific capital-asset which, even though it be on precarious evidence, impresses him as the most promising investment available to him' (GT, p. 161). However, these solutions, suggested in the past by a host of money cranks such as Gesell and Douglas, are eventually discarded by Keynes for two basic reasons:

(a) in a pure market economy investment would be discouraged: 'If individual purchases of investment were rendered illiquid, this might seriously impede new investment' (GT, p. 160);

(b) liquidity is a property possessed in different degrees by many assets, so that any intervention aiming to reduce the liquidity of one or a few of them would only shift the portfolios towards other assets.

Thus a remedy can come only from outside the market, through state interventions designed to undo the pathological consequences of liquidity preference. Sometimes excessive liquidity preference may be simply offset by monetary policy, but this is unlikely to work in all circumstances, precisely because of the expectational fragility induced by sophisticated financial relations. The only general remedy may be found in a bold 'socialization of investments' in order to curb the influence of speculative expectations and restore the dominance of entrepreneurial expectations. This is the main reason why Keynes expects 'to see the state, which is in a position to calculate the marginal efficiency of capital-goods on long views and on the basis of the general social advantage taking an ever greater responsibility for directly organising investment' (GT, p. 164).

Keynes's analysis of the peculiarities of a money economy is very perceptive and deserves to be reappraised and further developed. The remedy, however, is insufficiently argued, for the state cannot be considered simply as a *deus ex machina* acting in the higher interest of all citizens.

13

Keynes's heuristic model: methodological aspects

We do not know what the future will bring, except that it will be quite different from anything we could predict. (Keynes, CW, vol. 27, p. 62)

13.1 Introduction

Keynes's fundamental contribution in the *General Theory* is the exposition and application of the heuristic model of a monetary economy whose results differ from those of the classical model, both at the level of factual interpretation and at the level of economic policy. The brief digressions of a strictly analytical nature are quite unsatisfactory.[1] Other digressions, meant to give a more precise idea of the 'vision' underlying the *General Theory*, are doubtless of considerable interest.[2] But Keynes's 'vision' of capitalist dynamics is in many ways irremediably dated, not to say idiosyncratic. The fairy-tale of overcoming the scarcity of capital in one or two generations, the naive notion of 'socialization of investment', the simplistic analysis of tendencies to stagnation under capitalism, are a few examples of the limitations of his 'vision' of the capitalist system.

If the *General Theory* offered only an articulated 'vision' of the capitalist system, accompanied by a few analytical insights, it would be rightly considered as a historically important but hopelessly dated work which can no longer serve as a direct source of inspiration.[3] But between Schumpeter's two poles – *vision* of the economic system and economic *analysis* – there is an intermediate level which in the *General Theory* plays a decisive role: the construction and utilization of a general heuristic model that suggests a 'method' for dealing with economic problems. Such a heuristic model

---

[1] As is well known, in the *General Theory* there is only one graph, on page 159, showing Keynes's criticism of the classical theory of interest rates in a Cartesian diagram. This graph is borrowed from a letter written by Harrod (CW, vol. 13, p. 557).
[2] For an analysis of this aspect of Keynes's contribution, see among others Vicarelli, 1984.
[3] This is Lucas's position (1981, p. 276; it also appears in Klamer, 1984, pp. 50–1).

generates and coordinates more specific analytical models, and helps to indicate which is the right one to suit the circumstances: 'Economics is a science of thinking in terms of models joined to the art of choosing models which are relevant to the contemporary world. It is compelled to do this, because unlike the typical natural science, the material to which it is applied is, in too many respects, not homogeneous through time' (CW, vol. 14, p. 296).

What is still really alive in Keynes's work is the heuristic model, and especially its methodological and epistemological implications.

In section 13.2 I will emphasize the fundamental role of the probabilistic nature of economic argument in Keynes's heuristic model. I will then discuss which concepts of equilibrium and disequilibrium are used in it (section 13.3). The crucial property of Keynes's general heuristic model is structural instability rather than dynamic instability, as I will argue in section 13.4. This depends mainly on shifts of long-run expectations which do not necessarily contradict the rationality of economic behaviour properly understood (section 13.5). Conclusions follow in section 13.6.

13.2   The heuristic model and the probabilistic argument

Keynes's heuristic model is a general scheme of argument whose purpose is to find solutions for particular problems, both in terms of theory and in terms of economic policy:

The object of our analysis is not to provide a machine, or method of blind manipulation, which will furnish an infallible answer, but to provide ourselves with an organised and orderly method of thinking out particular problems; and, after we have reached a provisional conclusion by isolating the complicating factors one by one, we then have to go back on ourselves and allow, as well as we can, for the probable interactions of the factors amongst themselves. This is the nature of economic thinking. (GT, p. 31)

The first stage refers to the particular heuristic model constructed in the first 18 chapters of the *General Theory*, under the hypothesis of fixed wages, while the second (discussed in Book V, chapters 19–21) analyses the additional relations involved in the general heuristic model, under the hypothesis of flexible wages. The division of the economic argument into two stages is itself explained and justified elsewhere in the *General Theory* and in other works. Particularly significant in the present context is the following passage from a letter written to Harrod in 1938: 'The object of a model is to segregate the semi-permanent or relatively constant factors from those which are transitory or fluctuating so as to develop a logical way of thinking about the latter, and of understanding the time sequences which they give rise [to] in particular cases' (CW, vol. 14, p. 297).

While the probabilistic nature of the arguments in the second stage is quite explicit, the arguments in the first stage are not always expressed in probabilistic language, but that is only because Keynes wished to avoid unnecessary pedantry. In fact the difference between the first-stage and second-stage arguments is purely one of degree: the former are more reliable because the phenomena to which they refer are relatively more stable. Effects follow causes with a higher degree of probability, and above all the 'weight of the argument' is definitely more compelling. However, even the first-stage arguments must in general be understood as probabilistic.

This does not mean that the reasoning should not be formal and demonstrative wherever possible. Demonstrative argument is simply an extreme form of probabilistic argument. The aim of an argument is to persuade every rational individual that certain conclusions can be drawn from certain premises with a given degree of probability. When this degree of probability assumes extreme values (zero or one) the conclusion is considered certain and the argument can be called demonstrative. However, according to Keynes, demonstrative argumentation is possible only in certain scientific disciplines:

In most branches of academic logic, such as the theory of the syllogism or the geometry of ideal space, all the arguments aim at demonstrative certainty. They claim to be conclusive. But many other arguments are rational and claim some weight without pretending to be certain. In metaphysics, in science, and in conduct, most of the arguments, upon which we habitually base our rational beliefs, are admitted to be inconclusive in a greater or less degree . . . Thus . . . the study of probability is required. (TP, p. 3)

If demonstrative arguments play little part in the natural sciences themselves, they have even less chance in a discipline like economics which has to do with a highly variable and inhomogeneous body of material, strongly influenced by subjective and inherently unpredictable factors.

So it is not surprising that in most cases economic reasoning cannot be completely formalized. We must be content with a semi-formalized language like that used by Keynes to expound his heuristic model:

When we write economic theory, we write in a quasi-formal style; and there can be no doubt, in spite of the disadvantages, that this is our best available means of conveying our thoughts to one another. But when an economist writes in a quasi-formal style, he is composing neither a document verbally complete and exact so as to be capable of strict legal interpretation, nor a logically complete proof. (CW vol. 13, p. 469)

Moreover, even when it is possible to produce a total or partial mathematical formulation of the argument, strong precautions are necessary to avoid misleading results:

It is a great fault of symbolic pseudo-mathematical methods of formalising a system of economic analysis . . . that they expressly assume strict independence between the factors involved . . . whereas, in ordinary discourse, where we are not blindly manipulating but know all the time what we are doing and what the words mean, we can keep 'at the back of our heads' the necessary reserves and qualifications and the adjustments which we shall have to make later on . . . too large a proportion of recent 'mathematical' economics are merely concoctions, as imprecise as the initial assumptions they rest on, which allow the author to lose sight of the complexities and interdependencies of the real world, in a maze of pretentious and unhelpful symbols. (GT, pp. 297–8)

By this criticism Keynes does not mean to rule out the use of formalization, but only to dissociate himself from the formalism and operationalism which were then becoming prevalent both in epistemology (logical positivism) and in the empirical sciences, especially economic disciplines. He wants above all to emphasize the importance of continuous intuitive awareness of the meaning and the limits of the manipulations involved in any process of formalization.[4] Keynes thus anticipates the results of certain recent developments in epistemology which have turned sharply away from formalism and re-evaluated the constructivist and semantic aspects of scientific practice.[5]

The above considerations make it clear why, in Keynes's view, 'in economics you cannot convict your opponent of error; you can only convince him of it' (CW, vol. 13, p. 470). Thus the aim of economic reasoning can only be to persuade a rational interlocutor. It is no coincidence that Keynes entitled one of his books *Essays in Persuasion*. The

[4] The following passage gives a balanced judgment on these topics:
There are occasions for very exact methods of statement, such as are employed in Mr Russell's *Principia Mathematica*. But there are advantages also in writing the English of Hume. Mr Moore has developed in *Principia Ethica* an intermediate style which in his hands has force and beauty. But those writers, who strain after exaggerated precision without going the whole hog with Mr Russell, are sometimes merely pedantic. They lose the reader's attention, and the repetitious complication of their phrases eludes his comprehension, without their really attaining, to compensate, a complete precision. Confusion of thought is not always best avoided by technical and unaccustomed expressions, to which the mind has no immediate reaction of understanding; it is possible, under cover of a careful formalism, to make statements, which, if expressed in plain language, the mind would immediately repudiate. There is much to be said, therefore, in favour of understanding the substance of what you are saying all the time, and of never reducing the substantives of your argument to the mental status of an x or y. (TP, p. 20)
[5] A detailed survey can be found in Suppe, ed., 1977, and also, with particular attention to economics, in Caldwell, 1982.

art of persuasion, however, was based for Keynes on a rigorous discipline: the theory of probability which underlies any rational argument, whether it is non-demonstrative, as in most cases, or demonstrative, as in some extreme cases. In fact according to Keynes the theory of probability coincides with the broadest conception of logic. Economics, in turn, is considered by Keynes as a branch of logic in the sense outlined above.[6] Thus economics must be seen as an inherently probabilistic discipline. This is a fundamental key to understanding Keynes's economic ideas. The probabilistic nature of his economic reasoning may not be evident at first sight because the conception of probability used in the economic arguments is close to that implicit in ordinary language.[7]

In fact probability plays a part not only in most arguments conducted in ordinary language, but also in those involving scientific language. In the empirical sciences, such as economics, arguments are based on epistemic causal relations between propositions. As we have seen in more detail in chapter 7, these causal relationships must be interpreted in terms of probabilistic causal links. A proposition (an event)[8] is considered as the cause of another proposition (another event) whenever the occurrence of the first corroborates the belief that the second will occur. The causal link, therefore, is generally conceived as epistemic (*causa cognoscendi*), while the link between epistemic cause and ontological cause (*causa essendi*) is left indeterminate (see TP, p. 183). Only very rarely, according to Keynes, does the truth of the first proposition (or the occurrence of the first event) make us certain that the second will be true or will occur (necessary or sufficient cause, or 'casuality in the strict sense'): 'Those antecedent circumstances, which we are usually content to accept as causes, are only so in strictness under a favourable conjunction of innumerable other influences' (TP, p. 306). Hence for Keynes the term 'cause' in its strictest sense is useless not only in ordinary language but also in most scientific disciplines.[9] Economics in particular, as a moral discipline, is inherently probabilistic, and its arguments are based on epistemic causal links of a probabilistic nature (see chapter 7, in particular footnote 11).

Economics, then, is not based exclusively or even predominantly on any uniformity of nature. On this point Keynes's disagreement with Lucas and

---

[6] 'Economics is a branch of logic, a way of thinking' (CW, vol. 14, p. 296).

[7] This position was already clearly expressed in the preface to the typewritten version of 1908. The same position is reaffirmed in the final version of the *Treatise on Probability*, where the logic of probability is reconnected to the 'actual exercise of reason' (p. 3) and to 'the practice of ordinary argument' (p. 37).

[8] Remember that the concept of 'event' used in Suppes's version of probabilistic causality is substantially equivalent to Keynes's concept of 'proposition' (see chapter 7 above).

[9] According to Keynes the theory of probabilistic argument applies 'in metaphysics, in science, and in conduct' (TP, p. 3).

the other new classical economists could not be more radical: 'States of the universe, identical in every particular, may never recur, and, even if identical states were to recur, we should not know it' (TP, p. 276). In economics, as in all disciplines whose object is influenced by the psychology of the agents, one cannot count on any assumption of continuity and empirical uniformity: 'economics is essentially a moral science and not a natural science' (CW, vol. 14, p. 297).[10] Keynes's heuristic model serves to bring out not only empirical regularities (such as the consumption function or the link between real wages and employment), but also the main points of discontinuity (the shifts of the functions of liquidity preference and the marginal efficiency of capital).

At this point we can understand why and in what sense Keynes insists on the methodological and argumentative nature of political economy in general, and macroeconomics in particular. This position is already clearly stated in the 'Introduction' to the 1922–3 series of *Cambridge Economic Handbooks*: 'the theory of economics does not furnish a body of settled conclusions immediately applicable to policy. It is a method rather than a doctrine, an apparatus of the mind, a technique of thinking, which helps its possessors to draw correct conclusions' (CW, vol. 12, p. 856). The same idea is expressed several times later on: for example in his exchange of letters with Harrod on the nature of economic science (1938; CW, vol. 14, part II, pp. 295–301), and in his review of Tinbergen (1939). So any doctrinal or fundamentalist interpretation of Keynes clearly contradicts his theoretical and methodological position.

13.3 Equilibrium and disequilibrium

The concept of equilibrium plays a fundamental role in the *General Theory*. For Keynes the primary aim of the heuristic model is certainly to work out the equilibrium position which corresponds with maximum probability to the values of the exogenous variables (including economic policy rules and the state of long-term expectations).[11] Moreover, in several passages of the *General Theory* he makes it clear that he considers the analysis of

---

[10] This thesis is repeated in other circumstances. In any discipline involving the psychology of agents, 'we are faced at every turn with the problems of organic unity, of discreteness, of discontinuity – the whole is not equal to the sum of the parts, comparisons of quantity fail us, small changes produce large effects, the assumption of a uniform and homogeneous continuum are not satisfied' (1933b, p. 262). These pregnant observations negate many of the methodological principles that characterize classical economic thought, old and new, particularly those of regularism, structural stability, and methodological individualism.

[11] In the case of the generalized heuristic model the exogenous components of expectations must be taken as given in order to analyse their endogenous variations (see below, section 13.5).

adjustment processes leading to equilibrium to be of secondary importance. The dynamic instability of equilibrium, if not completely eliminated, is certainly relegated to the background of the analysis. Indeed Keynes, not only in the *General Theory* but also in previous works and in discussions after its publication, often argued against those writers who gave the examination of disequilibrium adjustment processes a central place in their analysis: in particular members of the Swedish school, as well as his own *Treatise on Money*.

One may wonder why there should have been this sharp change in methodological direction. The main reason is to be found in the need to give the greatest possible prominence to the heterodox concept of underemployment equilibrium. As long as deviations from classical equilibrium can be interpreted as disequilibrium positions, their importance may be doubted because of their more transitory nature relative to the equilibrium position. The solution explored by Keynes in the *Treatise on Money* is to insist on the dynamic instability of the economic system. Beyond certain limits, however, one cannot insist on the dynamic instability of the capitalist system without coming into glaring contradiction with the facts. This point is very well argued by Keynes himself in the *General Theory*: 'it is an outstanding characteristic of the economic system in which we live that, whilst it is subject to severe fluctuations in respect of output and employment, it is not violently unstable' (GT, p. 249; see also section 4 of the same chapter). Thus Keynes realizes that the phenomenon of persistent unemployment, if it is to be taken seriously, must be considered as an equilibrium phenomenon. This implies a much more radical break with classical theory, as it proves necessary to substitute a different equilibrium theory. So it is quite comprehensible that Keynes should choose to put the analysis of disequilibrium behaviour in the background in order to bring out fully his different analysis of equilibrium.[12] This need leads Keynes to introduce some simplifying assumptions of doubtful validity: for example the identity between savings and investment, the essentially static version of the multiplier, the assumption that short-term expectations are always satisfied. But he does achieve his basic aim of concentrating attention on the equilibrium positions, while avoiding distractions arising from secondary details.

In the GT, therefore, the concept of equilibrium plays a fundamental role which is profoundly different from the role it plays in classical thought. This has led to endless misunderstandings and controversies. In particular, to many economists of the 'classical' school, from Patinkin (1948, 1965) to

---

[12] The theme of the instability of capitalism does not disappear; it is reformulated in terms of structural instability (see section 13.4 below).

Lucas (1981), the concept of 'underemployment equilibrium' has seemed to be a contradiction in terms. But in reality there is no contradiction in the Keynesian concept of underemployment equilibrium. That is clear if we recognize that Keynes, unlike his classical critics, generally uses the concept in a strict dynamic sense. The economic system, as reconstructed in Keynes's heuristic model, does not involve any endogenous dynamic tendency when it settles on an underemployment equilibrium. In other words, in that situation there is no endogenous adjustment mechanism that can bring the system back towards a full-employment equilibrium. For this reason Keynes denies that the economic system is able to regulate itself, and is compelled to uphold the necessity of suitable forms of external market regulation.

Alternative meanings of equilibrium undoubtedly exist, according to which positions of 'underemployment equilibrium' would be redefined as disequilibrium positions. Two significant examples are the definitions of equilibrium proposed by Patinkin and Lucas. For Patinkin an equilibrium situation is one in which 'nothing changes in the system'. In fact, unless fixed prices are assumed, a situation of excess supply in a competitive labour market would have to be associated with a reduction in money wages, which would contradict Patinkin's definition of equilibrium. If prices were to vary in the same sense and to the same extent, as Keynes maintained, then according to Keynes's concept of equilibrium neither real wages nor employment would vary. On the other hand, if like Lucas and the new classical economists we assume a Walrasian concept of equilibrium, there is no doubt that an equilibrium position with unemployment must be redefined as a disequilibrium position.

More specifically, the concept of underemployment equilibrium leads Keynes to move away from the classical analysis of equilibrium in a few crucial points:

(a)   The existence, in general, of a plurality of equilibrium positions. A classical economist would probably not deny that in particular conditions (for example peculiar assumptions regarding the form of the supply and demand curves) there could be a plurality of equilibrium positions. But Keynes holds that this is the norm under general hypotheses regarding the form of the functions. Moreover, a classical economist would not deny that on the hypothesis of fixed prices the economy might temporarily be stuck in a position characterized by unemployment. But Keynes, as we have seen, presents his theory as general and anti-classical precisely because he is convinced that its implications for unemployment will not substantially change in the case of flexible prices.

(b)   The concept of equilibrium is disassociated from that of optimum. Keynes believes that this is the case even in the long period, since 'there is no reason to suppose that positions of long-period equilibrium have an inherent tendency or likelihood to be positions of optimum output. A long-period position of optimum output is a *special case* corresponding to a special kind of policy on the part of the monetary authority' (CW, vol. 29, p. 55). This is nothing but a corollary of the economic system's incapacity to regulate itself. The task of economic policy may thus be conceived as the choice of that rule or set of rules capable of restoring or maintaining the optimum equilibrium positions.[13]

(c)   Keynes sees equilibrium as transitory. This has nothing to do with the distinction between long and short-period equilibrium. Short-period equilibrium is certainly transitory, if only because the effects of investment on the quantity and quality of the capital stock in themselves significantly alter the parameters of the system.[14] But even long-period equilibrium, insofar as it enters Keynes's analysis, is to be understood as transitory. This is because the structure of the economic system's parameters is considered unstable. In particular, long-term expectations, based as they are on conventional factors, may suffer sudden and radical revisions.

(d)   Moreover, the variation of equilibrium at a given moment depends on the actual dynamic behaviour which has occurred previously. The structural instability of the parameters is manifested in the form of successive bifurcations whose nature depends on preceding bifurcations. Path dependence in this case is the rule rather than the exception. So it is quite impossible to adopt the classical methodology, carried to its extreme consequences by Lucas and the other new classical economists, which distinguishes between transitory and permanent equilibria in order to disregard transitory phenomena and concentrate exclusively on permanent equilibria.

[13] New classical economists do not necessarily deny the possibility of a sub-optimal equilibrium (see e.g. Sargent in Klamer, 1984, p. 68). They do however, generally deny that a non-optimal equilibrium can be important and/or permanent. In these circumstances there are in fact unexploited opportunities, which they believe cannot but be discovered and exploited by economic agents. But this assertion is not sufficiently argued to be compelling (for a convincing criticism, see Akerlof and Yellen, 1985a).

[14] This also depends on the structural interactions examined in the general heuristic model: 'The position of equilibrium will be influenced by these repercussions; and there are other repercussions also. Moreover, there is not one of the above factors which is not liable to change without much warning, and sometimes substantially. Hence the extreme complexity of the actual course of events' (GT, p. 249).

13.4   Dynamic and structural instability

Throughout his scientific career Keynes often referred to the instability of capitalism. In the *General Theory* this theme is of crucial importance, but interpreters – even those most sensitive and attentive to this aspect of Keynes's work – have always found it difficult to pin down the exact nature and implications of the concept of instability in Keynes's major work. This difficulty, I believe, arises from a basic misunderstanding about Keynes's conception of instability in his mature works. The concept has always been understood in the traditional terms of dynamic instability. While such an interpretation is acceptable with regard to Keynes's early works, up to the *Treatise on Money*, it cannot be applied to the *General Theory*. In fact in the latter work Keynes clearly expresses the view that the capitalist system is characterized by a high, though not extreme, degree of dynamic stability. Keynes maintains that there is a 'continuum' of possible equilibria with full employment at one end, and at the other a minimum level of employment below which life would be endangered (GT, p. 254). Inside this 'corridor' (Leijonhufvud, 1981) turbulences may occur, but the set of trajectories possible within it is dynamically stable (in the set-stability sense; see appendix 3A above). Keynes also dwells with unusual meticulousness on the reasons for this substantial degree of stability exhibited by the capitalist system. Among others, he mentions the following factors:

(a)   The multiplier, while greater than one, is not very large. This condition 'provides that a moderate change in the rate of investment will not involve an indefinitely great change in the demand for consumption goods' (GT, p. 252).

(b)   The growing cost of producing an increasing quantity of capital goods. This condition 'provides that a moderate change in the prospective yield of capital assets or in the rate of interest will not involve an indefinitely great change in the rate of investment' (*ibid.*).

Instability, however, plays a crucial role in the arguments of the *General Theory*, as we saw in the last chapter when reconstructing Keynes's heuristic model. Without it an economic policy of the classical type would have to be considered as a perfectly adequate remedy for a depression. In particular, if instability were unimportant, Keynes's arguments for the view that an inflationary monetary policy is insufficient, and in any case less reliable than an expansionary budget policy, would not stand up (see section 11.2.2 above). These arguments, developed especially in chapter 19 of the *General Theory*, suggest that at least here Keynes had in mind a concept of instability which today we would call *structural* (see above, chapter 4). The problems arise from variations in the functional structure of the system, brought about by economic policy interventions that modify long-period expectations and cause a shift of the two 'psychological' schedules of liquidity preference and marginal efficiency of capital.

The problem, from the logical point of view, is the same as that brought out with extreme clarity by the 'Lucas critique' of the so-called 'Keynesian' large-scale econometric models. But the criticism of ignoring the structural instability of the parameters does not apply to Keynes's heuristic model, which in fact shows full awareness of the problem. Indeed he draws from the structural instability of a competitive market in a monetary economy some crucial implications for the understanding of how a mature capitalist system works, and for the choice of suitable economic policy rules to deal with involuntary unemployment. The basic source of structural instability, for Keynes as for Lucas, lies in the way expectations react to variations in the economic environment, particularly economic policy rules. To explore this theme further, therefore, we need to analyse the role played by expectations in Keynes's *General Theory*, a vexed question to which the next section is dedicated.

Meanwhile we may observe that in his famous critique Lucas, paradoxically, rediscovers a Keynesian argument from which he draws completely opposite conclusions. For Lucas the structural instability of the parameters arises from the use of an erroneous model – that of Keynes – which he considers unable to take account of the hidden 'deep' structure which is invariable with respect to economic policy interventions. For Keynes structural instability is a property that should be attributed to capitalist reality itself. This imposes a conception of economic science opposed to the classical one: a methodology of probabilistic argumentation aiming to persuade a rational audience.

13.5   Expectations

The role of expectations in the *General Theory* has always been a source of difficulty for interpreters. While Keynes undoubtedly saw expectations as playing a crucial role, his observations (developed especially in chapter 12 of the *General Theory*) are brilliant but impressionistic, and when reduced to strictly analytical terms they seem to boil down to a pair of not very convincing assumptions:

(a)   short-period expectations are always fulfilled;
(b)   long-period expectations are exogenous and subject to discontinuous and unpredictable changes.

Put this way, these assumptions are open to objections on several grounds. The first assumption is undoubtedly meant to repudiate what

Keynes saw as the excessive importance[15] attributed to short-period expectations in various analyses, including his own *Treatise on Money* and the works of the Swedish school.[16] This point, already clearly presented in the *General Theory*, is repeated in even stronger terms in the polemics that followed its publication:

The theory of effective demand is substantially the same if we assume that short-period expectations are always fulfilled ... I now feel that if I were writing the book again I should begin by setting forth my theory on the assumption that short-period expectations were always fulfilled; and then have a subsequent chapter showing what difference it makes when short-period expectations are disappointed. (CW, vol. 14, p. 181)

This initial assumption may prove more or less convincing, but it presents no particular interpretative or methodological problems. The second assumption, however, has given rise to innumerable perplexities and controversies. Even such a careful and basically sympathetic interpreter as Hicks has made no secret of the fact that he considers the assumption unacceptable for at least two reasons:[17]

(a)   The assumption of complete exogeneity makes the influence of long-period expectations altogether arbitrary;
(b)   The emphasis on sudden and discontinuous changes in long-period expectations ultimately gives too much weight to irrationality in the behaviour of economic agents.

However, these criticisms are not entirely justified if applied to Keynes's heuristic model as we have reconstructed it in the preceding section. First of all, in the generalized version of the heuristic model, long-period expectations are not totally exogenous. Indeed endogenous variations arising from changes in economic policy rules play a central role, absolutely vital to the argument. Such causal links (structural feedbacks) are of a probabilistic

[15] Keynes did not mean to deny that short-period expectations have a certain importance. But he did mean to emphasize that they were far less important than the analysis of equilibrium positions and of long-period expectations.
[16] The following passage from a letter to Hawtrey, dated 15 April 1936 (CW, vol. 14, p. 27), is particularly revealing:
You are usually concerned with the higgling of the market, the short-time lags lasting a few weeks during which everybody is discovering what the demand really is; whereas I am concerned with the forces determining the demand ... and I am not very much interested myself in the brief intermediate period during which the higgling of the market is discovering the facts.
[17] Although Hicks later moved away in many respects from the classical positions and came closer to those of Keynes, on the specific question of expectations his criticisms of the *General Theory* became if anything progressively stronger. The observations that first appeared in his 1936 review were later developed and repeated in even more critical terms (see, for example, Hicks, 1983b, p. 351).

type, like all the causal links in Keynes's heuristic model, though in this case the probability nexus is considered particularly unreliable. But it does not fall into total indeterminacy and arbitrariness. If nothing else, different degrees of probability can be assigned to the qualitative direction of changes. If that were not true the crucial arguments developed by Keynes in chapter 19 would completely collapse.

Long-term expectations, then, are not totally exogenous, nor are their variations totally arbitrary. Still, the indications that can be traced in the *General Theory* can be developed in the spirit of Keynes only in terms of qualitative probability and probabilistic causal links. Up to now this line of investigation has been completely neglected, but in fact it is extremely important for clarifying the nature and consequences of the structural instability that characterizes the capitalist system – an instability which depends crucially on long-period expectations.

At this point, however, it should be made clear that the structural instability arising from long-period expectations does not necessarily contradict the hypothesis of rationality in the behaviour of economic agents. Paradoxically, the many recent studies on rational expectations prove useful in clarifying this point. One possible interpretation of rational expectations in its weak version is precisely in conventionalist terms not very far from those suggested by Keynes. The uniformity of average expectations of economic agents, assumed by the hypothesis of rational expectations, may be understood as a common adherence to a conventional interpretation of reality which is codified in the relevant model. In any case it is not necessarily irrational on the part of the single agent to adjust, in conditions of uncertainty, to the conventional market valuations. On rather general assumptions, such behaviour could minimize the probability of error for the single agent:

In making a decision we have before us a large number of alternatives, none of which is demonstrably more 'rational' than the others, in the sense that we can arrange in order of merit the sum aggregate of the benefits obtainable from the complete consequences of each. To avoid being in the position of Buridan's ass, we fall back, therefore, and necessarily do so, on motives of another kind, which are not 'rational' in the sense of being concerned with the evaluation of consequences, but are decided by habit, instinct, preference, desire, will, etc. (CW, vol. 29, p. 294)

The convention adopted is influenced by certain opinion-leaders who are considered especially well informed and skilled at processing information. The equilibrium between the 'conventional valuation' and the results of actions can only be temporary, as it will necessarily be modified by new information introduced by exogenous mechanisms, or by effective transformations of the environment.

The preceding observations also bring out why and in what sense conventional expectations imply the structural instability of the economic system. The 'Lucas critique', in fact, can be used in the above perspective to clarify Keynes's arguments on the structural instability of a monetary economy. Obviously there is a basic difference: Lucas sees the property of structural instability as a defect in Keynes's model, whereas for Keynes it is a property of the real system which has to be somehow incorporated in his heuristic model.

In an argument of this type rational expectations cannot be interpreted in terms of strong substantive rationality, and the method of solution must not arbitrarily exclude instability and indeterminacy. Moreover, such an interpretation conflicts with a use of the hypothesis of rational expectations within demonstrative arguments aiming to give an unequivocal and conclusive solution to the problem under discussion. But these difficulties would not bother Keynes – indeed he would draw from them further arguments in confirmation of his own methodological convictions.

All this suggests that, contrary to a widespread view, Keynes's observations on the unpredictable and discontinuous dynamics of long-term expectations do not necessarily imply irrationality on the part of agents. What he puts in doubt is not the rationality of single agents but macroeconomic rationality. This is one of Keynes's basic ideas, which runs through all his works, from the earliest to the *General Theory*. In a market economy the individual optimum may be in conflict with the collective optimum: hence the constant polemic tones against *laissez faire* which we find in all his works.

From the point of view of principle I find Keynes's arguments on the nature and dynamics of long-period expectations perfectly legitimate and essentially correct, though they have been the object of much incomprehension and misunderstanding. Undeniably Keynes's own arguments on the subject are more impressionistic than analytic. But modern developments of 'information economics' and the theory of endogenous mechanisms of expectation formation open new avenues for clarifying and developing this crucial part of Keynes's contribution on the analytical level. To do this it is necessary to give up the hypothesis of the representative agent, which at once eliminates the basic problem of coordination between the individual plans of economic agents making conventional behaviour altogether unintelligible.

13.6   Conclusions

The heuristic model suggested by Keynes in the *General Theory* is still alive. Many of its most innovative features may be appreciated better today than in the past decades, as they are in tune with recent developments in epistemology and formal languages. The probabilistic nature of its causal texture, the basic indeterminacy and structural instability attributed to a monetary economy, and the role of conventional long-run expectations in an environment characterized by k-uncertainty are among the ideas which have not yet exhausted their heuristic potential. They point out a way of understanding economic regularities at the system level which is radically different from the classical one. The hypothesis of rationality is not rejected but broadened from a purely adaptive form to a properly human conception which includes a creative effort directed to improve the conditions of economic behaviour.

Such a path of analysis will certainly lead *beyond* Keynes, but even now it offers a useful direction for research and provides a fertile source of inspiration.

14

Conclusions

Whenever a theory appears to you as the only possible one, take this as a sign that you have neither understood the theory nor the problem which it was intended to solve. (Popper, 1972, p. 266)

14.1   Introduction

Lucas maintains that macroeconomics can now rest on what he considers to be the firm ground of general equilibrium. What this actually means is a reduction of macroeconomics to Walrasian microeconomics. Macroeconomics, which was founded by Keynes as an autonomous discipline in opposition to classical reductionism, would lose not only its original anticlassical inspiration but also its own autonomy. This striking implication of new classical economics has been explicitly pointed out by Lucas himself:

The most interesting recent developments in macroeconomic theory seem to me describable as the reincorporation of aggregative problems such as inflation and the business cycle within the general framework of 'microeconomic' theory. If these developments succeed, the term 'macroeconomic' will simply disappear from use and the modifier 'micro' will become superfluous. We will simply speak, as did Smith, Ricardo, Marshall and Walras, of economic theory. (Lucas, 1987, pp. 107–8)

A theoretical statement is thus defined as 'macro' just because it refers to the economy considered as a whole and hence involves aggregate variables. In this view macroeconomic theory overlaps with Walrasian microeconomic theory; the only difference is that in this case decision-makers are conceived as 'representative agents'. As a consequence, any theoretical statement that cannot be immediately reduced to Walrasian microeconomics is rejected as hopelessly wrong or at least as non-scientific. Thus according to Lucas there is no room for macroeconomic theory conceived as an autonomous discipline.

234

According to the new classical economists, the main effect of the Keynesian revolution has been to cut the ties anchoring macro statements to the required general equilibrium discipline. In their opinion it is now time to undo the misleading consequences of the Keynesian revolution and restore the 'classical' discipline of general equilibrium. Macroeconomics should thus be freed from its Keynesian inspiration, and in particular from its unjustified presumption of scientific autonomy. Thus, in this view, in modern macroeconomics there is no need for Keynes after Lucas.

From the vantage point of the preceding arguments we are now in a position to evaluate the soundness of these theses. This appraisal is very important because their acceptance or rejection is bound to have far-reaching repercussions on research strategy and policy interventions in macroeconomics.

14.2   Macroeconomics as an autonomous discipline

Paradoxically, the main result obtained by the new classical economists is the demonstration – against their wishes and expectations – that a satisfactory *synthesis* of macroeconomics and microeconomics is not yet mature. As a matter of fact, the micro-foundations of macroeconomics which they suggest are by now far from satisfactory. They rely on the heroic assumption that the decision-makers of the models are representative agents, whose behaviour fairly well approximates the aggregate behaviour of the economy. Unfortunately this assumption surreptitiously eliminates the main object that should be studied by macroeconomics: aggregation problems and failures of coordination between the behaviour of individuals. Even so, the suggested micro-foundations work only under very special assumptions which actually deny any importance to the main problems considered by Keynes's macroeconomics: uncertainty, disequilibrium, instability, structural change, etc. As we have seen, disequilibria are assumed to be non-intelligible and are therefore ignored; uncertainty is emasculated by the 'certainty equivalence' hypothesis; instability is defined away by arbitrarily restricting the analysis to stationary and ergodic processes and taking account only of the subset of stable solutions (see chapters 5 and 6).

The failure of this reductionist research programme may be due to the immaturity of current macroeconomics, but it may also be due to weaknesses in existing microeconomic theory. Notwithstanding the widespread belief in its intrinsic solidity, the micro theory currently accepted by the new classical economists may prove on closer examination to be insufficiently powerful to provide solid foundations for a satisfactory macroeconomics. To take the preliminary steps towards a real synthesis between macro and

Conclusions

micro theories, it is necessary to consider not only the micro-foundations of macroeconomics but also the macro-foundations of microeconomics (Hicks, 1983a).

The history of scientific thought shows that whenever a synthesis between different disciplines has been successfully accomplished, the result has been a new discipline with features not reducible to those of the original disciplines.[1] Such a synthesis between micro and macroeconomics, if it is possible, is still far away. In the meantime the reciprocal autonomy of both disciplines should be carefully safeguarded. It is particularly important to defend the autonomy of macroeconomics, as today this is greatly jeopardized by views like those mentioned above. Therefore we should revert to the original Keynesian concept of macroeconomics as an autonomous discipline. This does not imply that we should give up making serious efforts to provide rigorous micro-foundations for our macroeconomic statements,[2] if that means searching for greater consistency between the two disciplines. In other words we should continue to pursue a full synthesis between microeconomics and macroeconomics. Many things have been learned from past attempts, unsuccessful as they were, and many others may be understood through further efforts.

But in the meantime one should not reject as non-scientific any contribution that lacks proper 'micro-foundations', particularly in the restricted sense of a 'reduction to current Walrasian microeconomics'. As a matter of fact, though it may be found impossible to provide proper micro-foundations to a given macroeconomic statement, this might become possible in the future. Such developments have occurred many times in the past[3] and it could happen again, especially if microeconomics extends its range well beyond its Walrasian bounds. To reject this view would be as irrational as to reject as non-scientific any biological statement not yet reducible to chemical statements. Unfortunately, as has been wisely remarked, the only known way to reduce biology to chemistry is murder.

[1] This has been clearly emphasized by the great epistemologist Jean Piaget (1967, p. 1249):
Any reduction brings about a reciprocal assimilation ... the features of the superior system are not eliminated but appear as the product of a composition rule whose discovery will eventually attribute to the inferior system new features still unknown. For instance, any progress in biochemistry develops organic chemistry not less than biology to such an extent that it is difficult to say which discipline 'reduces' and which discipline is reduced.
[2] It should be noticed, however, that this terminology is most unfortunate because it seems to prejudge this very complex issue as one of mere reduction to current Walrasian microeconomics.
[3] A case in point is the consumption function which was introduced by Keynes without any serious attempt at a proper micro-foundation and which has since found many suggested micro-foundations (e.g. that of Modigliani, 1944, or that of Clower, 1965).

14.3   The legacy of Keynes

I have argued so far in favour of the survival of macroeconomics conceived as an autonomous discipline. But does this imply that such a discipline should be developed along Keynesian lines? I would not deny that many features of the *General Theory*, more than fifty years since its first publication, appear old-fashioned, weak or altogether wrong. The Keynesian view of the capitalist system appears questionable in many respects. This reflects not only the evolution of capitalism itself in the last fifty years, but also certain intrinsic weaknesses in Keynes's own point of view. The insufficient attention given to long-run, supply and real conditions *vis-à-vis* short-run, demand and financial conditions, the excessive reliance on public intervention as a *deus ex machina*, the Utopian perspective of 'euthanasia of *rentier*' – these are just a few examples of perplexing features in Keynes's view of the capitalist system (see above, section 13.1). Moreover, the *General Theory*'s contributions to economic analysis in the strict sense of the word (see chapter 1) must today be considered very poor, as the few analytical suggestions which are still of some interest are often fuzzy and confusing.

Keynes's major heritage, therefore, lies in his heuristic model which has been at the centre of the foregoing analysis. Even here, however, his contribution should not be taken too literally. As has already been shown in chapter 13, the dubious notion of a necessary identity between investment and saving, the misplaced emphasis on the static version of the multiplier, the uncritical juxtaposition of relations in logic time (as in the case of the static multiplier) and relations in historical time (as in the case of liquidity preference), the narrow strait-jacket of the short period, show the existence of weaknesses in the heuristic model itself. Nevertheless it contains many concepts and methodological hints that are undoubtedly 'alive'. The concept of unemployment equilibrium, the principle of effective demand, the liquidity preference schedule, the influence of long-run expectations, the crucial role of money wages, and above all the fundamental idea that a market economy is unable to self-adjust, are still a major source of inspiration for economic research, and rightly so.

At the root of these fruitful ideas lies the method that generates and coordinates them. An anti-formalist constructivism inspires the gradual building up of the heuristic model as well as its critical utilization, which never loses a proper intuitive control over the economic meaning of symbolic operations and formal manipulations. This method has been completely neglected by mainstream economics, which has been heavily influenced by mathematical formalism. Recent developments in the philosophy of science have in a sense vindicated Keynes's point of view. For example it has been clarified how strict the limits of formalization are in empirical sciences (see e.g. Suppe, ed., 1977, or Caldwell, 1982). In addition the epistemology of mathematics has become increasingly critical of Hilbert's formalist programme, giving more and more credit to the constructivist point of view (see e.g. Kline, 1980 and Popper, 1972). Keynes's constructivism and anti-formalism are much less out of tune with prevailing epistemology now than they were before. Moreover, this methodological approach rests on a basis of probabilistic causality which should be recognized as particularly congenial to economic reasoning. The recent advances in the theory of probabilistic causality (mentioned in chapter 7) lend themselves to a reappraisal of the remarkable potentialities of Keynes's heuristic model.

One of the main advantages of Keynes's probabilistic constructivism is that we are led to take seriously the structural instability of a modern economy. Once Lucas's idea of finding a set of 'structural' parameters invariant to changes in policy rules is recognized as illusory, some sort of sequential method able to trace the path of shifts in the parameters will be found necessary in order to analyse structural changes in the economic system. Such a method is just hinted at in a few passages of the *General Theory* (in particular, in chapter 19) but it is not adequately developed either in Keynes's works or in those of his followers. However it should be recognized that he laid down a few important methodological premises for its development.

14.4   Macroeconomics as a discipline founded on rational non-demonstrative arguments

The liveliest part of Keynes's message may perhaps be found in his conception of the nature and role of economics. This is conceived as a truly human (or moral) discipline which is profoundly influenced by the motivations affecting the decisions of economic agents. Economics is thus conceived as a 'non-Euclidian' discipline, since its conclusions cannot be taken as certain but only as the most probable in given circumstances. Thus its aim cannot be to give conclusive demonstrations, but only to give arguments meant to persuade a rational audience. Economics, in particular macroeconomics, should never be doctrinaire or presumptuous:[4] on the contrary it should always be tolerant and open to criticism and innovation (see chapter 13). On the other hand it should be stressed that like any

---

[4] As Keynes remarked in his essay 'Economic Possibilities for our Grandchildren': 'if economists could manage to get themselves thought of as humble, competent people, on a level with dentists, that would be splendid!' (CW, vol. 9, p. 332).

argumentative discipline it has to be founded on a proper concept of rationality because all arguments must appeal to the reason of the audience.

Such a rigorous style of reasoning cannot rely on a narrow conception of rationality as substantive rationality which is preferred by Lucas and many mainstream economists. It must be based on a broader conception capable of coordinating substantive rationality (which refers to equilibrium configurations) with procedural rationality (which refers to processes of learning and discovery) and with creative rationality (which refers to the moulding of the environment to satisfy human needs). As a matter of fact, macroeconomics cannot restrict its scope to the study of optimal adaptation to a given environment, which expresses a limited form of rationality that may be found in the behaviour of all living beings. The main problem is that of adapting the environment to human needs, which is a function of the specifically human aspect of rationality. The scope of economics must thus encompass the choice of an 'institutional environment' conducive to the solution of economic problems.[5] In addition, macroeconomics should not neglect the arduous themes of environmental control in the ecological sense. While I cannot attribute any merit to Keynes in this latter research area, today the perspective of a designing rationality – as defined in section 6.2 – implicit in his writings necessarily involves problems of environmental control, not only in the institutional sense but also in the ecological sense.

14.5   The contributions of new classical economics

It would be interesting to sketch an appraisal of the contributions made by Lucas and other new classical economists. At the moment such an enterprise would be premature, as this school of thought is still in its infancy and its limits are still to be clarified. Moreover, like any school of thought it has undergone a significant evolution, which is still going on and will

---

[5] Lucas blames Keynes for having distracted the economic profession from this sort of problem (1981, p. 216):

> Accompanying the redirection of scientific interest occasioned by the Keynesian Revolution was a sharp change in the nature of the contribution to policy . . . The effort to 'explain business cycles' had been directed at identifying institutional sources of instability, with the hope that, once understood, these sources could be removed or their influence mitigated by appropriate institutional changes . . . the abandonment of the effort to explain business cycles accompanied a belief that policy could effect immediate, or very short-term, movement of the economy from an undesirable current state, however arrived at, to a better state.

This accusation is definitely unjust as far as Keynes himself is concerned. He always put this sort of problem at the centre of his reflections. Even a superficial reading of the *General Theory* immediately reveals that the book ultimately aims at a radical institutional reform of capitalism, which Keynes believed necessary to assure its survival. However, it is difficult to deny that Lucas's accusation may find some justification in reference to subsequent versions of Keynesianism, for example the fine-tuning macroeconomics fashionable in the sixties.

certainly continue in the future. Since I do not think this evolutionary process is a stationary and ergodic stochastic process, I believe that surprising developments should be expected. For the time being I feel able to indicate a few contributions that are likely to last, but I cannot avoid pointing out a substantial failure as far as its main past objectives are concerned.

Among the long-lasting contributions I would reckon a few criticisms and a few constructive suggestions. Among the criticisms, two are particularly important. The first concerns the weaknesses of the so-called 'neoclassical synthesis', the prevailing macroeconomic school of the sixties and early seventies. In particular it was argued that the alleged 'synthesis' between Keynesian macroeconomics and neoclassical microeconomics is not at all satisfactory because these two positions remain inconsistent in many crucial respects (as is shown by theoretical constructs such as involuntary unemployment, adaptive expectations, the Phillips curve, fine tuning, etc.). Moreover, the so-called 'Lucas critique' correctly emphasized the problems connected with the structural instability of parameters in econometric models.

Both criticisms are substantially sound as far as the destructive side is concerned, but the constructive suggestions built on them are much less convincing. The new alleged synthesis between classical macroeconomics and Walrasian microeconomics is very weak, since it rests on very special assumptions which condemn to irrelevance all the most interesting macroeconomic problems (see chapter 9). In addition, as far as the second criticism is concerned, the problems raised by the structural instability of parameters are not really overcome by the new classical models.

This is not meant to imply that new classical economics has been altogether barren of constructive contributions. I should mention first the systematic attention given to the role of information in macroeconomics. Its importance had been recognized before in general terms, particularly by Hayek, and had been explored in analytical terms by a few pioneers such as Alchian and Machlup. However, information economics became an integral part of macroeconomic theory only with new classical economics, although the modalities of that integration are still not at all satisfactory (see e.g. the criticisms raised by Stiglitz, 1984).

A very important corollary of this first contribution is the systematic study of the interaction between cognitive and decisional processes through the simplistic but powerful hypothesis of rational expectations. Although the prevailing interpretation and use of rational expectations is very questionable, this hypothesis has shown a remarkable heuristic value and remains the first systematic attempt at studying endogenous formation of expectations without violating economic rationality. The existing models incorporating rational expectations should be considered only as a first step in a promising direction. I would guess that the future generations of models with endogenous expectations will only vaguely resemble the first generation of rational-expectations models. Even so, future historians of economic analysis will have to recognize the great impetus given to this subject by the application of this hypothesis to macroeconomics.

Along with a few positive contributions like those just mentioned, I have to point out some negative influences exerted by the new classical economists (intentionally or not) on professional and academic circles and perhaps to some extent on public opinion as well. The main bad influence has been the spread, in many university departments of economics and in specialized journals, of a doctrinaire attitude which is not at all conducive to a desirable degree of scientific and methodological pluralism. This does not necessarily come from a doctrinaire attitude taken subjectively by Lucas and other new classical economists. As a matter of fact on many occasions they have declared an open attitude towards different points of view.[6]

Whatever the *subjective* attitude, however, the 'flavour' of theoretical and methodological rigidity derives from the acceptance of methodological and theoretical principles which are *objectively* rigid. In particular, the crucial conception of economics as an exact science leaves hardly any room for alternative theoretical and methodological options. The object of economic analysis is limited to strictly recurring events which are interpretable as realizations of stationary and ergodic stochastic processes. Any point of view prepared to give scientific relevance to non-recurring events is rejected as non-scientific by definition. Moreover, the rigid requirement that each scientific statement be explicitly founded on the so-called market fundamentals – i.e. on the principles of current Walrasian microeconomics – leaves no actual alternative. Hence it is not surprising that the new classical economists feel in their bones that there are no really viable alternative options, either theoretical or methodological.[7]

By contrast, Keynes's point of view is objectively open to different theoretical and methodological options, whatever subjective attitude may have been taken by him and his followers.[8] However, in this respect there is

---

[6] I could mention, for instance, the following passage often quoted in this connection: 'I have tried to avoid claiming too much for the particular examples of equilibrium models that now exist. There is no point in letting tentative and, I hope, promising first steps harden into positions that must be defended at all cost' (Lucas, 1981, p. 292).

[7] A case in point is Lucas who declares in the introduction to his famous book, 'if there is a single, main theme to this introduction, it is a sense of having severely limited theoretical options, which I feel very strongly' (1981, p. 17).

[8] Neither Keynes nor his followers have always been consistent with their open-minded theoretical point of view. There are many anecdotes on this subject, not always edifying: for example see Hicks's introduction to Robertson, 1940, where the intolerant attitude taken by the Cambridge Circus against Robertson is elegantly recalled.

Conclusions

a fundamental asymmetry between Keynes and Lucas. Keynes's conception of economics as an argumentative discipline does not exclude the use of demonstrative arguments whenever possible, provided that the limits of their validity are always kept in mind. On the other hand Lucas's conception of economics as a rigorously exact demonstrative discipline excludes the scientific validity of any non-demonstrative argument. This considerably restricts the theoretical and methodological flexibility of economic theory. According to Keynes, by contrast, the behaviour of the economic system need not be the same in different institutional environments.[9]

From all this we may conclude that Keynes's point of view, at least in this context, is more general than that of Lucas. In any case a rigid position on theory and method is today both unjustified and dangerous. It is unjustified because a synthesis between macro and micro is not around the corner. It is dangerous because the conception of economics as a demonstrative discipline considerably narrows not only the range of theoretical options but also the range of empirical applications of 'economic reasoning'. This widens the gap between economic theory and actual problems. It is dangerous, moreover, because a doctrinaire attitude discourages much-needed serious attempts at innovation in theory and method in order to cope with real problems.

14.6   Which Keynesianism today?

From the preceding considerations it is clear that it would be a mistake to counter the rigidity of new classical economics by relying on an opposite fundamentalism of a Keynesian type. On the contrary, the crucial message of Keynes which I think should be recovered today is a lay conception of economic disciplines. This is particularly true of macroeconomics, which should always remain open to basic theoretical innovation, and should be concerned with the solution of real problems. Macroeconomics should thus be conceived in the way that Keynes conceived it, as an autonomous discipline founded on arguments, not necessarily demonstrative, which aim to find reasonable solutions for real problems.

It seems justified, therefore, to take an attitude towards new classical economics which is close to that taken by Keynes towards the classical economics of his day. Now, as then, we have to liberate the economic profession from a discipline which limits the scope of theoretical and

[9] This is made crystal clear by the Keynesian distinction between a cooperative economy and an entrepreneur economy (see chapter 12).

242

methodological options without successfully solving the problems posed by both economic theory and policy. In this sense Keynes today, after Lucas, is no less up to date than he was after Pigou. We have to open our minds to new theoretical and methodological options, struggling – as Keynes urged us to do many years ago – against the old ideas 'that ramify in any corner of our mind' (Keynes, GT, 'Introduction').

The same attitude must be taken towards Keynesian macroeconomics and Keynes's own contributions. We still need Keynesian macroeconomics, in the sense that has been specified, but we have to rethink it in a courageous and radical way. After all, if Keynes were writing the *General Theory* in the eighties he would probably have chosen Lucas rather than Pigou as his Turk's head. In other words, the ever-new metamorphoses of classical thought demand a continuous adjustment of the critical part of Keynesian thought.

The evolution of real problems is a second fundamental reason for a ceaseless effort to develop Keynesian theory. The need for a courageous rethinking of Keynesian macroeconomics is clearly shown by ideas like the assumption of a closed economy in a world more and more affected by international relations, or by the naive confidence in the superior foresight and even-handedness of public intervention after a long experience of disillusion, to mention only two examples.

Lastly, we cannot neglect the analytical inadequacies of the *General Theory*, which since the very beginning have weakened the impact of the Keynesian message on both economic theory and economic policy, and many of which even now have not been really overcome. However it is not the aim of this work either to survey the shortcomings of Keynes's thought or to outline the most promising research programme for Keynesian macroeconomics.

I conclude by observing that Keynes conceived of macroeconomics as an autonomous discipline founded on the category of possibility, in open disagreement with the reductionist classical conception founded on the category of necessity (see Carabelli, 1984 and 1988). The economic system is ruled, according to old and new classical economists, by natural laws which are eventually bound to prevail against any kind of interference. Thus any attempt at controlling the economy would only worsen the situation because of their side effects. Keynes, on the contrary, stresses the artificial character of economic phenomena, whose appearance depends on the institutional framework, and in general on past and present human interventions (see Vicarelli, 1985–6). The working and the evolution of the economic system are thus conceived by Keynes as always open to different possibilities and to unexpected innovations. This gives room for a con-

Conclusions

scious action of control, not in the sense of fine-tuning but as a project continually adjusted to changing reality and gradually realized. Whether intentional or unintentional, the actions of economic agents have a crucial influence on the behaviour of the economic system. We cannot escape the need to design policies aimed at rational control of the economic system and of the ecological and institutional environment.

References

Abbreviations

AM Abraham, R., and Marsden, J.E., *Foundations of Mechanics*, 2nd edn,
    Reading, Mass., Benjamin and Cummings, 1980.
CW Keynes, J.M., *The Collected Writings of J.M. Keynes*, edited by Mog-
    gridge, D.E. and Johnson, E., London, Macmillan, 1971– .
GT Keynes, J.M., *The General Theory of Employment, Interest and Money*,
    1936, reprint as vol. 7 of CW.
KP Kydland, F.E. and Prescott, E.C., 1982, Time to build and aggregate
    fluctuations, *Econometrica*, 50, 1345–70.
TP Keynes, J.M., *A Treatise on Probability*, 1921, reprint as vol. 8 of CW.

Abraham, R. and Marsden, J.E., 1980, *Foundations of Mechanics*, 2nd edn
    (abbreviated AM), Reading, Mass., Benjamin and Cummings.
Abraham, R. and Smale, S., 1970, Nongenericity of Ω-stability, in Chern and
    Smale, eds., 1970.
Adelman, I. and Adelman, F.L., 1959, The dynamic properties of the Klein-
    Goldberger model, *Econometrica*, 27, 4, 596–625.
Akerlof, G.A., 1979, The case against conservative macroeconomics, *Economica*,
    46, 219–38.
Akerlof, G.A. and Yellen, J.L., 1985a, Can small deviations from rationality make
    significant differences to economic equilibria?, *American Economic Review*, 75,
    708–20.
    1985b, A near-rational model of the business cycle, with wage and price inertia,
    Quarterly Journal of Economics, Supplement, 100, 823–38.
Ammassari, P., 1977, Causality and probability in social research, *Epistemologia*, 5,
    187–204.
Andronov, A.A. and Leontovich, E., 1938, A contribution to the theory of the
    qualitative structure of the partition of a plane by paths, *Doklady Akademii
    Nauk SSSR*, 21, 427–30.
Andronov, A.A., Leontovich, E., Gordon, I. and Maier, A., 1967, *Theory of
    Bifurcations of Dynamical Systems in the Plane*, Jerusalem, Israel Program of
    Scientific Translations.

References

Andronov, A.A. and Pontryagin, L., 1937, Structurally stable systems, *Doklady Akademii Nauk SSSR*, 14, 5, 247–51.

Andronov, A.A., Vitt, A. and Khaikin, S., 1937, *Theory of Oscillations*, translated into English by Lefschetz, S., 1949, Princeton, N.J., Princeton University Press. (Page references are to the English edition of 1949.)

Arnold, V.I., 1978, *Geometrical Methods in the Theory of Ordinary Differential Equations*, English translation, Berlin, Springer, 1983. (Page references are to the English edition of 1983.)

1984, *Catastrophe Theory*, Berlin, Springer.

Arrow, K.J., 1958, Toward a theory of price adjustment, in Abramovitz, M. *et al.*, eds., *The Allocation of Economic Resources: Essays in Honour of B.F. Haley*, Stanford, Stanford University Press.

Arrow, K.J. and Hahn, F.H., 1971, *General Competitive Analysis*, San Francisco, Holden-Day.

Ashenfelter, O., 1984, Macroeconomic analyses and microeconomic analyses of labour supply, in Brunner and Meltzer, eds., 1984, 117–56.

Aumann, R., 1976, Agreeing to disagree, *Annals of Statistics*, 4, 1236–9.

Azariadis, C., 1981, Self-fulfilling prophecies, *Journal of Economic Theory*, 25, 380–96.

Azariadis, C. and Guesnerie, R., 1982, Prophéties créatrices et persistance des théories, *Revue Economique*, 33, 787–805.

Banks, J. and Sobel, J., 1985, Equilibrium selection in signalling games, mimeo, Cambridge, Mass., MIT.

Barnett, W.A. and Singleton, K.J., eds., 1987, *New Approaches to Monetary Economics: Proceedings of the Second International Symposium in Economic Theory and Econometrics*, Cambridge, Cambridge University Press.

Baumol, W.J., 1970, *Economic Dynamics*, 3rd edn, New York, Macmillan.

Begg, D.K.H., 1982, *The Rational Expectations Revolution in Macroeconomics*, Oxford, Allan.

1984, Rational expectations and bond pricing: modelling the term structure with and without certainty equivalence, *Economic Journal*, 94, Supplement, 45–58.

Bernheim, D., 1984, Rationalizable strategic behaviour, *Econometrica*, 52, 1007–28.

Bewley, T., 1986–7, Knightian decision theory, I and II, *Cowles Foundation Discussion Papers*, nos. 807 and 835, New Haven, Conn., Yale University.

Binmore, K.G., 1986, Remodeled rational players, manuscript, London, LSE.

Binmore, K.G., and Dasgupta, P., 1987, *The Economics of Bargaining*, Oxford, Blackwell.

Black, F., 1982, General equilibrium and business cycles, *NBER Working Paper*, no. 950.

Blatt, J.M., 1978, On the econometric approach to business-cycle analysis, *Oxford Economic Papers*, 30, 2, 292–300.

1983, *Dynamic Economic Systems: A Post-Keynesian Approach*, Armonk, N.Y., Sharpe.

Blaug, M., 1980, *The Methodology of Economics*, Cambridge, Cambridge University Press.

References

Blinder, A.S., 1986, Keynes after Lucas, *Eastern Economic Journal*, 12, 209–16.

Bouligand, G., 1935, Sur la stabilité des propositions mathématiques, *Académie Royale de Belgique, Bulletin Classe Science*, 21, 5, 227–8; 776–9.

Box, C.E.P. and Jenkins, G.M., 1970, *Time Series Analysis, Forecasting and Control*, San Francisco, Holden-Day.

Bray, M.M., 1982, Learning, estimation, and the stability of rational expectations, *Journal of Economic Theory*, 26, 318–39.

1983, Convergence to rational expectations equilibrium, in Frydman and Phelps, eds., 1983.

Bray, M.M. and Kreps, D., 1986, Rational learning and rational expectations, in Heller, W., Starret, D. and Starr, R., eds., *Essays in Honour of K.J. Arrow*, Cambridge, Cambridge University Press.

Bronfenbrenner, M. and Holzman, F.D., 1963, Survey of inflation theory, *American Economic Review*, 53, 593–661.

Brunner, K. and Meltzer, A.H., eds., 1984, *Essays on Macroeconomic Implications of Financial and Labour Markets and Political Processes*, Carnegie-Rochester Conference Series on Public Policy, vol. 21, Amsterdam, North-Holland.

Bruno, S., 1987, Micro-flexibility and macro-rigidity: some notes on expectations and the dynamics of aggregate supply, *Labour*, 1, 2, 127–51.

Bruns, H., 1887, Über die Integrale des Vielkörper-problems, *Acta Mathematica*, 11, 25–96.

Buiter, W.H., 1980, The macroeconomics of Dr Pangloss: a critical survey of the new-classical macroeconomics, *Economic Journal*, 90, 2, 34–50.

1982, The superiority of contingent rules over fixed rules in models with rational expectations, *NBER Technical Paper*, no. 9.

Bunge, M., 1963, *Causality. The Place of the Causal Principle in Modern Science*, 2nd edn, Cambridge, Mass., Harvard University Press.

1982, The revival of causality, in Fløistad, G., ed., *Contemporary Philosophy*, vol. 2, The Hague, M. Nijhoff, pp. 133–55.

Burmeister, E., 1980, On some conceptual issues in rational expectations modeling, *Journal of Money, Credit, and Banking*, 12, 4, 800–16.

Burmeister, E., Flood, P.R. and Garber, P.M., 1983, On the equivalence of solutions in rational expectations models, *Journal of Economic Dynamics and Control*, 5, 311–21.

Cagan, P., 1956, The monetary dynamics of hyperinflation, in Friedman, M., ed., *Studies in the Quantity Theory of Money*, Chicago, University of Chicago Press.

Caldwell, B.J., 1982, *Beyond Positivism: Economic Methodology in the Twentieth Century*, London, Allen and Unwin.

Calvo, G., 1978, On the indeterminacy of interest rates and wages with perfect foresight, *Journal of Economic Theory*, 19, 321–37.

Cameron, R.E., 1967, *Banking in the Early Stages of Industrialization; a Study in Comparative Economic History*, New York, Oxford University Press.

Carabelli, A., 1984, Causa, caso e possibilità in J.M. Keynes, in Lunghini *et al.*, 1984.

1988, *On Keynes's Method*, London, Macmillan.

References

Carnap, R., 1950, *Logical Foundations of Probability*, Chicago, University of Chicago Press.

Casarosa, C., 1981, The microfoundations of Keynes's aggregate supply and expected demand analysis, *Economic Journal*, 91, 188–94.

Champernowne, D.G., 1953, A model of income distribution, *Economic Journal*, 63, 318–51.

Chern, S.S. and Smale, S., eds., 1970, *Proceedings of the Symposium in Pure Mathematics: Global Analysis*, Providence, R.I., American Mathematical Society.

Chick, V., 1983, *Macroeconomics after Keynes. A Reconsideration of the* General Theory, Oxford, Philip Allan.

Clower, R.W., 1960, Keynes and the classics: a dynamical perspective, *Quarterly Journal of Economics*, 74, 312–323.

   1965, The Keynesian Counter-revolution: A Theoretical Appraisal, in Hahn, F.H. and Brechling, F.P.R., eds., *The Theory of Interest Rates*, London, Macmillan.

Clower, R.W., ed., 1969, *Monetary Theory*, Harmondsworth, Penguin.

Coddington, A., 1976, Keynesian economics: the search for first principles, *Journal of Economic Literature*, 14, 1258–73.

Conway, R.K., Swamy, P.A.V.B. and Yanagida, J.F., 1983, The impossibility of causality testing, *Federal Reserve Board, Special Studies Papers*, no. 178, Washington, D.C.

Cooley, T.F. and LeRoy, S.F., 1985, Atheoretical macroeconometrics: a critique, *Journal of Monetary Economics*, 16, 3, 283–308.

Cottingham, J., 1984, *Rationalism*, London, Paladin.

   1988, *The Rationalists*, Oxford, Oxford University Press.

Cugno, F. and Montrucchio, L., 1982, Cyclical growth and inflation: a qualitative approach to Goodwin's model with money prices, *Economic Notes*, 11, 3, 93–107.

Davidson, P., 1982–3, Rational expectations: a fallacious foundation for studying crucial decision-making processes, *Journal of Post-Keynesian Economics*, 2, 182–98.

Day, R.H. and Shafer, W., 1983, Keynesian chaos, *Journal of Macroeconomics*, 7, 277–95.

De Finetti, B., 1980, Foresight: its logical laws, its subjective sources, in Kyberg, H.E. and Smokler, H.E., eds., *Studies in Subjective Probability*, New York, R.E. Krieger, pp. 53–118.

Descartes, R., 1637, *Discourse on the Method*, in Descartes, R., *Selected Philosophical Writings*, translated by Cottingham, J., Stoothoff, R. and Murdoch, D., Cambridge, Cambridge University Press, 1988, pp. 20–56. (Page references are to the English edition of 1988.)

Destouches, J., 1935, Les Espaces abstraits en logique et la stabilité des propositions, *Académie Royale de Belgique, Bulletin Classe Science*, 21, 5, 780–6.

Devaney, R.L., 1987, *An Introduction to Chaotic Dynamical Systems*, Menlo Park, Calif., Addison-Wesley.

Diamond, P.A., 1984, *A Search Equilibrium Approach to the Microfoundations of*

Macroeconomics, Cambridge, Mass., MIT Press.

Diaz-Giménez, J. and Prescott, E.C., 1989, Asset returns in computable general equilibrium heterogeneous agent economies, Minneapolis, Federal Reserve Bank of Minneapolis, Research Department, mimeo.

Duhem, P., 1906, *The Aim and Structure of Physical Theory*, English translation, Princeton, N.J., Princeton University Press, 1954. (Page references are to the English edition of 1954.)

Egidi, M., 1981, *Schumpeter. Lo sviluppo come trasformazione morfologica*, Milan, Etas Libri.

Eichenbaum, M. and Singleton, K.J., 1986, Do equilibrium real business cycles theories explain postwar US business cycles?, in Fischer, S., ed., *NBER Macroeconomics Annual 1986*, Cambridge, Mass., MIT Press.

Ellsberg, D., 1961, Risk, ambiguity, and the Savage axioms, *Quarterly Journal of Economics*, 75, 643–69.

Engle, R.F., Hendry, D.F. and Richard, J.-F., 1983, Exogeneity, *Econometrica*, 51, 2, 227–304.

Farmer, R.E.A. and Woodford, M., 1984, Self-fulfilling prophecies and the business cycle, *CARESS Working Paper* 12.

Fay, J.A. and Medoff, J.L., 1985, Labor and output over the business cycle: some direct evidence, *American Economic Review*, 75, 3, 638–55.

Fischer, B., 1982, General equilibrium and business cycles, *NBER Working Paper*, no. 950.

Fischer, S., ed., 1980, *Rational Expectations and Economic Policy*, Chicago, University of Chicago Press.

Fisher, F.M., 1983, *Disequilibrium Foundations of Equilibrium Economics*, Cambridge, Cambridge University Press.

Fitoussi, J.-P., 1983, Modern macroeconomic theory: an overview, in Fitoussi, J.-P., ed., *Modern Macroeconomic Theory*, Oxford, Basil Blackwell.

Friedman, M., 1968, The role of monetary policy, *American Economic Review*, 58, 1, 1–17.

Friedman, M. and Schwartz, A.J., 1963, *A Monetary History of the United States, 1867–1960*, Princeton, N.J., Princeton University Press.

Frydman, R. and Phelps, E.S., eds., 1983, *Individual Forecasting and Aggregate Outcomes*, Cambridge, Cambridge University Press.

Futia, C.A., 1981, Rational expectations in stationary linear models, *Econometrica*, 49, 171–92.

Galavotti, M.C. and Gambetta, G., eds., 1983, *Causalità e modelli probabilistici*, Bologna, CLUEB.

Gandolfo, G., 1983, *Economic Dynamics: Methods and Models*, 2nd edn, Amsterdam, North Holland.

Gärdenfors, P., 1979, Forecasts, decisions and uncertain probabilities, *Erkenntnis*, 14, 159–81.

Gärdenfors, P. and Sahlin, N.-E., 1982, Unreliable probabilities, risk-taking, and decision-making, *Synthèse*, 53, 361–86.

1983, Decision-making with unreliable probabilities, *British Journal of Mathematical and Statistical Psychology*, 36, 240–51.

References

Garegnani, P., 1979, *Valore e domanda effettiva*, Turin, Einaudi.

Geweke, J., 1984, Inference and causality in economic time series models, in Griliches, Z. and Intriligator, M.D., eds., *Handbook of Econometrics*, Amsterdam, North Holland, vol. 2, pp. 1101–44.

Good, I.J., 1961-2, A causal calculus I-II, *British Journal of the Philosophy of Science*, 11, 305–18; 12, 43–51.

Goodwin, R.M., 1947, Dynamical coupling with especial reference to markets having production lags, *Econometrica*, 15, 181–204.

Goodwin, R., Krüger, M. and Vercelli, A., eds., 1984, *Nonlinear Models of Fluctuating Growth*, Berlin, Springer.

Gourieroux, C., Laffont, J.J. and Monfort, A., 1982, Rational expectations in dynamic linear models: analysis of the solutions, *Econometrica*, 50, 2, 409–26.

Grandmont, J.-M., 1985, On endogenous competitive business cycles, *Econometrica*, 53, 995–1045.

Granger, C.W.J., 1963, Economic processes involving feedback, *Information and Control*, 6, 28–48.

1969, Investigating causal relations by econometric models and cross-spectral methods, *Econometrica*, 37, 424–38.

1980, Testing for causality: A personal viewpoint, *Journal of Economic Dynamics and Control*, 2, 329–52.

Greenwald, B. and Stiglitz, J.E., 1987, Keynesians, new-Keynesians and new classical economics, *Oxford Economic Papers*, 39, 119–32.

Grossman, S.J. and Stiglitz, J.E., 1976, Information and competitive price systems, *American Economic Review*, 66, 246–53.

1980, On the impossibility of informationally efficient markets, *American Economic Review*, 70, 393–407.

Hadamard J., 1898, Les Surfaces à courbures opposées et leur lignes géodésiques, *Journal de mathématiques pures et appliquées*, 5.

Hahn, F., 1973, *On the Notion of Equilibrium in Economics*, Cambridge, Cambridge University Press.

1981a, *Money and Inflation*, Oxford, Basil Blackwell.

1981b, General Equilibrium Theory, in Bell, D. and Kristol, J., eds., *The Crisis in Economic Theory*, New York, Basic Books.

1984, *Equilibrium and Macroeconomics*, Oxford, Blackwell.

1987, On involuntary unemployment, *Economic Journal*, Supplement, 97 (Conference 1987), 1–16.

1989, *The Economics of Missing Markets, Information and Games*, Oxford, Clarendon Press.

Hahn, F. and Negishi, T., 1962, A theorem on non-*tâtonnement* stability, *Econometrica*, 30, 463-9.

Hansen, A.H., 1951, *Business Cycle and National Income*, London, Allen and Unwin.

Hansen, L.P. and Sargent, T.J., 1980, Formulating and estimating linear rational expectations models, *Journal of Economic Dynamics and Control*, 2, 7–46.

Harsanyi, J., 1975, The tracing procedure: a Bayesian approach to defining a solution for n-person noncooperative games, *International Journal of Game Theory*, 5, 61–94.

Hawking, S.W., 1988, *A Brief History of Time*, New York, Bantam Books.

Hayek, F.A. von, 1933, *Monetary Theory and the Trade Cycle*, London, Jonathan Cape.

1974, *The Pretence of Knowledge*, Nobel Memorial Lecture.

Heiner, R.A., 1983, The origin of predictable behaviour, *American Economic Review*, 73, 3, 560–95.

Hicks, J., 1950, *A Contribution to the Theory of the Trade Cycle*, Oxford, Clarendon Press.

1974, *The Crisis in Keynesian Economics*, Oxford, Blackwell.

1979, *Causality in Economics*, Oxford, Blackwell.

1980–1, IS-LM: an explanation, *Journal of Post-Keynesian Economics*, 3, 2, 139–54.

1982, *Money, Interest and Wages, Collected Essays on Economic Theory*, vol. 2, Oxford, Blackwell.

1983a, *Classics and Neoclassics, Collected Essays on Economic Theory*, vol. 3, Oxford, Blackwell.

1983b, Review of *Microfoundations: The Compatibility of Microeconomics and Macroeconomics*, by E. Roy Weintraub (Cambridge, 1979), in Hicks, 1983a, 349–52.

Hogart, R.M. and Reder, M.W., eds., 1987, *Rational Choice. The Contrast between Economics and Psychology*, Chicago, University of Chicago Press.

Hoover, K.D., 1984, Two types of monetarism, *Journal of Economic Literature*, 22, 58–76.

1988, *The New Classical Macroeconomics. A Sceptical Inquiry*, Oxford, Basil Blackwell.

Intriligator, M., 1971, *Mathematical Optimization and Economic Theory*, New York, Prentice Hall.

Jones, R.A., and Ostroy, J.M., 1984, Flexibility and uncertainty, *Review of Economic Studies*, 51, 13–32.

Kahn, R.F., 1931, The relation of home investment to unemployment, *Economic Journal*, 41, 173–98.

Kaen, R.F. and Rosenman R.E., 1986, Predictable behaviour in financial markets: some evidence in support of Heiner's hypothesis, *American Economic Review*, 76, 1, 212–20.

Kahneman, D., Slovic, P. and Tversky, A., eds., 1982, *Judgement under Uncertainty: Heuristics and Biases*, Cambridge, Cambridge University Press.

Keynes, J.M., CW; *The Collected Writings of J.M. Keynes*, edited by Moggridge, D.E. and Johnson, E., London, Macmillan, 1971– . (Page references are to CW where a CW reprint is cited.)

1921, *A Treatise on Probability* (abbreviated TP), reprint as vol. 8 of CW.

1930, *A Treatise on Money*, 2 vols., reprint as vol. 4 of CW.

1931, *Essays in Persuasion*, reprint in vol. 9 of CW.

1933a, The means to prosperity, reprint in vol. 9 of CW, pp. 335–66.

References

1933b, *Essays in Biography*, reprint as vol. 10 of CW.

1936, *The General Theory of Employment, Interest and Money* (abbreviated GT), reprint as vol. 7 of CW.

1937, The general theory of employment, *Quarterly Journal of Economics*, 51, 209–23.

1939, Professor Tinbergen's method, *Economic Journal*, 49, 34–51.

Kim, J., 1973, Causation, nomic subsumption and the concept of event, *Journal of Philosophy*, 70, 8.

King, R.G. and Plosser, C.I., 1987, Nominal surprises, real factors, and propagation mechanisms, in Barnett and Singleton, eds., 1987.

King, R.G., Plosser, C.I. and Rebelo, S.T., 1988a, Production, growth and business cycles: I. The basic neoclassical model, *Journal of Monetary Economics*, 21, 195–232.

1988b, Production, growth and business cycles: II. New directions, *Journal of Monetary Economics*, 21, 309–41.

King, R.G., Plosser, C.I., Stock, J. and Watson, M., 1987, Stochastic trends and economic fluctuations, *NBER Working Paper* no. 2229.

Kirzner, I.M., 1973, *Competition and Entrepreneurship*, Chicago, University of Chicago Press.

Klamer, A., 1984, *The New Classical Macroeconomics. Conversations with New Classical Economists and their Opponents*, Brighton, Harvester Press.

Kline, M., 1980, *Mathematics: The Loss of Certainty*, New York, Oxford University Press.

Knight, F.H., 1921, *Risk, Uncertainty and Profit*, Boston, Houghton and Mifflin.

Kolmogorov, A.N., 1933, *Grundbegriffe der Wahrscheinlichkeitsrechnung*, Berlin, Springer; English translation, *Foundations of the Theory of Probability*, New York, Chelsea, 1950. (Page references are to the English edition of 1950.)

Koopman, B.O., 1940, The basis of probability, *Bulletin of the American Mathematical Society*, 46.

Kregel, J., 1976 Economic methodology in the face of uncertainty: the modelling methods of Keynes and the post-Keynesians, *Economic Journal*, 86, 209–25.

Kreps, D. and Wilson, R., 1982, Sequential equilibria, *Econometrica*, 50, 863–94.

Kuhn, T.S., 1977, *The Essential Tension. Selected Essays in Scientific Tradition and Change*, Chicago, University of Chicago Press.

Kydland, F.E. and Prescott, E.C., 1982, Time to build and aggregate fluctuations, *Econometrica*, 50, 1345–70.

Laidler, D., 1986, The new classical contribution to macroeconomics, *Banca Nazionale del Lavoro Quarterly Review*, 39, 1, 27–55.

Latsis, S.J., 1972, Situational determinism in economics, *The British Journal of the Philosophy of Science*, 23, 207–45.

Leijonhufvud, A., 1966, *On Keynesian Economics and the Economics of Keynes*, Oxford University Press.

1981, *Information and Coordination: Essays in Macroeconomic Theory*, Oxford, Oxford University Press.

LeRoy, F.S. and Singell, L.D., Jr, 1987, Knight on risk and uncertainty, *Journal of Political Economy*, 95, 2, 394–406.

References

Lombardini, S., 1982, Economics: past and future, in Szegö, ed., 1982, pp. 29–75.

Long, J.B. and Plosser, C.I., 1983, Real business cycles, *Journal of Political Economy*, 91, 36–69.

Lorenz, H.-W., 1989, *Nonlinear Dynamical Economics and Chaotic Motion*, Berlin, Springer.

Lovell, M.C., 1986, Tests of the rational expectations hypothesis, *American Economic Review*, 76, 1, 110–24.

Lucas, R.E., Jr, 1972a, Econometric testing of the natural rate hypothesis, in Eckstein, O., ed., *The Econometrics of Price Determination*, Washington, D.C., Board of Governors of the Federal Reserve System, pp. 50–9.

1972b, Expectations and the neutrality of money, *Journal of Economic Theory*, 4, 103–24.

1973, Some international evidence on output–inflation trade-offs, *American Economic Review*, 63, 326–34.

1975, An equilibrium model of the business cycle, *Journal of Political Economy*, 83, 1113–44.

1976, Econometric policy evaluation: a critique, in Brunner, K. and Meltzer, A.H., eds., *The Phillips Curve and Labour Markets*, Carnegie-Rochester Conference Series, 1, 19–46; reprint in Lucas, 1981. (Page references are to the reprint of 1981.)

1977, Understanding business cycles, in Brunner, K. and Meltzer, A.H., eds., *Stabilization of the Domestic and International Economy*, Carnegie-Rochester Conference Series, 5, 7–29.

1981, *Studies in Business-Cycle Theory*, Cambridge, Mass., MIT Press.

1984, Money in a theory of finance, in Brunner and Meltzer, eds., 1984.

1986, Adaptive behaviour and economic theory, *The Journal of Business*, 59, 4; reprint in Hogart and Reder, eds., 1987. (Page references are to the reprint of 1987.)

1987, *Models of Business Cycles*, Yrjö Jahnsson Lectures, Oxford, Basil Blackwell.

1988, On the mechanics of economic development, *Journal of Monetary Economics*, 22, 3–42.

Lucas, R.E., Jr. and Rapping, L., 1969, Real wages, employment and inflation, *Journal of Political Economy*, 77, 721–54.

Lucas, R.E., Jr and Sargent, T.J., 1979, After Keynesian macroeconomics, *Federal Reserve Bank of Minneapolis Quarterly Review*, 3, 2, reprint in Lucas and Sargent, eds., 1981. (Page references are to the reprint of 1981.)

Lucas, R.E., Jr and Sargent, T.J., eds., 1981, *Rational Expectations and Econometric Practice*, London, Allen and Unwin.

Lucas, R.E., Jr and Stokey, N.L., 1987, Money and interest in a cash-in advance economy, *Econometrica*, 55, 3, 491–513.

Lunghini, G. *et al.*, 1984, *La scienza impropria*, Metamorfosi, Milan, Angeli.

Machlup, F., 1963, *Essays on Economic Semantics*, Englewood Cliffs, N.J., Prentice-Hall.

Mankiw, N.G., Rotemberg, J.J. and Summers, L.H., 1985, Intertemporal substitution in macroeconomics, *Quarterly Journal of Economics*, 100, 1, 225–51.

References

Manuelli, R. and Sargent, T., 1988, Models of business cycles: a review essay, *Journal of Monetary Economics*, 22, 523–42.

Marcet, A. and Sargent, T.J., 1988, The fate of systems with 'adaptive' expectations, *American Economic Review*, 78, 2, *Papers and Proceedings*, 168–72.

Marro, G., 1979, *Fondamenti di teoria dei sistemi*, 3rd edn, Bologna, Patron.

May, R.M., 1976, Simple mathematical models with very complex dynamics, *Nature*, 261, 459–67.

Medio, A., 1979, *Teoria non lineare del ciclo economico*, Bologna, Il Mulino.

Minsky, H.P., 1975, *John Maynard Keynes*, New York, Columbia University Press.

1982, *Inflation, Recession and Economic Policy*, Brighton, Wheatsheaf.

Modigliani, F., 1944, Liquidity preference and the theory of interest and money, *Econometrica*, 12, 45–88.

1977, The monetarist controversy or, should we forsake stabilization policies?, *American Economic Review*, 67, 1–19.

Morishima, M., 1980, *Dynamic Economic Theory*, London, ICERD, LSE.

Muth, J.F., 1961, Rational expectations and the theory of price movements, *Econometrica*, 29, 315–35.

Myerson, R.B., 1978, Refinements of the Nash equilibrium concept, *International Journal of Game Theory*, 7, 73–80.

Nash, J., 1950, The bargaining problem, *Econometrica*, 18, 155–62.

1951, Non-cooperative games, *Annals of Mathematics*, 54, 286–95.

Neary, P. and Stiglitz, J.E., 1983, Towards a reconstruction of Keynesian economics: expectations and constrained equilibrium, *Quarterly Journal of Economics*, Supplement, 199–228.

Nishimura, K.G., 1982, A new concept of stability and dynamical economic systems, *Journal of Economic Dynamics and Control*, 6, 25–40.

Olson, M., 1984, Beyond Keynesianism and monetarism, *Economic Inquiry*, 22, 3, 297–322.

Palis, J. and Smale, S., 1970, Structural stability theorems, in Chern and Smale, eds., 1970.

Papoulis, A., 1984, *Probability, Random Variables, and Stochastic Processes*, Auckland, McGraw-Hill.

Pasinetti, L.L., 1974, *Growth and Income Distribution. Essays in Economic Theory*, Cambridge, Cambridge University Press.

1981, *Structural Change and Economic Growth. A Theoretical Essay in the Dynamics of The Wealth of Nations*, Cambridge, Cambridge University Press.

Pasquinelli, A., 1958, *I presocratici. Frammenti e testimonianze*, Turin, Einaudi.

Patinkin, D., 1948, Price flexibility and full employment, *American Economic Review*, 38, 543–64.

1965, *Money, Interest and Prices*, 2nd edn, New York, Harper and Row.

Pearce, D.G., 1984, Rationalizable strategic behaviour and the problem of perfection, *Econometrica*, 52, 1029–50.

Peixoto, M., 1959, On structural stability, *Annals of Mathematics*, 69, 199–222.

1962, Structural stability on two-dimensional manifolds, *Topology*, 2, 101–21.

Peixoto, M., ed., 1973, *Dynamical Systems*, New York, Academic Press.

Pesaran, M.H., 1987, *The Limits to Rational Expectations*, Oxford, Basil Blackwell.

References

Petitot, J., 1979, Locale/globale, in *Enciclopedia*, vol. 8, Turin, Einaudi.

Phelps, E.S., 1967, Phillips curves, expectations of inflation and optimal unemployment over time, *Economica*, NS, 34, 3, 254–81.

1968, Money wage dynamics and labour market equilibrium, *Econometrica*, 29, 315–35.

1970, *Microeconomic Foundations of Employment and Inflation Theory*, New York, Norton.

Piaget, J., 1967, Logique et connaissance scientifique, in *Enciclopédie de la Pléiade*, vol. 22, Paris, Gallimard.

Piaget, J. and Garcia, R., 1971, *Les Explications Causales*, Paris, Presses Universitaires de France.

Pizzi, C., 1983, *Teorie della probabilità e teorie della causa*, Bologna, CLUEB.

Popper, K.R., 1945, *The Open Society and its Enemies*, London, Routledge.

1957, *The Poverty of Historicism*, London, Routledge.

1969, *Conjectures and Refutations*, London, Routledge.

1972, *Objective Knowledge. An Evolutionary Approach*, New York, Oxford University Press.

1982a, *Realism and the Aim of Science*, London, Hutchinson.

1982b, *The Open Universe. An Argument for Indeterminism*, London, Hutchinson.

1982c, *Quantum Theory and the Schism in Physics*, London, Hutchinson.

Prescott, E.C., 1977, Should control theory be used for economic stabilization?, in Brunner, K. and Meltzer, A.H., eds., *Optimal Policies, Control Theory and Technology Exports*, Amsterdam, North Holland.

1986, Theory ahead of business cycle measurement, *Federal Reserve Bank of Minneapolis Quarterly Review*, 3, 9–22.

Prigogine, I., 1974, L'Ordre par fluctuations et le système social, Brussels, mimeo.

1980, *From Being to Becoming*, San Francisco, Freeman.

Prigogine, I. and Stengers, I., 1984, *Order Out of Chaos. Man's New Dialogue with Nature*, London, Fontana.

Reichenbach, H., 1956, *The Direction of Time*, Berkeley, University of California Press.

Robertson, D.H., 1940, *Essays in Monetary Theory*, London, P.S. King and Son.

Rotemberg, J.J., 1987, The new Keynesian microfoundations, in Fischer, S., ed., *NBER Macroeconomics Annual 1987*, Cambridge, Mass., MIT Press, pp. 69–105.

Salmon, W.C., 1984, *Scientific Explanation and the Causal Structure of the World*, Princeton, N.J., Princeton University Press.

Samuelson, P.A., 1947, *Foundations of Economic Analysis*, Cambridge, Mass., Harvard University Press.

1968, What classical and neo-classical monetary theory really was, *Canadian Journal of Economics*, 1, 1–15, reprint in Clower, ed., 1969, pp. 170–90.

1972, *The Collected Scientific Papers*, vol. 3, Cambridge, Mass., MIT Press.

Sargent, T.J., 1979, *Macroeconomic Theory*, New York, Academic Press.

1984, Autoregressions, expectations and advice, *American Economic Review*, 74, 2, 408–15.

References

Sargent, T.J. and Sims, C.A., 1977, Business cycle modelling without pretending to have too much *a priori* economic theory, in Sims, ed., 1977.

Saunders, P.T., 1980, *An Introduction to Catastrophe Theory*, Cambridge, Cambridge University Press.

Savage, L.J., 1972, *The Foundations of Statistics*, New York, Dover.

Schumpeter, J.A., 1911, *Theorie der wirtschaflichen Entwicklung*, Leipzig, Duncker and Humblot; English translation, *The Theory of Economic Development*, Oxford, Oxford University Press, 1934. (Page references are to the English edition of 1934.)

——— 1928, The instability of capitalism, *The Economic Journal*, 3, 361–86.

——— 1936, Review of Keynes's *General Theory*, *Journal of the American Statistical Association*, 31, 791–5.

——— 1939, *Business Cycles: a Theoretical, Historical, and Statistical Analysis of the Capitalist Process*, New York, McGraw-Hill.

——— 1952, *Ten Great Economists*, London, Allen and Unwin.

——— 1954, *History of Economic Analysis*, London, Allen and Unwin.

Selten, R., 1975, Re-examination of the perfectness concept for equilibrium in extensive games, *International Journal of Game Theory*, 4, 22–5.

Shackle, G.L.S., 1972, *Epistemics and Economics*, Cambridge, Cambridge University Press.

——— 1982, Sir John Hicks' 'IS-LM: an explanation': a comment, *Journal of Post-Keynesian Economics*, 4, 3, 435–8.

Sheffrin, S.M., 1983, *Rational Expectations*, Cambridge, Cambridge University Press.

Shiller, R.J., 1978, Rational expectations and the dynamic structure of macroeconomic models, *Journal of Monetary Economics*, 4, 1–44.

Siljak, D., 1978, *Large-scale Dynamic Systems. Stability and Structure*, New York, North-Holland.

Simon, H.A., 1952, On the definition of the causal relation, *The Journal of Philosophy*, 49, 517–28.

——— 1953, Causal ordering and identifiability, in Hood, W.C. and Koopmans, T.J., *Studies in Econometric Methods*, New York, J. Wiley, pp. 49–74.

——— 1954, Spurious correlation: a causal interpretation, *Journal of the American Statistical Association*, 49, 267, 467–79.

——— 1956, Dynamic programming under uncertainty with a quadratic criterion function, *Econometrica*, 24, 74–81.

——— 1982, *Models of Bounded Rationality*, Cambridge, Mass., MIT Press.

Simons, H.C., 1948, *Economic Policy for a Free Society*, Chicago, University of Chicago Press.

Sims, C.A., 1972, Money, income and causality, *American Economic Review*, 62, 540–52.

——— 1977, Exogeneity and causal ordering in macroeconomic models, in Sims, ed., 1977.

——— 1980a, Macroeconomics and reality, *Econometrica*, 48, 1–48.

——— 1980b, Comparison of interwar and postwar business cycles: monetarism reconsidered, *American Economic Review*, 70, 2 (Papers and Proceedings), 250–7.

References

1982, Policy analysis with econometric models, *Brookings Papers on Economic Activity*, 1, 107–52.

1986, Are forecasting models usable for policy analysis?, *Federal Reserve Bank of Minneapolis Quarterly Review*, 10, 1, 2–15.

1987, A rational expectations framework for short-run policy analysis, in Barnett and Singleton, eds., 1987.

Sims, C.A., ed., 1977, *New Methods in Business Cycle Research*, Minneapolis, Federal Reserve Bank of Minneapolis.

Smale, S., 1959, Diffeomorphisms of the two sphere, *Proceedings of the American Mathematical Society*, 10, 621–6.

1966, Structurally stable systems are not dense, *American Journal of Mathematics*, 88, 491–6.

1980, *The Mathematics of Time*, New York, Springer.

Spohn, W., 1983, Probabilistic causality: from Hume via Suppes to Granger, in Galavotti and Gambetta, eds., 1983.

Stahl, D.O., 1988, On the instability of mixed-strategy Nash equilibrium, *Journal of Economic Behaviour and Organization*, 9, 59–69.

Steindl, J., 1965, *Random Processes and the Growth of Firms*, London, Griffin.

Stiglitz J.E., 1984, Information and economic analysis: a perspective, *Economic Journal*, Supplement, 95, 24–41.

Summers, L.H., 1986, Some skeptical observations on real business cycle theory, *Federal Reserve Bank of Minneapolis Quarterly Review*, 10, 4, 23–7.

Suppe, F., ed., 1977, *The Structure of Scientific Theories*, Urbana, Ill., University of Illinois Press.

Suppes, P., 1970, *A Probabilistic Theory of Causality*, Amsterdam, North-Holland.

1981, *La logica del probabile*, Bologna, CLUEB.

1984, *Probabilistic Metaphysics*, Oxford, Blackwell.

Swamy, P.A.V.B., Barth, J.R. and Tinsley, P.A., 1982, The rational expectations approach to economic modelling, *Journal of Economic Dynamics and Control*, 4, 125–48.

Szegö, G., ed., 1982, *New Quantitative Techniques for Economic Analysis*, New York, Academic Press.

Taylor, J.B., 1977, Conditions for unique solutions to stochastic macroeconomic models with rational expectations, *Econometrica*, 45, 1377–85.

Termini, V., 1984, Sequenze e tempo nel ragionamento economico, in Lunghini *et al.*, 1984.

Thom R., 1974, *Modèles mathématiques de la morphogenèse*, Paris, Union générale d'éditions.

1975, *Structural Stability and Morphogenesis: an Outline of a General Theory of Models*, Reading, Mass., Benjamin and Cummings.

1980, *Parabole e castrofi*, Milan, Il Saggiatore.

Tinbergen, J., 1939, *Les Cycles économiques aux Etats-Unis d'Amérique de 1919 à 1932*, Geneva, League of Nations.

Tobin, J., 1958, Liquidity preference as behaviour towards risk, *Review of Economic Studies*, 25, 65–86.

References

1970, Money and income: *post hoc ergo propter hoc?*, *Quarterly Journal of Economics*, 84, 301–17.

1980a, Are new classical models plausible enough to guide policy?, *Journal of Money, Credit and Banking*, 12, 788–99.

1980b, *Asset Accumulation and Economic Activity: Reflections on Contemporary Macroeconomic Theory*, Chicago, University of Chicago Press.

Tonveronachi, M., 1982, Monetarism and fixed rules, in H.C. Simons, *Banca Nazionale del Lavoro Quarterly Review*, 35, 181–203.

1983, *J.M. Keynes. Dall'instabilità ciclica all'equilibrio di sottoccupazione*, Rome, NIS.

Vasari, G., 1568, *Lives of the Artists, a Selection Translated by G. Bull from the Second Edition*, vol. 1, Harmondsworth, Penguin, 1988. (Page references are to the English edition of 1988.)

Velupillai, K., 1982, Linear and nonlinear dynamics in economics: the contributions of Richard Goodwin, *Economic Notes*, 3, 73–92.

Vercelli, A., 1979, *Equilibrio e dinamica del sistema economico. Semantica dei linguaggi formalizzati e modello keynesiano*, Discussion Paper, Department of Political Economy, University of Siena.

1981, Equilibrio e disequilibrio nella *Teoria Generale* di Keynes: il ruolo dei salari monetari e le difficoltà di un metodo di puro equilibrio, in Graziani, A., Jossa, B. and Imbriani, C., eds., *Studi di economia keynesiana*, Naples.

1982, Is instability enough to discredit a model?, *Economic Notes*, 4, 173–90.

1984a, Fluctuations and growth: Marx, Schumpeter, Keynes and the structural instability of capitalism, in Goodwin, R., Krüger, M. and Vercelli, A., eds., 1984.

1984b, Il complesso di Euclide nella filosofia della scienza e nella metodologia economica, in Lunghini, *et al.*, 1984.

1985a, Keynes, Schumpeter, Marx, and the structural instability of capitalism, *Cahiers d'économie politique*, 10–11, 279–304.

1985b, Money and production in Keynes and Schumpeter: two dichotomies, in Arena, M. and Graziani, A., eds., *Money and Production*, Paris, Presses Universitaires de France.

1986a, Stagflation and the recent revival of Schumpeterian entrepreneurship, in Frisch, H. and Gahlen, B., eds., 1986, *Causes of Contemporary Stagnation*, New York, Springer.

1986b, La 'lunga crisi': interpretazioni e prospettive, in Ente Einaudi, ed., *Oltre la crisi. Le prospettive di sviluppo dell'economia italiana e il contributo del sistema finanziario*, Bologna, Il Mulino.

1988, Technological flexibility, financial fragility and the recent revival of Schumpeterian entrepreneurship, *Recherches économiques de Louvain*, 54, 1, 103–32.

1989, Uncertainty, technological flexibility and long-term fluctuations, in Di Matteo, M., Goodwin, R. and Vercelli, A., eds., *Technological and Social Factors in Long-term Fluctuations*, Berlin, Springer.

Vicarelli, F., 1984, *Keynes: The Instability of Capitalism*, Philadelphia, University of Pennsylvania Press.

1985–6, Natural laws and economic policy: some considerations on the theoretical foundations of the new classical macroeconomics, *Journal of Post-Keynesian Economics*, 8, 2, 298–314.

Vicarelli, F., ed., 1985, *Keynes's Relevance Today*, London, Macmillan.

Vilar, P., 1971, *Oro e moneta nella storia*, Bari, Laterza.

Voltaire, 1759, *Candide: or, All for the Best*, London, J. Nourse.

Wallace, N., 1980, The overlapping generations model of fiat money, in Kareken, J.H. and Wallace, N., eds., *Models of Monetary Economics*, Minneapolis, Federal Reserve Bank of Minneapolis, vol. 1, pp. 49–82.

Weatherford, R., 1982, *Philosophical Foundations of Probability Theory*, London, Routledge and Kegan.

Wiener, N., 1958, The theory of prediction, in Beckman, E.F., ed., *Modern Mathematics for Engineers*, series 1, New York, McGraw-Hill, chapter 8.

Williams, R.F., 1970, The 'DA' maps of Smale and structural stability, *Proceedings of the Symposium on Pure Mathematics (Global Analysis)*, American Mathematical Society, 14, 329–34.

Wilson, A.G., 1981, *Catastrophe Theory and Bifurcation: Applications to Urban and Regional Systems*, London, Croom Helm.

Wittgenstein, C., 1980, *Culture and Values, Vermischte Bemerkungen*, edited by G.H. von Wright, Oxford, Blackwell.

Wold, H.O., 1949, Statistical estimation of economic relationships, *Econometrica*, 17, Supplement, 1–21.

1954, Causality and econometrics, *Econometrica*, 22, 162–77.

Yoshizawa, T., 1966, *Stability Theory by Liapounov's Second Method*, Tokyo, Mathematical Society of Japan.

Zeeman, E.C., 1977, *Catastrophe Theory. Selected Papers 1972–1977*, Reading, Mass., Addison-Wesley.

Zellner, A., 1979, Causality and econometrics, in Brunner, K. and Meltzer, A.H., eds., *Carnegie-Rochester Conference Series on Public Policy*, vol. 10, Amsterdam, North Holland.

1982, Comment on J. Geweke, 'Measurement of linear dependence and feedback between multiple time series', *Journal of the American Statistical Association*, 77, 313–14.

Subject index

accelerator, 152
anti-Keynesian counter-revolution, 2n, 4–5,
   99, 128–9
arguments
   demonstrative, 45, 140–2, 221–3, 232,
      238–9, 242
   probabilistic, 176, 220–4, 229, 238–9

behaviourism, 80
black boxes, 110
business cycle
   and equilibrium, 11, 20n, 128–42, 151–2,
      163–5, 170–5
   and impulses, 134–6, 165
   and instability, 37
   and monetary policy, 131, 134–6
   and propagation mechanisms, 135, 152,
      165, 170–1
   Lucas's definition, 132–6, 154
   monetary (MBC), 2n, 136n, 164, 168,
      170, 172–3, 175
   monetary-real (MRBC), 2n, 171–2, 174–5
   real (RBC), 128, 136, 139, 164–75

causa cognoscendi, see causality, epistemic
causa essendi, see causality, ontological
causality
   according to Granger, 106–7, 109,
      116–23, 135, 136n, 147–8, 158–61, 165
   according to Suppes, 107–17, 119–22
   and business cycle, 134–6
   and causal production, 110
   and 'conditionality', 120–1, 147
   and empiricism, 110
   and events, 111–12
   and Keynesian economists, 106, 123
   and new classical economists, 106, 117,
      120, 123, 158
   and qualitative probability, 111, 231
   and stationarity, 119

contemporaneous, 112–16, 119
deterministic, 107, 111, 114–16, 223
efficient, 69–70
epistemic, 115–16, 223
formal, 45, 69–70
genuine, *see* causality, spurious
in Keynes, 106–7, 109, 114–17, 120, 122,
   176–93, 198, 200, 223, 231, 233
inhibitory, 116
ontological, 115–16, 223
prima facie, definition, 108
probabilistic, 106–23, 200, 223, 231, 233,
   238
sequential, 114, 199–200
spurious, 108–10, 113, 118–19, 121
cause, *see* causality
cause, sufficient, *see* causality, deterministic
certainty equivalence, 145–6, 157, 165,
   235
chaos, 79
circular flow, 33, 202–9, 212
classical postulates, *see* market, labour
coherence criterion, 75
constructivism, 177, 222, 237–8
consumption, 166–8, 171, 181–4, 189, 192,
   194, 207, 224, 228, 236n
credit, 37, 203–6, 210, 212, 216

demand
   and Say's Law, 110, 180, 207
   effective, 14, 154, 180–3, 188–9, 191–4,
      197–8, 230, 237
   for capital, *see* market, capital
   for labour, *see* market, labour
   for money, *see* liquidity, preference
determinism, 107, 114–15, 119
   causal, *see* causality, deterministic
   scientific, 45, 61
   situational, 157
development, 202–6, 208, 210–12

Subject index

dichotomy
  classical, 185, 201–2
  Keynesian, 202, 206–12
  Schumpeterian, 202–6, 209–12
disequilibrium, 31–4, 130, 137–9, 152–5
  and Keynes, 32–3, 224–6
  and Lucas, 32, 152–4
  intelligibility of, 4, 20–2, 25, 32, 153–5,
    159, 235

econometrics, 37, 117–18, 153
  atheoretical, 149, 159
  rational expectations, 18n, 159
  vector autoregression (VAR), 18n, 41,
    159–62, 165
economic policy, 1, 4, 22, 32, 36–9, 55, 75,
  96, 102, 122, 128, 130, 136, 150, 172–3
  in Keynes, 177, 188–93, 194n, 200, 208n,
    219–20, 224, 227–9, 243
  ineffectiveness of, 131, 142, 156
  rules of, 104, 127–59, 190, 200, 224,
    229–30, 238
economic vision, 111
  in Keynes, 3–6, 219, 242–4
  in Lucas, 3–6, 80, 127–32, 138–42, 151,
    175, 235
  in RBC, 164–5, 174
  in Schumpeter, 5–6
economics (conception of)
  in Keynes, 176, 220–4, 238, 242
  in Lucas, 140–2, 239–42
economy
  barter, 207
  cooperative, 202, 206–9, 212, 242n
  entrepreneur, 202, 206–10, 211–12, 242n
  monetary, 71, 85, 207, 211, 216–19, 229,
    232–3
  neutral, 208–9
environment,12–13, 24, 27, 33n, 71, 79,
  81–2, 84, 86, 88, 92, 93n, 95–6, 104–5,
  137–9, 143–59, 167, 173, 213–14, 229,
  231, 233, 239, 242, 244
equilibrium
  and attractors, 67–8
  and singularities, 66–8
  cognitive-decisional, 98, 100, 105
  daily, 181
  dynamic interpretation, 11–14, 16–17,
    23–7, 29, 151–2, 183n
  general economic, 2, 33, 99, 128–32, 138,
    150–1, 174–5, 204–5, 234–5
  in Keynes, 14–15, 23, 182–3, 224–9
  in Lucas, 14–15, 23, 130, 136, 150–2, 154,
    224
  in Patinkin, 15, 226
  Keynes's semantic interpretation, 14–15
  long-period, 19, 213, 227

Lucas's semantic interpretation, 14–15,
  151–2
Nash, 27–9
non-Walrasian, 19
reasons for, 16–18
reification of, 17–18
relativity of the distinction between
  equilibrium and disequilibrium, 11–12,
  18–20, 151
saddle point, 43, 100–2, 103n, 156
short period, 19, 181, 227
stochastic, 34–5, 150–1
syntactic interpretation, 12, 17, 23, 27–9,
  151, 183n, 184n
temporary, 19
Walras's semantic interpretation, 12, 14
with under-employment
  (unemployment), *see* unemployment
ergodicity, 31n, 35, 40–2, 78–9, 81n, 100,
  104, 154–5, 159, 235, 241
errors
  and uncertainty, 231
  cumulative character of, 152
ethology, 97, 145
events, 108–9, 111–12, 223
  chunk, 112
  dispositional, 109, 120
  instantaneous, 112
  single, 109, 120
  types of, 109, 120
expectations
  adaptive, 153, 240
  and effective demand, 181
  and equilibrium, 97–9
  entrepreneurial, 217–18
  long-term, 199, 217, 224, 227, 229–33,
    237
  rational (*see also* rationality, and
    expectations), 3, 22, 33, 35n, 43, 53, 81,
    117, 127, 132, 134, 136n, 141–2, 146,
    149–50, 156–7, 159, 165–7, 213n,
    231–2, 240–1
  short-term, 181, 183, 225, 229–30
  speculative, 217–18

flexibility, 71–90
  allocative, 216
  distributional, 216
  exchange, 88, 90, 215–17
  financial, 90
  functional, 88
  intertemporal, 84, 89–90, 217
  labour, 214–15
  macroeconomic, 88, 90
  micro-structural, 89–90
  microeconomic, 88–90
  public policy, 90

Subject index

multiplier, 17, 182–3, 194n, 228
  and equilibrium, 182–3
  and stability, 56, 182
  dynamic, 56, 114, 152, 183n
  static, 114, 183n, 225, 237

neoclassical synthesis, 1n, 2, 4, 149, 193, 240

Pareto efficiency, 102
path dependence, 32, 33n, 227
Phillips curve, 1, 140, 193, 240
predictability, 40, 45–6, 53, 61, 71–90, 98, 100, 157
principle of retarded action, 113
process
  cognitive-decisional, 97, 144, 146, 240
  ergodic, *see* ergodicity
  Markov, 166
  of learning, 93n, 155, 239
  stationary stochastic, *see* stationarity
  stochastic, and equilibrium, 129, 133

rationality
  adaptive, 92, 95–6, 105, 233
  and causality, 157–8
  and equilibrium, 21, 92, 95, 97–100
  and expectations, 91–105, 232
  and *logos*, 44, 60, 70
  and Nash equilibrium, 28
  bounded, 95, 104
  collective, 102
  creative, 96, 104–5, 157–8, 239
  designing, 96, 239
  procedural, 28, 93–5, 96n, 99, 104, 157, 239
  substantive, 4, 28, 92–5, 97–9, 104–5, 150, 153n, 156–7, 232, 239
  utopic, 96
regularity, 72, 79–82, 89, 100, 103–4
reliability condition, 83, 86
representative agent, 142, 144, 164, 166, 173, 232, 234–5
research programme, *see* economic vision
rigidity
  price, 171–2
  structural, 214–15
  technological, 214
risk, *see* uncertainty

s-stability = structural stability, *see* instability
savings, 167, 183–4, 225, 237
Say's Law, 110, 180, 189, 207–8
scientific paradigm, *see* economic vision
shocks

exogenous, 20n, 134–5, 166–7
  external, 20, 47
  monetary, 134–6, 168–9, 172–3
  productivity, 170, 173
  random, 16, 37
  real, 165, 168, 170, 172–3
  stochastic, 101–2, 151, 166
  technology, 166–75
solidity
  financial, 214
  structural, 214
solution (procedure of)
  for functional dynamic equations, 13, 23–7
  for models with rational expectations, 100–4, 232
stability, *see* instability
stationarity, 16, 34–5, 39, 42, 78–82, 84, 98, 100, 104–5, 119, 129, 133, 141, 149–50, 154–5, 159, 235, 241
structural change, 35–8, 45–6, 49–51, 53, 55–6, 60, 68–9, 84–5, 99, 104, 148–50, 161, 203, 205–6, 210, 212–14, 235, 238
structure
  connective (or 'flow'), 54–5
  functional, 55, 204
  technological, 139, 156
supply
  labour (*see also* market, labour), 167, 169
  money, *see* market, money

technical change, 174, 203–4, 206, 210, 212, 214
technical progress, *see* technology
technology, 137–9, 142, 144, 146–7, 151, 156, 164–6, 168, 171–2, 175, 204, 210, 213, 216
time
  epistemic (or 'logical'), 89, 113–14, 237
  historical (or 'ontological'), 40, 52n, 89, 104, 113–14, 237
  to build, 136, 165, 169
trade, channels of, 204
traverse, 104
truth, 98

uncertainty, 71–90, 94, 104, 114, 117, 131, 133, 144, 146, 155–7, 187, 200, 208, 211, 217, 231, 233, 235
  and decision theory, 76, 84–90
  and flexibility, 82–4, 88
  and reliability of probability, 72–8, 80n, 85–6, 89
  environmental, 71
  genuine, 79, 80n
  simple (or 'risk'), 71–4, 76, 78, 80–2,

Author index

Author index

Author index